TECHNOLOGY AND OPERATIONS MANAGEMENT
FOR
AGRI-BUSINESS SECTOR

Technology
and
Operations Management
for
Agri-Business Sector

V.G. Dhanakumar

ANMOL PUBLICATIONS PVT. LTD.
NEW DELHI - 110 002 (INDIA)

ANMOL PUBLICATIONS PVT. LTD.
H.O.: 4374/4B, Ansari Road, Darya Ganj,
New Delhi-110 002 (India)
Ph.: 23278000, 23261597
B.O.: No. 1015, Ist Main Road, BSK IIIrd Stage
IIIrd Phase, IIIrd Block
Bangalore - 560 085 (India)
Visit us at: www.anmolpublications.com

Technology and Operations Management for Agri-Business Sec

First Published, 2007
ISBN 81-261-3105-5

PRINTED IN INDIA

Printed at Mehra Offset Press, Delhi.

Contents

Contents

Preface

The aim of this book is to share with readers in agribusiness & plantation industry and academic, as well as policy makers, on how technology and operations management concept may be managed more purposefully within well defined agribusiness sector. The scope of the book is built around the fundamental premise of managing technology to fulfill business objectives within the framework of value chain. This book also explain practical dimension of different agribusiness area, discuss the economic importance to agribusiness industry, and explains basic principles of agribusiness, technology operations, world class business strategy, supply chain and cost minimization parameter. This book is divided into fifteen major sections, unit one includes comparison of technology and agri business, which sets the stage for the book. The principles, types and knowledge dimensions of technology and impact of agribusiness on economy are discussed. Units 2, 3 and 4 includes, chapters on operations strategy, features of future commodity parks and world class business management technology. Unit five to eight, explain the concept of supply chain and value chain and its relevance to agribusiness with special reference to diversification, venture technology and contract farming. Unit nine to eleven explained the global quality standards, warehousing and packaging technology & technology for concentrated to condensed product from farm to consumer. Units 12 to 14, concerns the management of innovation in the field of organic agriculture with special reference to WTO, HACCP and ready to eat food technology network for agri-business performance. The chapter 15, covers the area of biofuel and aromedic plantation with an emphasis on entrepreneurship led business. In this respect, some of the most proformed changes are taking place in agriculture and agribusiness industry. The remaining chapter includes a brief note on appropriate technology with reference to production, productivity, quality and profitability for agri-plantation sector viz., tea, coffee, spices, rubber, etc.

The chapters in this book will provide the upto date knowledge, advice and inspiration on how robust and resilient the agribusiness and associated sector will be in the era of globalization. This book is designed to help the readers to better understand their cognitive models about how the agribusiness does and should operate, allowing them to adopt more easily to the dynamics of world class business.

Acknowledgement

The author is indebted to many colloquies from the Commodity Boards of India, UPASI, Agri-plantation industry and IIPM that contributed to the completion of this work. Preparation of the manuscript for this work took a lot of time and efforts of quite a few people, especially I would like to recognize Mr. K. Narendran for contributing specific insights and work for the effectiveness of the book. My special thanks to Mrs. Shilpa and Mr. M. Aravind Kumar for the secretarial support. I am also grateful to anonymous reviewers.

1

Technology and Operations Management (TOM) for Agri-Business

Technology based agri-business organizations are constantly confronted with dynamic and unpredictable changes in production, marketing and profitability. How do they stay competitive in a rapidly changing environment? Obviously, such agri-business units compete on the basis of their technological strength. A challenge of what makes one company stronger than the other in terms of technological capabilities is the scope of the business. As an example, when Hindus-O Company entered into food processing business in the early 1990s, it certainly had the skilled manpower and electronic system. But a key ingredient was missing: Hindus realized that it did not have appropriate processing unit to produce maximum capacity of production within the unit of cycle time to meet the requirements. This allowed the company to make the essential quick decision and develop its new product line exceptionally fast enough to its customer and competitors. As the example show, whether a technology-based company is contemplating a strategic change or evaluating its existing strategy, it must critically examine its capacity to exploit change based on the core operational technology.

The words in the title of this book have special meaning. Strategy relates to the steps important in the initiation, conduct and completion of agri-business long-term plan; technology is the state-of-the art method and techniques of achieving a practical purpose in agri-business; management is the tact of accomplishing an agri-business mission, its objectives, and its goal through planning, organising and controlling; and the term operations is a regulatory interacting and interdependent group of activities forming a holistic approach in totality perspective. When combined, these words begin to take form as important concepts in the Mastering of Business in Agriculture (MBA). Apart from this, a partnering the technology to agri-business goal is the subject most discussed by both technical and non-technical managers. It also focussed on the need for increasing the managers' understanding of the issues related to technology and its management in agriculture.

What is Technology?

The word technology usually conjures up many different images and generally refers to what had been described as the "high-tech". Limiting technology to high-tech industries such as computers, chips, superconductivity, genetic engineering, robotics, and so on focuses excessive attention on what the media consider newsworthy. Limiting technology to science, engineering and mathematics also loses sight of other supporting technologies. Technology includes more than machines, processes and inventions. There are many different manifestations of technology; some are very simple and others, very complex. A description of technology in the context of agri-business should go beyond the traditional. Technology can be described in the following ways:

- Technology is the means for accomplishing a task – it includes whatever is needed to convert nature based agri-resources into products or services.
- Technology includes the knowledge and natural resources that are required to achieve an objective.
- Technology is the body of scientific and engineering

knowledge, which can be applied in the design of products and/or processes or in the search for new knowledge.

Technology is a know-how, physical things and procedures used to produce products and services.

Within this context of management of technology, regardless of whether the decision involves a major financial investment or the introduction of some new human resource programme. Both involve allocation of resources to the extent of management and technology can be defined as:

> "Management as a technology can be described as the process of integrating the agri-business unit resources and infrastructure in the fulfillment of its defined purposes, objectives, strategies and operations."

This is a simple statement with significant implications for management of technology. If the broader descriptions are accepted, then management definitely is a technology. If the restrictive approach of description is used, management would probably not be considered as a technology.

According to Gaynor (2001)[1], it could be argued that descriptions on Management and Administration are so broad that they encompass all of management and further that considering management as a technology is stretching the description of technology. It is true that the broad perspective is all-encompassing, but then technology in one form or another or to a greater or lesser extent drives most organizations, especially those that are concerned about the future. If it does not drive the product base, it does drive the distribution process from order entry to customer satisfaction. Technology cannot be restricted to the manufacturing industries. It encompasses not only the manufacturing sector but all industries—agriculture, airlines, banks, communication, entertainment, fast food, clothing, hospitals, insurance, investment, and so on – and determines future viability of the business unit as well as the industry.

There is no limit to the way in which organizations can describe technology. The important point is that organizations define what they mean by technology.

Technological Classification

Managing technologies requires some delineation of the technologies into categories. There are no agreed-on approaches for classification. Technologies can be classified according to any of the following categories:

- State-of-the-art technologies: those technologies that equal or surpass the competitors
- Proprietary technologies: those technologies protected by patents or secrecy agreements that provide a measurable competitive advantage
- Known technologies: those technologies that may be common to many organizations but are used in unique ways
- Core technologies: those technologies that are essential to maintain a competitive position
- Leveraging technologies: those technologies that support the core technologies
- Pacing technologies: technologies whose rate of development controls the rate of product or process development
- Emerging technologies: technologies that are currently under consideration for future products or processes
- Scouting technologies: formal tracking of potential product and process technologies for future study or application
- Idealized unknown basic technologies: technologies

that, if available, would provide a significant benefit in some aspect of life

[Source: T&I Management Academy]

Primary Areas of Technology

Inventing a new technology on an existing one is important for the feasibility of the technology. The shares of companies bringing a new agri-business based technology to market get uncharitably referred to as "binary events", they can either be worth nothing, or a lot, nothing in between. There are no simple answers, and each technology's history is unique in some ways. Yet, seeking answers is key by understanding the different types (or) areas of technology to reassuring business unit that are looking for new growth opportunities from mind to market. The classification and types of technologies given below are drivers of evolutionary iteration of primary importance for the business in agriculture.

The Three Primary Areas of Technology are,

- *Product Technology*

  Production system must be designed to produce products and services spawed by technological advances. Product technology translates ideas into new products and services. It develops primarily by engineers and researchers and needs co-operation with marketing & operations department

- *Process Technology*

  Process Technology is a technique, which improves the methods used in production system, is called as process technology. For example, Mango processing with Kaizan Unit to avoid wastage and zero-in microbial contamination.

- *Information Technology*

  Used to operate the production system. E.g., Telecommunications system, word processing, computer spreadsheets, computer graphics, e-mail, online databases, the Internet, etc. to assess value of the products and market demands. It might be mentioned that specification process for the selective technology includes case of manufacture, case of usability and practical testability as well as use of a minimum number of tolerance components. To overcome such tolerances of technology, business managers had to select the technology based on the following criteria's.

- *Absolute Technology (AT)*

  The principle of containing fully (or) perfectly developed technology within the design based on the utility cycle is called as *Absolute Technology.*

- *Obsolete Technology (OT)*

  The principle of containing imperfectly developed (or) rudimentary in design and fallen into disuse is called *Obsolete Technology.*

- *Obsolescence Technology (ObT)*

The state, process, condition of being (or) becoming a technology into "*Obsolete*" is called *Obsolescence Technology.*

GUIDELINES FOR TECHNOLOGY IMPLEMENTATION

Technology Acquisition

Technology acquisition deals with how far back in the R&D stream a firm gets involved to secure new technologies and which options its uses. The three options for acquiring new technology are:

- Internal sources
- Inter-firm relationship
- Purchasing from the suppliers

Internal Sources

Available sources within the companies for acquiring technology. Suitable for earliest research stage of R&D. E.g., Amul gets >50% of its milk based value added product technology within the company.

Inter-firm Relationships

To acquire technology, a firm might build co-operative inter-firm relationships. Firms choose outside sources to acquire technology. Company with no R&D prefer inter-firm relationship. An alternate option for technology acquisition is:

- Firms outsource research grants to universities or laboratories. E.g., Pepsi, Indo-American Firm.
- Firm may obtain license for technology to get legal right. E.g., Innovative product from American Sweet Corn.
- Enter into a joint venture or alliance to produce a technology. E.g., Tata and Tetley for marketing of premium Tea.
- A firm can buy another firm which has desired technological know-how.

Suppliers

Firm can buy new technology from outside. Supplier can be source of parts for firms own technological product. Operation manager must be alert to new technologies available from the suppliers that will enhance performance of industry.

Human Side of Technology

Largely technology determine the jobs that people actually perform. Now technology affects job, people and efficiency.

Technology Forecasting (TF)

Technology Forecasting (TF) is a process of predicting the future performance characteristics of technology. It identifies:

- Future trends in technology
- Identify alternative products
- Analyse to meet corporate objective

Technology Absorption

The term integration is used to signify the rate of absorption of technology by the industry by import of technology. E.g. Import of food processing machinery at Food Park (or) Agri-Export Zone level in India and its absorption rate. The Thumb Rule for absorption rate of technology is given below:

a) Semi-knock down condition : 10-20%

b) Completely-knock down condition : 50-60%

c) Full integration : 90-100%

Formula for percentage of integration

$$I = \frac{FG - RM \times 100}{FG}$$

I = Integration percentage

FG = Price of finished goods

RM = Cost of important materials & cost of components to produce in factory.

Role of Technology

Within this context, technology is probably the most important force driving the increase in global competition.

As various studies show, agri-business companies that invest in and apply new technology tend to have stronger financial position than companies that don't. At the same time, the relationship between technology and competitive advantage is often misunderstood. This paradox raises the question: One view is that the agri-business manager merely needs to understand what a technology can do, including its cost and performance possibilities. An alternative view is that such an understanding isn't enough; that the effective manager must also understand how the technology works and what goes on in the technology's "black box". Therefore, a firm must not only look at its immediate competitors, but also at its invisible competitors outside the industry that have the technological capability to enter the industry sometime in the future. Here, the stakes are high because such choices affect the human as well as the technical aspects of operations. A firm must examine how technology should be chosen and how these choices link with strategy to create a competitive advantage. As such, an appropriate technology is one that fits agri-business sector and operations strategies and gives the firm a sustainable advantage.

Technology and Knowledge Management

The way in which organizations use technology to manage knowledge has quickly emerged as the single most important discriminator between success and failure in this intensely competitive global economy. Nonaka and Takeuchi,[2] authors of The Knowledge – Creating Company, confidently predict that a company's ability to create, store and disseminate knowledge will become absolutely crucial for staying ahead of the competition in quality, speed, innovation, and price. Only by developing and implementing systems and mechanisms to assemble, package, promote, and distribute the fruits of its thinking will a company be able to transform knowledge into corporate power.

Thomas Stewart,[3] in his classic Intellectual Capital: The New Wealth of Organizations, writes, "Knowledge has become more important for organizations than financial resources, market position, or any other company asset." Knowledge is now seen as the main resource needed for performing work in an organization since all the organization's traditions, culture, management, operations, systems, and procedures are all based on knowledge.

Intelligent organizations recognize that only one asset grows more valuable as it is used – the knowledge skills of people. Unlike machinery that gradually wears out, materials that become depleted, patents and copyrights that grow obsolete, and trademarks that lose their ability to comfort, the knowledge and insights that come from the learning of employees actually increase in value when used and practiced.

Technological Resource as Knowledge

As per the norms of WTO-IPR, unless and until a company determines what "knowledge" is and what type of knowledge is important, there is no way it can manage its agri-business. The most important factor of business now is not land, labour or capital, but knowledge. In the market, patents are a way of converting knowledge into wealth. In a business environment, the knowledge is not merely power, but also wealth. If, a knowledge becomes wealth, we know who acquires it, seeks to monopolize it. "Know-how" consists of knowledge and experience acquired for practical application of a technique. The notion of property (patents) is employed by those deal in technical know-how. Until it is patented, it can be treated only as know-how. In a technological dimension, knowledge can be recognized as knowledge, only if it is wealth creator in a business setting. A pace of change is a comprehensive systems approach for the management of corporate knowledge through technological support.

Future Challenges for Agri-business

The importance of integrating technology, learning and organizational performance has become increasingly obvious to corporate leaders around the globe. In this book, we will explore the capacity of technology for strengthening agri-business performance and building corporate success in agriculture. Technology provides firms with many opportunities for improving competitive performance. But gaining such effectiveness and efficiency comes with a wealth. The cost of entry into "Wealth Creating Agri-business" (not a profit built business) requires a change in thinking, a new agri-business management model, a novel techno-strategy, a focus on the integration of the business system and an executives of MBA, i.e., Masters of Business in Agriculture. Here, we view technology as a tool for management. It is a means for accomplishing a wealth creating business continuum in agriculture through techno-management. Today's competition requires all industries to improve the strategic management of their technology. In the final analysis, what make a company a learning organization is, its capacity to have its people learn faster and better and its ability to effectively manage wealth-creating knowledge. Technology is absolutely necessary to accomplish each of these functions. World Class companies view advanced technology as a competitive weapon that can be used to capture shares of world markets. In the remaining chapters of the book, we will examine in depth on implicit knowledge to explicit technology and its support to agri-business industry.

Conclusion

Investment in technology and management is the key to the companies' success. Well-designed techno-strategy and executed system for agri-business is not only a critical means for the business performance to be a good steward of the companies' resources, it is also a rewarding business experience.

Getting an agri-business to realise the benefits of techno-management of planning, requires the techno-manager to oversee the process of evolving nature of business system. It is believed that, techno-managers can use the points covered in this book to help to formulate agri-business strategies towards achieving its goal.

REFERENCES

1. Buffa, S.E. (1994). *Modern Production/Operations Management.* John Wiley & Sons. Toranto.
2. Dhanakumar, V. G, (2004). Technology and Operations for Agri-Plantation Sector, *PGDABPM Manual,* IIPM, Bangalore.
3. Dosi, G., Teece, J.D., and Chytry, J. (1998). *Technology, Organization and Competitiveness.* Oxford University Press, New York.
4. Gaither, N and Frazier, G (2002). Operations Management. Thomson Asia Pvt. Ltd., Singapore.
5. Szakonyi, R. (1999). *Handbook of Technology Management.* Viva Books Private Limited, New Delhi.
6. Kathuria, S. (1996). *Competing through Technology and Manufacturing.* Oxford University Press, Bombay.

NOTES

1. Gaynor, G.H., 2002. *Management of Technology.* G.H.Associates, Inc. Minnesota.
2. Nonaka, I. and Takeuchi, H. 1995. *The Knowledge – Creating Company,* NY: Oxford University Press.
3. Stweart, T. 1977. Intellectual Capital. NY: Doubleday.

2

Operations Strategy for Agri-business

The term 'strategy' has been derived from the Greek word *Strategos* which means 'General' of Army. Literally, strategy implies the art of the General to improve the probability of winning a war as the term strategy originated in military science. In agri-business, a strategy refers to a 'complex plan' designed to bring the organization from a given posture to a desired posture in a future period of time. Learned et.al., defined strategy as the pattern of objectives, purposes or goals and major policies and plans for achieving these goals stated in such a way as to define what business the company is in or to be in and the kind of company it is or is to be. A strategy is a contingent plan formulated in the light of the present and potential activities of competitors. It is basically an administrative course designed to achieve success. In the words of Smith, "it is the plan for getting the best return from resources, the selection of the kind of business to engage in and the scheme for obtaining a favourable position in the business world. It is the arrangement for dealing with the ever-changing outer world".

Operations Strategy

The concept of an operations strategy has received much recent attention in agri-business literature. Nevertheless, there remains much speculation as to the purpose, role, composition and evolution of such strategies. An effective strategy is critical in competitive markets to sustain business performance. There are four broad approaches to conceptualizing a strategy: strategic planning, competitive strategy, emergent views about strategy, and the resource-based view of strategy. Texts tend to argue that good strategic management should reflect different aspects of all four contingents upon the context, and that a strategy should be unique for competitive advantage: strategy is about the difference that creates value.

The important role of an operations strategy has been well documented; less clear, however, is its exact nature. Michael Porter (1996) offers us some guidelines when he describes activities as the basic units of competitive advantage. An organization, he suggests, will adopt a distinct 'strategic positioning'; it will compete on the basis of flexibility, cost, quality, speed, diversity and variety, etc,. Here, strategic positioning means: 'performing different activities from rivals' or performing similar activities in different ways'. In contrast, Porter describes 'operational effectiveness' as 'performing similar activities better than rivals'. We suggest that operational effectiveness does, in fact, depend upon the correct operations strategy: a 'fusion' of various building blocks. A number of definitions can be found concerning the nature of an operations strategy. The following from Lowson, 2001 attempts to encapsulate the various views:

> '..... major decisions about, and strategic management of: core competencies, capabilities and processes; technologies; resources; and key tactical activities necessary in any supply network, in order to create and deliver products and services and the value demanded by a customer/consumer. The strategic role involves blending these various building blocks into one or more unique, organizational specific, strategic architectures.'

A notion of an operations strategy as compared to long

term pattern of strategic decision making regarding combination of components that have been fused together as a result of the contingent circumstances. The examples are given below with reference to agri-business sector. Here, we see the important notion of an operations strategy for agri-business as composed of a long-term pattern of strategic decisions made regarding a combination of components that have been fused together as a result of the contingent circumstances. We now to learn the exact nature of an operations strategy and examine how it reflects these strategic perspectives in agri-business.

Operations strategy is a long range game plan for agri-business products & services and provides a road map for what the production (or) operations function must do if business strategies are to be achieved. Moreover, all elements of agri-business led operations strategy (positioning strategies, product plans, outsourcing, process and technology plans, strategic allocation of resources, and facility plans) must be carefully linked. The examples are given below with reference to agri-business sector would facilitate the firms to choose the right operations strategy.

Core competency; Capabilities & Process. These are:

a) Process based

Derived from transformation of important food process by natural transformation activities. Examples are organic farming, indigenous way of processing wine as a nature added product and Parmesan cheese.

b) Systems of Coordination based

Across the entire operating system of Darjeeling Tea processing unit, strategic approach for hygiene management is required in order to maintain World Class Quality of product to fetch premium price.

c) Organization based

A strategic operations across the entire organization to prevent pesticide residue in product. Eg. Farm to fork strategy for pesticide residue management.

d) Network based

Covering the whole supply network from supplier to customer to minimize cost of operations of production unit.

Resources

Depend upon the type of agribusiness firm, which can be considered at two levels.

a) Individual resource of the farm

Value added equipment, brand added product. Eg. Mysore Nuggets Coffee, Guntur Chilli and so on.

b) The way to work together to create competitive advantage are classified as below.

1) Tangible

Type of cultivable land, appropriate technology and infrastructure

2) Intangible

Taste and quality of the product, SPS-TBT information system, brands, culture and customer delight

3) Human

Specialized skill and knowledge of the people

Tappers in rubber

Pluckers in Tea

Honey extractors for the mountain hive

Technology

In addition to being renounced in agribusiness, technology

will have increasingly important role to play in product, process, market and consumption across the organizational network. Eg. Fertigation, Capsulation of product ingredients (or) enzymes etc.

Tactical Activities

Key activities that are vital in order to support for particular strategy or position.

The continuation of certain core and tactical activities such as food safety, diversification for risk management and specialty products will be vital to sustain particular strategy or business position.

An operations strategy aims to ensure that key operational management activities are performed better than rivals so as to provide support for the overall strategy of agri-business as well as serving as its distinctive competence.

Returning to role of an operations strategies, it is our contention that an agri-business units may adopt an operations strategies with certain common components given below in the table No. 1 based on the relevant literature on operations strategy types (Harrison, 1993).

To achieve the above strategies, we posit that a strategy must be unique and closely aligned to the individual firm circumstances – strategy is about the difference that creates value. It may be appropriate, at an operations strategy level, for organizations to seek quick response as well as time-based competition and strategic postponement. Lean production, Six sigma efficiency, JIT, TPM, Technology and SCM strategies are frequently combined for the effectiveness of the business in agriculture.

TABLE NO.1

Operations Strategies & its examples in Agribusiness

Operation Strategies	Theoretical Foundation and Rationale
Quick Response (QR) or Planned Product Response (PR)	The QR philosophy links all activity to real-time or appropriate time. Eg. Availability of seeds and fertilizer during sowing season for contract farming.
Time-Bound Competition (TBC)	Time based competition requires expanded variety, flexible manufacturing and increased innovation. Eg. Mango slice, Mango juice, Mango puree, Mango bar, Mango flavour etc. The strategy involves more than just speed of product response. It is concerned with reducing delays throughout business cycle.
Supply Network Strategy (including supply chain, value chain and value stream)	A supply network strategy seeks close links between production and inventory through network of partnership. Eg. Links between production and inventory through network of partnership can reduce wastage by 11% in coffee. (ICAR Project, 2004)
Just-in-Time	JIT can be considered the philosophy of waste reduction and continuous improvement. Eg. Drying of coconut kernel within 4 hours of breaking nuts for Copra preparation. Otherwise leads to microbial contamination and quality detoriation.

World Class Manufacturing (WCM)	The capabilities that have to compete in export markets globally. The key attributes of WCM are: Becoming the best Quality producer in spices Able to manufacture quality and decisively Adopting zero- break down, TPM, 5S , HACCP etc.

Strategic Support for Technology

In successful companies, there is growing acceptance that "technology" goes beyond the traditional R&D function. It is perceived as a "practical way of doing things", believed to be part of all products and processes.

Education and training in successful companies reflects strategic technology management. Successful companies keep abreast of technological changes and put much effort into finding, understanding, and transferring technology as part of their integrated technological and business strategy.

The strategic direction of the organization depends on corporate leaders' expectations for new product and process technology. We believe that successful management of technology depends as much on the attitude of managers and professionals as on the technology itself. Thus, organizational culture is an important factor in the successful management of technology.

The senior management of successful companies recognizes the importance of the strategic management of technology. They know it helps a company remain competitive with its products and it supports organizational processes. These executives are continually involved in planning for and watching over the selection of technology-based strategic initiatives. In addition, they ensure that the organizational hardware, software, information systems, and culture are in place, effectively supporting the company's technology-based mission, objectives and goals. Senior management, often led by chief technology officer who understands the force and trajectory of evolving technology ideas, actively supports both product and process development. Top management provides the resources as well as the supportive culture that encourage creativity, innovation and acceptance of a new product and process technology.

Service Quality as an Operations Strategy

A service is a result that customers want. Services are generally obtained by engaging in an interactive process with the provider. A product is something tangible that customers use to derive a desired result. Companies that sell goods generally offer many services to help them to do so such as customer training, information services and field service.

Search Qualities

Verifiable (sampling) attributes of a product

Experimental Qualities: Can only be ascertained through usage

Services are generally *low in search* qualities and *high in experimental quality.* "Word of mouth" is particularly important in services.

Customers seeking to reduce their risk before purchasing can do by listening to credible people who have experienced the product? The best way for company to get new customers is to satisfy existing customer base. Satisfied customer is the company's greatest revenue – generating *asset* and every unsatisfied customer is liability to the firm.

Operations Strategy for service in agri-business refers to positioning of strategies for service should be based on the following two elements:

(A) Type of service Design Standard and custom, amount of customer contact, mix of physical good and intangible service.

(B) Type of Production Process: Quasi-manufacturing, customer as participants and customer as product.

(1) Quasi Manufacturing

Under this service operations, emphases is on production cost, technology, physical material, quality and prompt delivery. In case of McDonald's, restaurant will have Quasi manufacturing operations in backroom and customer as a participant in the front room. Similar examples are referred to coffee day and Barrista.

(2) Customer as a Participant

There is a high degree of customer involvement in this type of service operation. Eg., cup tasting, wine tasting and sample quality assessor.

(3) Customer as a Product

The Customers are so involved that the service is actually performed on the customer. Eg., Aroma therapy for a customer with an agri-business products of aloe vera.

Operations Strategy for Agri-business service

Branding, as an operations strategy is one of the hottest topics in agri-business. Indeed, some refers to it as a "Farmgate Branding Revolution" (FBR). The paramount role that FBR play now has been accompanied by major shifts in the field of agri-business. Brands in FBR are not seen to be much more on names or logos. FBR are referred as natural product promotion and raced with emotion. For example, promotion and marketing of hill banana either from Himalayas (or) Thandigudi in Tamil Nadu (or) marketing of fresh fish from seabed and promotion of Basmati rice at farmgate as branded product: a means to an end, not an end in itself.

Because brands are largely perceptions, even though corporate bodies today increasingly count brand strength as a key corporate strategy, it makes sense to argue that brands are not exclusively owned by organizations. They are co-owned by the producers and consumers / organizations. Operations strategy for branding in agri-business is no longer predominantly measured by how many consumers recognize or are aware of brands and their logos or slogans but by now strongly consumers feel connected to the products from nature.

Conclusion

The dominant strategic management approaches with special reference to agri-business are discussed in this chapter. Technology centered approaches in business have been emerged as an organisational action to view appropriate strategic management. The conceptual building blocks of the organisation can be traced with the application of appropriate science and technology interpretive paradigm to techno-strategic management. Techno-strategy in an organisation is viewed as the combination of handful and central ideas concerned with agri-business firm performance. Leadership is crucial in achieving techno-strategic flexibility. An effective leader of the future agri-business sector will be able to develop techno-strategic vision that can motivate and inspire the managers and employees, to develop a true empowerment to build the learning organisation that can manage the knowledge to enable continous creativity for the success of the business.

REFERENCE

1. Ackermann, F., Eden, C and Brown, I. (2005). The Practice of Making Strategy. Response Books, New Delhi.
2. Allio, J. R, (1994). The Practical Stratigist. Gopsons Papers Private Limited, Noida.
3. Harrison, M. 1993. Operations Management Strategy. Financial Times. Pitman Publishing: London.

4. Heracleous, L. (2003). Strategy and Organization. Cambridge University Press, Cambridge.
5. Lowson, R.H., "Customised Operations Strategies, International Journal of Retal. Vo. 11, No. 2, pp. 201-224.
6. Porter, M.E., 1996. "What is strategy?" Harward Business Pesource, Nov. Dec., pp. 61-81.

3

Features of Future Agri-Business in India: Commodity Parks and LEAN Management Dimensions

The first part of this section is to explain the term Features of Agri-business approaches for establishing a joint business venture between the corporate and the farming community, as a potential source of information. The second purpose is to review critically the concept of "LEAN" management and its application in agri-business for Cost Minimization and Profit Maximization (CM&PM). Indian agriculture, agri-business and agri-export have its own inherent strengths. The burgeoning market opportunities in the wake of liberalization of the economy since 1991 have encouraged the growth of the Food Processing Industries (FPI). FPI ranks fifth in size in the country and employs 1.6 million workers, which constitutes 19 percent of the country's industrial labour force. It accounts for 14 percent of the total industrial output with only 5.5 percent of total industrial investment and contributes 18% to the GDP. The turnover of this industry is estimated to be US$ 36 billion.

There are over 27,500 units, large and small, operating in the food-processing sector. According to a study made by the Confederation of Indian Industry (CII) and the management consultants, Mckinsey and Co., India can be the *"worlds largest food factory"*. Food processing activity is poised for rapid expansion. The green revolution in food grains, the white in milk, the yellow in oil, the rainbow in horticulture and the blue revolution in fish and other marine foods have laid the foundation for rapid expansion of the FPI. At the same time, now we have an equal opportunity to tap the global markets to emerge as winner in agri-export focussed value-chain from the farm to the consumer's plate by establishing commodity parks viz., tea park, coffee park, spices park, coconut park etc.

Government Initiatives

The Government of India has established a full-fledged ministry, especially for the food processing industries along with export promotion councils for agri-processed products. Exclusive commodity boards have been established for the promotion of agri-commodity. A good number of industry associations are also activated in the country to represent the requirements of the industry. Special schemes have also been advised for 100 percent export oriented units located in the export processing zones enabling duty free import of capital goods and raw materials and other inputs, full convertibility of foreign exchange earnings at market rate, tax holiday for 5 years and the facility for selling 50 percent in the domestic tariff area. The concept of FPI is a boom for entrepreneurs, farmers, corporate units, self-help groups (SHGs) as they get a better platform for their business and appropriate channel to market their products with regulated duty as per government norms. FPI is likely to be another milestone in the national & industrialization vision.

Agri-resources of the Nation

Agriculture has been growing at 3.3% compared to industry's 7.5% an year. India stands second in fruit production after Brazil and also second in vegetable production after China. Thirty three million tonnes of fruits and 70 million tonnes of vegetables are produced in India with a global market share of 11% and 17.5% respectively. The fruits and vegetables are processed to an extent of 1 to 2% in India, compared to 70 to 80% by the developed countries. The

Government of India is offering many incentives for the food processing industries treating it as a thrust area. Horticultural crops in India are currently grown in 12 million hectares, which represents 7 percent of India's total cropped area. Annual horticultural production is estimated at 100 million metric tonnes, which are over 18% of India's gross agricultural output.

India's share of world trade in this sector is only around one percent. India's major exports are fruit pulps, pickles, chutneys, canned fruits and vegetables, concentrated pulps and juices, dehydrated vegetables and frozen fruits and vegetables. This sector has attracted a total investment of US$ 1954.2 million since the initiation of the liberalization process, including foreign investment of US$ 219.7 million. Export of fruit, vegetable seeds and other products (in quantity) to the United States has grown up considerably in 2002-03. The details are given below:

Agricultural Products	*2000-01 (Quantity in MTs)*	*2001-02 (Quantity in MTs)*	*2002-03 (Quantity in MTs)*
Floriculture	7336.16	5110.35	9663.466
Fruits and Vegetable Seeds	191.224	381.534	801.375
Fresh Onions	180	169.982	1715.271
Other Fresh Vegetables	10408.726	18639.378	22240.8
Milled Products	144.997	289.233	1581.26
Fresh Mangoes	716.433	730.689	467.912
Fresh Grapes	47.341	30.602	17.628
Other Fresh Fruits	858.232	901.13	1391.636
Dried and Preserved Vegetables	16283.34	20999.399	25150.63
Mango Pulp	2591.01	2829.821	3028.384
Pickles and Chutneys	6296.15	5081.608	9596.196
Other Processed Fruits and Vegetables	11477.883	8528.847	12544.136
Animal Casing	—	50.000	6524.519
Dairy Product	116.028	753.732	2210.248

Source: Indian Food Exports to US, Agri Business & Food Industry, Pp. 22-24, July 2004-APEDA.

It is this chain of sequences that needs to be implemented through integration of the entrepreneurs who plays a pivotal role in processing and the telescoping effect of the conventional and traditional practices synergising into the modern food processing concept that can extend the shelf-life and add value to the agri material and help further utilization of byproducts.

Growth Potential

The food processing industry will be one of the hinges of the Indian economy in the next century. India is among the leading producers of sugar, tea, coffee, milk, fruits and vegetables. Agricultural production and food processing account for 30 percent of India's GDP and employ more than 70 percent of its workforce.

This anomaly can be corrected by channeling more investment towards the farm sector and related agri-based industries. The need is to adopt an integrated approach to agriculture, procurement, Supply Chain Management (SCM) and food processing. The study entitled *"Food and Agriculture Integrated Development Action (FAIDA)"* suggests that, over the next 10 years, agriculture and food processing will need an investment of about Rs. 1,40,000 crores. This huge investment will be attracted by market opportunities but will materialize only with a conducive policy framework to promote Business Partnership in Agriculture (BPA) between small scale and corporate agriculture within the dimensions of post WTO.

India, in the world indicates that there is lot of scope of developing agri-based industries. The agri-based industry is perceived as high-risk industry and therefore, the entrepreneurs are not coming forward to establish such type of industries. The perceived risks are:

- It is seasonal industry

- It has to depend upon natural functioning and vagaries of nature
- The raw material is perishable and shelf life of finished product is limited
- Inconvenient location of industry
- Non-availability of trained managers and operators
- Lack of incentives from the government.

Therefore, the Ministry of Commerce and Industries and its allied ministries undertaken a number of FPI based development programmes like creation of Food Parks (FPs), Agri Export Zones (AEZs) and Agri-Business Centers (ABCs) for production, processing, value addition, storage, market, inviting officials and business delegation from abroad, arranging buyers-sellers meet, etc for the sustainability of FPI in India. It also playing a pivotal role in ensuring a bounteous future for the Indian agriculture industry. Already companies like HLL, TATA, Pepsi, Coca Cola, FME Asia Pacific, BGP International along with farmers, entrepreneur and individual have initiated their work on business partnership in agriculture (BPA) programme with help of FP, AEZ and ABC. A host of other agri-based companies from the US, Europe, Germany, Hong Kong, Belgium and Far East are coming in regularly to join in the events. The following paragraph illustrates the structure and functional aspects of FPI such as FP, AEZ & ABC and its benefits to entrepreneurs.

Food Parks (FPs)

The concept of Food Park in India was introduced with the objective to encourage agripreneurs from the private sector to set up small units for processing of all agri-products, a food park is an endeavor to eventually prevent wastage of agri commodities.

The skepticism around food parks notwithstanding, the Ministry of Food Processing Industries (MFPI) plans to propose an increase in the quantum of assistance given to food parks in the Tenth Five Year Plan. The quantum of the existing assistance and plans are to extend more infrastructures services such as power, water, packaging and incubator facilities. State FPI has added to the list of common infrastructural facilities that would be available to the parks. In addition to the laboratory, effluent treatment, incubator facilities and storage facilities that are made available at the parks. Plans are also a foot to synergise the parks along with the APEDA-promoted Agri-Export Zones (AEZs).

A market is also being developed to facilitate farmers to sell their fruits and vegetables to the processing units. Moreover, a common center is being constructed for the promotion of products. For example, Punjab Food Park (PFP) is extensively promoting the cultivation of certain exotic vegetables like excalibar onions, bird's eye chilli, sweet corn, snap peas, cherry tomato, yellow/red capsicum, etc. PFP promoted jointly with NRI's & MNCs to bring a horticultural revolution in Punjab by breaking the ancient wheat-paddy cycle. The government will provide support to both the suppliers and buyers by giving out incentives and subsidies. The benefit of which will ultimately reach the buyers by way of providing them quality goods at highly competitive price.

Agri – Export Zones (AEZs)

In line with a policy initiated by the Indian government in 2001, 48 Agri Export Zones have been set up in the country, covering 19 states. The AEZs boost agri exports by effecting end-to-end integration of the production, processing and marketing activities through partnership among different agencies and convergence of their resources, technologies and services. Investments to the tune of Rs. 4.75 billion have already been made in these AEZs and exports worth of Rs. 3.8 billion have taken place. One of the initiatives taken by the Government of India is to boost exports through introduction of AEZs in the Exim Policy announced for 2002-07 for an end-to-end development for export of specific products from a geographically contiguous area that have their own competitive advantage. In an AEZ, there is no physical demarcation of boundaries and there is no export obligation for the processing units established in the zone. AEZ provides a completely focused approach to agri-export, thus enabling a quicker resolution of these issues. The steps for the creation of FPI zone and its aims are illustrated in *Figure. 1.* Strategies on how to invest, install and operate processing modular units at FP and AEZ can be obtained from www.fao.org/docrep/V5030E/V5030E0v.htm.

The Government is following a two pronged strategy to promote and boost exports of agricultural and allied products from the country. It is also trying to create domestic awareness and raise the question of safety, quality and productivity concerns through a coordinated multi-pronged approach. This includes promoting Good Agricultural Practice (GAP), Good Manufacturing Practices (GMP), Hazard Analysis Critical Control Point (HACCP) though export promotional bodies such as Export Inspection Council of India which initiates an awareness, education and training on Quality and Safety Management, upgrading systems to meet international requirements.

Agri- Business Centers (ABCs)

Agri-Business Center (ABC) concept is primarily based on modern concepts of relationship marketing and networking. It would therefore be pertinent to note that it is not just the investment and physical facilities that can ensure the success. On the other hand a "SMART AGRI-PRENEUR" even without any investment of his own can also make a beginning. However, few basic resource mobilization and physical facilities can reduce the problems in initial phase and would also simultaneously improve the revenue generation right in the beginning of ABC.

A potential agripreneur could preferably be with an agriculture background (both qualification and experience) must have location-specific intentions to setup ABC. The ABCs have been conceptualized to generate revenues in the initial phase itself. The operational and resource mobilization requirements for ABC are available in www.morakango.com/agri_business.html.

In order to ensure the integrated business partnership in agriculture between FPI and small-scale agri-sector, a new model of farm business and processing should be advocated in the near future. The concept of FP, AEZ, ABC would orient the activities of post-harvest management & marketing in agri-business chain. On the other hand, a model to integrate pre-harvest processing in agriculture is required to sustain industry, as a whole. A leading method is that of family farming, corporate farming, farming by SHG, etc., would enter into contract with FPI. The recent tenth five year plan on agri-policy of the government also champion's the small scale farmers' participation in FPI to promote agri-business partnership between small scale and corporate agriculture. Such models are already in practice in the country. IIPM has reviewed such cases in Tamil Nadu, Andhra Pradesh, Karnataka including the performance of contract farming undertaken by HLL, Pepsi and Nijjer.

Operational Dimensions of Food Processing Industries (FPI)

An operational dimension is the management aspect of FPI's productive resources or its production system, which converts input into FPI's appropriate product and services. It is important to understand what the best managed FPI companies in the world are doing relative to the competitors. We call such FPI, as a world class processing industry. Focussing on their approach will give an insight into the most of advanced approaches to structure, layout, work design, processing technique, quality and operational system. It is mandatory to use operational management concept in FP, AEZ, ABC such as TQM, ISO, HACCP, OHSAS, SA 18001, LEAN, Six Sigma, SCM, TPM, CRM, ERP, etc., to allow FPI a thorough integration of latest thinking about important issue that FPI entrepreneurs face today. World-class agri-business partnership programmes excel in developing FPI business and operations capturing global market.

The corporate bodies are in a position to achieve commercial agricultural objectives better than individual entrepreneurs, they could be encouraged to promote small scale agri-sector as a commercial proportion. IIPM under the sponsorship of the Division of Agriculture Extension of the Indian Council of Agricultural Research (ICAR) had taken-up a project assignment to develop a Sustainable Agri-business Model (SAM) for the livelihood of small scale mixed farming agripreneurs in coffee, coconut and chilli sector.

Implications

FPI schemes are formulated by Ministry of Commerce and Industries and aimed at pronding facilities and incentives for setting up of FPI in all parts of the country. However, the extension service to FPI network is limited to the sector from Ministry of Agriculture, ICAR, National Institute, etc. In order to facilitate FPI promotion, the extension network of the country (e.g., KVK) should be provided a capacity building exercise on extension led agri-business partnership programme to meet the demands from field operations to the customer, to sustain FPI in the country. To assure coherence and efficiency

Fig. 1. Steps for the Creation of FPI Zones and its Functions

<table>
<tr><th><u>Food Parks (FPs)</u></th><th><u>Agri Export Zone's (AEZs)</u></th><th><u>Agri Business Centers (ABCs)</u></th></tr>
<tr><td>Development of area-specific agri food parks by Ministry of Food Processing Industries for the predominant Produce of the area
↓
Call for project proposal sent by entrepreneurs, central/state government organization, education and training institutions, NGOs, cooperaties, etc
↓
Selection of food park promoter based on the fulfillment of specified criteria
↓
Setting-up of infrastructure facilities and small/medium processing unitts
↓
Call to the small/medium entrepreneurs for developing small units inside the Food Park
↓
Selection of small/medium entrepreneurs for developing small units.</td><td>Feasibility report to Central Government by State through APEDA
↓
Preliminary evaluation and consideration of interdepartmental steering committee
↓
If approved, Memorandum of Understanding between APEDA and State Government
↓
Advertisement by the State Government to solicit private sector investment
↓
Private sector entrepreneurs will be selected
↓
Private Sector Export zone with the governemnt and agencies providing Committed support</td><td>Enrollment prospective agri preneur
↓
Selection of agri-preneur based on location, qualification, aptitude and investment capacity
↓
Training and capacity building of agri-preneur
↓
Resource mobilization, linkages and tie-ups for agri-business center
↓
Procurement and marketing of farm produce.</td></tr>
</table>

Food Park	*Agri Export Zone*	*Agri Business Center*
Promoted by Ministry of Food Processing Industries Encourage corporate for establishing food park with common facilities like cold storage, warehouse, etc. To encourage entrepreneur to set up small units for processing Minimum areas of 30 acres and 20 units in small and medium scale Grant-in-aid to the project to the extent of 25-33% 20 – 25% of losses can be minimized	Promoted by Commerce Ministry through APEDA Identification of an agricultural produce which could be developed for exports through cluster approach Zone could be a block/group of blocks or a district / group of districts There has to be close relationship between the central government, state government, farmer, processor, and their exporter for the success of an AEZ.	Promoted by Ministry of Agriculture Basically, relationship marketing and networking of agri-products Backward linkage with the farmers Some physical facilities for value addition, processing, packaging and storage

of FPI, the farming community should form and establish Self- Help Groups (SHGs) based on the availability of specialty products of the region. The farming community led institutions should develop partnership with FPI, MNC, family farm units and entrepreneurs to bridge the linkage between production and marketing sector in order for agri-business to remain both competitive and profitable.

As indicated earlier, the following section provides an insight on the evolution and emergence of the LEAN Management in Agribusiness (LEMA) and shared conclusions about the future of LEMA from the perspective of academic, R&D and practitioners. Management based on LEAN production has enabled enterprises to attain very high levels of efficiency, competitiveness and cost minimization in production system. This section proposes a methodology for implementation of LEAN management in an agribusiness sector for management measures aimed at moving from a conventional approach to one of LEAN to determine the level of improvement to be attained.

Concept of "LEAN to Manage" is a workable combination of philosophy and procedure, a very real way of identifying and shaping the development of potential opportunities in agribusiness viz., quality, safety and Cost Minimization & Profit Maximization (CM&PM) attainability. Looking at the concept at the whole system of agribusiness sector might first seem overwhelming, but once we understand the pieces of LEAN, the puzzle will fit together perfectly and the system will help us look at decision making in an entirely new way. LEAN method reflects more as a scientific management than an arts approach, because only with the power of a scientific approach can a firm reliably predict future product requirements beyond the customer's knowledge with the understanding needed to cope with the changing technological and market environment. Thus, in a logical and practical way, LEAN spans and provides necessary tools from policy plans to tactical action involving an innovation needed to implement long-range objectives. The books & papers on LEAN management written by different authors focus on technical methods and offer a picture of what a LEAN system should look like. It also provides snapshots of before and after effects of LEAN inter-related system. This is the first paper to provide techno-managerial descriptions of successful solutions for agribusiness performance improvements.

What is LEAN?

LEAN production, LEAN manufacturing and LEAN management is termed as "LEAN" because it used less of every resources compared with mass production (i.e.), half the human effort in field & factory; half the manufacturing space, half the investment in tools and half the engineering hours (cycle time of manufacturing) to make value added in agribusiness products. Also, it requires keeping far less than half the needed inventory on site, results in many fewer defects, and produces a greater and ever growing variety of products.

LEAN based procedure, set its rights explicitly on perfection, continuously declining costs, zero defects, zero inventories and endless product variety.

According to Norman Bodek (1996), LEAN management is about operating the most efficient and effective organization possible, with least cost and zero waste. It is an approach that requires companies to make smart use of their resources i.e., technology, and equipment and above all, the knowledge and skills of their people. LEAN means no fat -no waste, but adopts the zero-waste.

Evolution of LEAN

U.S. manufacturers have always searched for efficiency

strategies that help reduce costs, improve output, establish competitive position, and increase market share. Early process oriented, mass production manufacturing methods common before World War II shifted afterwards to the results-oriented, output-focused, production systems that control most of today's manufacturing businesses.

Japanese manufacturers, re-building after the Second World War were faced with declining human, material, and financial resources. The problems they faced in manufacturing were vastly different from their Western counterparts. These circumstances led to the development of new, lower cost and manufacturing practices. Ohno, and Shingeo Shingo of TQM guru's developed a disciplined, process-focused production system now known as the "Toyota Production System", or "LEAN production." The objective of this system was to minimize the consumption of resources that added no value to a product.

The "LEAN manufacturing" concept was popularized in American factories in large part by the Massachusetts Institute of Technology study of the movement from mass production toward production as described in The Machine That Changed the World, (Womack, Jones & Roos, 1990), which discussed the significant performance gap between Western and Japanese automotive industries. It described the important elements accounting for superior performance as LEAN production. The term "LEAN" was used because Japanese business methods used less human effort, capital investment, floor space, materials, and time in all aspects of operations. The resulting competition among U.S. and Japanese automakers over the last 25 years has lead to the adoption of these principles within all U.S. manufacturing businesses. (MAMTC, 2002).

The aim of LEAN Manufacturing is the elimination of waste in every area of production including customer relations, product design, supplier networks, and factory management. Its goal is to incorporate less human effort, less inventory, less time to develop products, and less pace to become highly responsive to customer demand while producing top quality products in the most efficient and economical manner possible. Essentially, a "waste" is anything that the customer is not willing to pay for within a LEAN manufacturing system.

Why LEAN?

For years manufacturers have created products in anticipation of having a market for them. Operations have traditionally been driven by sales forecasts and firms tended to stockpile inventories in case they were needed. A key difference in LEAN Manufacturing, is that it is based on the concept that production can and should be driven by real customer demand. Instead of producing what you hope to sell, LEAN Manufacturing can produce what your customer wants with shorter lead times. Instead of pushing product to market, it's pulled there through a system that's set up to quickly respond to customer demand.

LEAN organizations are capable of producing high-quality products economically in lower volumes and bringing them to market faster than mass producers. A LEAN organization can make twice as much product with twice the quality and half the time and space, at half the cost, with a fraction of the normal work-in-process inventory. LEAN management is about operating the most efficient and effective organization possible, with the least cost and zero waste.

LEAN Production Requires LEAN Management

The majority of companies still clinging to mass production methods due to several reasons. First, the setup of a LEAN production system requires assistance and time. A Company that is not thinking in the direction of long-term growth will not have the patience to persevere until the new system is firmly in place. Second, the process of transforming a company from mass to LEAN requires many physical procedural changes, often accompanied by major upheavals in company structure and processes. A Company that doesn't have the courage will not feel a great compulsion to turn itself inside out and stick through the uncomfortable chaos known as change. Third, the metamorphosis into leanness undergone by a mass production company must be desired, decided upon, and – most important – driven by its leader. If the CEO, president, or owners are unaware of or uncommitted to LEAN management, LEAN production is not likely to happen (Jackson, 1996).

LEAN production techniques have contributed to a spectacular improvement in efficiency, speed of response and flexibility in production at many industrial enterprises, through *process-based* management, elimination of *waste* and the highly *flexible* implementation of these processes. LEAN management has allowed these enterprises to offer a *highly diversified range of products,* at the *lowest cost,* with high levels of *productivity, speed* of delivery, *minimum* stock levels and optimum *quality.*

LEAN Management Beyond Conventional Economic Aspects of Production

According to Arbos, 2002, the LEAN management makes it possible to obtain a product that is adapted to actual demand using the minimum amount of resources and therefore minimizing the cost, with the appropriate quality and very high speed of response. Since the production system must produce in accordance with demand, it cannot resort to economies of scale by dealing in large batches, as in the case of conventional management systems.

In order to attune production to demand and obtain high performance without recourse to economies of scale, LEAN management suggests two main inherent characteristics: Firstly, it operates with the least possible number of activities, thereby obtaining economies that are not economies of scale but rather of resources; for this purpose, all activities that do not add value, called wasteful, must be eliminated, including inappropriate processes, unnecessary carriage, unnecessary movement, stocks of all kinds which would result in increased costs, as well as quality defects and all manner of delays and times, which would be detrimental as regards the quality and response. Furthermore, production that is not attuned to demand is also wasteful (excess production), and avoiding this waste will result in a product or service that is faster, more appropriate and less costly.

The second aspect is covered by the characteristic of LEAN management, i.e., flexibility, which means that the system must be attuned at all times to the type and volume of production required by demand.

Understanding Concept of Agribusiness & Integrating LEAN

New economy is rapidly becoming a major force in world industry, where traditional approaches to agricultural change have been dominated by assumptions privileging stability, sustainability and serviceability. As a result, agricultural change has been verified and treated as exceptional (e.g., sustainable agriculture) rather than nature (agriculture by nature, it is sustainable and its sustainability depends on the interventions and usage of external influence).

The central issue we address is what is agribusiness and how we integrate the concept of LEAN? The importance of agribusiness is reflected throughout the world because agribusiness is the single most important contributor to the world's economy (Buston, 1998). Agribusiness worldwide represents approximately one-fourth of the total world economic production and provides employment for nearly half the population on the earth.

According to John David and Ray Goldberg, the term agribusiness is defined as the sum total of all operations involved in the manufacture and distribution of farm supplies; production operations on the farm; and the storage, processing, and distribution of the resulting farm commodities and items. A similar definition of agribusiness describes it as any profit-motivated enterprise that involves providing agricultural supplies and/or the processing, marketing, transporting, and distributing of agricultural materials and consumer products. Ewell Roy defines agribusiness as the coordinating science of supplying agricultural production inputs and subsequently producing, processing and distributing food and fibre.

Some exclude "farming" or the "production" of food and fiber from the definition of agribusiness. However, we would be mistaken to think that farming is not a business. A production agriculturist must make decisions, develop plans, and solve problems, all which require business-related skills. A typical farmer manages taxes, repair and replacement of equipment, fertilizers, wages, fuel, electricity, and many other items. Therefore, production agriculturists must be financial and business managers or they will fail. Production agriculture is indeed a business, that is the business of agriculture.

India is an agro based country with fruits and vegetables production exceeding 136 million tons, rice production exceeding 85 million tones, milk production exceeding 82 million tons and other production such as eggs, inland fish and spices, Indian stands in very high order. However, the post harvest losses is over 25%. (Prakash, 2002). The wastage cost of fruits and vegetables is Rs.23,000 crores per year (Anonymous, 2002). India is also a potential world player (second largest producer of food crop in the world in 2001).

Small farm enterprises produce good quality fruit and vegetables, but post harvest wastage in the distribution stage of the supply chain mishandled the produce due to improper storage facilities, improper means of distribution and seasonal overproduction adversely affect the marketability of the produce. (Dheeraj Singh and Hemant Mahure 2002).

The fundamental driver behind eliminating waste is *"true efficiency"*, a matter of doing work using the best method known, waste removal and management. The focus on waste (or Muda in Japanese) was pioneered by Taiichi Ohno. He demonstrated seven fundamental form of waste which are summarized below:

Overproduction – the making of too much, too early or just in case.

Waiting – where materials or information are waiting to produce to the next process. They are not moving or having value added

Transporting – where materials (or information) are being transported into, out of or around the factory. Transport cannot be fully eliminated, but the aim is to minimize it.

Inappropriate processing – using machinery or equipment which is inappropriate in terms of 'capacity' to perform an operation.

Unnecessary inventory – which ties up capital and space and prevents identification of problems

Defects – defined in terms of product defects, rework defects, scrap defects or service defects.

Unnecessary motion – the ergonomics of the work place.

Source: Shingo, 1989.

The evolution from the traditional management to the LEAN production that are illustrated in *Table 1* demands a group of actions, which aims at the development of Agribusiness Operations Management (AOM) strategies to minimize waste & post harvest loss. The principles of 7 waste management illustrated in Table 1 for agribusiness allow maximum elimination of waste and introduction of the required degree of flexibility in lean based production system. The rationale underlying the collection and use of LEAN tools is to help agribusiness to identify waste and to find out an appropriate route to removal, or at least reduction, of post harvest waste. The systematic attack on waste is also a systematic assault on the factors underlying for quality and fundamental management problems. *Table 2* shows an assessment on agribusiness market and customer demand based on cost/product value matrix to pouositige market segment. Priority markets, in which the customer focus and lean tools play a major role on agribusiness profitability and cost minimization.

The matrix also highlights high and low cost requirements and suggests possible development priorities in lean production. For example, customer C, is fairly strong in need of quality, safety and value added agri-products with optimum cost/unit value. The bottom-line of customers' requirement from the matrix are cost, as the focus of the value stream. In order to go lean to minimize cost, it is necessary to understand customer aspirations and what they value. In summary, matrix analysis of customizing the value stream shows that the true power of LEAN system is that to minimize the cost and it highlights that *"the more waste removed in agribusiness,* the more cost saved to delight customer and surprise the competitors". With the diagnostic criteria of matrix, an agribusiness company competes its profitability, product and market analysis as well as sharpens management's understanding of the company's future ability.

Conclusion

LEAN management system promotes LEAN production by providing a framework for integrating cost minimization and profit maximization through waste management in the direction appropriate to the sustainability of agribusiness.

TABLE 1

Operational Aspects of Lean

7 Lean Concepts to Manage Agribusiness Flow	5 Best Agribusiness Operations Management (AOM) for Maximization of Profit				
	Linear Flow	Customized Product Size	Technological Operations	Human Potential	Quality Maintenance
JIT – to avoid *over production*	Seasonal production & delivery; excess for value addition	Small and attuned to market demand	Planned harvest and rapid processing	Good skill in processing to packaging	Food engineering equipment should meet zero breakdown operations
First the Right Time and the Best Everytime Processing	Fewer processing steps for efficiency	Customized packing for ease of use	Automation from cleaning of product to customizing	Knowledge on process layout and cycle time	Sustainable process and equipment maintenance & setup time reduction
Zero Inventory With Best SCM	Operations with no accumulation fresh products	Batch and seasonal work cycle	Integrated SCM for no stock operations	Knowledge on SCM & in/out put requirement	Right time ordering and receiving
Best Timing to Avoid Waiting	No waiting for raw materials at work	Utilization of production site as market yard	Regular flow: maximize machine efficiency than utilization of worker	Work efficiency and time management	No stocks: prevent stoppage

7 Lean Concepts to Manage Agribusiness Flow	5 Best Agribusiness Operations Management (AOM) for Maximization of Profit				
	Linear Flow	Customized Product Size	Technological Operations	Human Potential	Quality Maintenance
Value of Movement and Transport	Nearby and short distance movement between lines	One unit of product/batch	Appropriate transport facilities and process layout	Understanding the nature of product persistability, versatile and its momentum	Quality maintenance to prevent backlogs & breakdown management
Zero Defects	On-time-delivery with no defects	Well predicted and best quality products	Avoid microbial, chemical and physical based contamination	Personnel hygiene	Quality and maintenance assurance: 100%
Quality	Agro-climatic and specialty product resourcing and rapid delivery	Small and attuned to market demand	TQM; ISO 9000/14000; HACCP; Value addition; upto date innovations	Well trained, qualified and committed group	Quality and maintenance assurance through TPM, 5S & 6 Sigma

The objective of this paper is to illustrate a management measure aimed at moving from a conventional approach to one of lean production in agribusiness sector. Production and manufacturing firms are exploring different ways to remain profitable in today's globally competitive market. Customer focus and cost minimization have been acknowledged as an important factor in developing sustainable competitive advantage. With an increased emphasis, corrective implementation of seven commonly accepted wastes (lean tools) such as over production, waiting, transport, inappropriate processing, unnecessary inventory, unnecessary motion and defects are regarded as the most serious value systems to agribusiness settings.

The capability of LEAN management in agribusiness to minimize waste lies at the heart of creating LEAN organization through LEAN thinking, with each of the value stream members working to reduce wasteful activity from production to consumption cycle. The practicality of LEAN management system works to raise quality, productivity, flexibility, marketshare and it relatively minimize cost through waste management and capital investment.

Lastly, an appropriate framework on LEAN reflection requires a Delta Zero mindset, a willingness to rethink the results desired as well as the factors required to achieve CM and PM aspects of agribusiness. LEAN enterprise owe their success in part to maintaining zero waste free, but also because they expect the unexpected and meet each new challenge with moves unexpected by customers and competitors through the power of delta zero. The term delta zero refers to the union of 2 concepts; *delta,* the Greek letter symbolizing incremental change, and *zero,* the Arabic numeral symbolizing, void. Essentially, Delta Zero refers to the paradox or learning. All learning, personal as well as organizational, which takes place within a normal and accepted paradigm of agribusiness and commodity parks.

TABLE 2

Customizing Agribusiness Products to Minimize Cost & Maximize Profit

Market Trend and Demand to Maximize Profit / Product Manufacturing Strategy to Minimize Cost	Customer A	Customer B	Customer C	Domestic	Export
Quality	M (750)	H (1000)	H (1000)	M (750)	H (1000)
Safety Aspects of Product	M (750)	H (750)	H (1000)	M (1000)	H (1000)
Value-Added	L (500)	L (500)	H (1000)	M (750)	H (1000)
Cost	L (500)	L (500)	M (750)	L (500)	M (750)
Total Expected Cost	Rs. 2500	Rs. 2750	Rs. 3750	Rs. 3000	Rs. 3750
	Customer Requirements			Cost of Production (Rs.)	
	L = Limited Level			500	
	M = Medium Level			700	
	H = Higher Level			1000	

Source: Adopted from Kenichi and modified to suite the article

REFERENCES

1. Anonymous (2002). Prospects of Food Processing Industry in India. Http://www.techno-preneur.net/timesis/technology/sirtech nov02/food indus.html
2. Anonymous (2004). Co-operative models to Help Farmers. Times Agricultural Journal. Http://111.etagriculture.com/jan-feb2002/news10html.
3. Anonymous. (2002). Food Processing Industry. *Science Tech Entrepreneur*, Jan. p. 68.
4. Anonymous. (2002). Giving Manufacturers the Edge. *History of LEAN*, MAMTC.
5. Buston, L. (1998). Agriscience and Technology.
6. Dhanakumar, V.G. (1999). *TQM for Plantation Industry*. Anmol Publications, New Delhi.
7. Dhanakumar, V.G. (2001). *Lean Management: Conceptual Paper*. Working Paper Series, Division of Extension Management, IIPM, Bangalore.
8. Dhanakumar, V.G. and Narendran, K. (2002). Aromedic Plantation for Agribusiness. Under Review for *Indian Journal of Arecanut, spices and Medicinal Plants*.
9. Dhanakumar, V.G. (2002). Lean to Manage Agribusiness. *Journal of Management Perception*, July – December, pp. 47-56.
10. Dhanakumar, V.G. (2004). Safety Management for Fruits & Vegetables. *Journal of Agri Business & Food Industry*, Vol. 1., Issue 6, pp. 19-23.
11. Dhanakumar, V.G. (2004). Quality in Supply Chain Management: The Case of Fruits and Vegetables Chain. *Working paper series of IIPM*, Bangalore.
12. Dheeraj Singh and Hemant Mahure, (2002). Redesigning the supply chain for fresh fruit and vegetables. *Agriculture Today*, June. P.45.
13. Ewell P. Roy. (1980). Exploring Agribusiness. Danville, Ill.: Interstate Printers and Publishers
14. Jackson, L.T. (1996). *A Lean Management System*. Productivity Press, Portland, Oregon.
15. Lluis Cuatrecasas Arbos. (2002). Design of a Rapid Response and High Efficiency Service by Lean Production Principles: Methodology and Evaluation of Variability of Performance.

16. Http://www.morarkango.com/agribusiness.html
17. Http://www.fao.org/docrep/v5030e/v5030eov.html
18. http://modpi.nic.in/venturesetup/exportzones/exportzones.html
19. Http://www.midcindia.org/sectfocus/parks/sectorshow.php?sectorid=65&healine=0
20. Mansingh, L. (2003). Welcome Advances. *Times Agricultural Journal.* September – October. Pp. 12-13.
21. Money, K.S. (2004). India's Agri Exports: Opportunities & Challenges. *Agri Business & Food Industry.* Vol. 1. Issue 8, pp. 16-18.
22. Norman Bodek. (1996). What is Lean? *In Lean Management Systems,* Production Press. Portland, Oregon.
23. Prakash, V. (2002). Food Processing Industry – Prospects & Challenges. *Agro India.* May. P.20.
24. Shingo, S. (1989). *A Study of the Toyota Production System from an Industrial Engineering Viewpoint,* Cambridge, MA: Productivity Press.
25. Taylor, D and Brunt, D. (2001). *The Lean Approach.* Vikas Publishing House, New Delhi.
26. Womack, et al., (1990). *The Machine That Changed the World,* New York: Rawsa Associates.

4

World Class Business Management (WCBM)

Managing for Quality in global level is the theme addressed in this chapter with managerial responsibility. The term world class is enormously powerful words where it express a wealth of meaning and entirely new level of work ethos. The concept of World Class Business Management (WCBM) is defined by or related to efficiency, effectiveness, high quality, cost minimization & profit maximization (CM&PM), built in quality and customer delight. WCBM concepts such as TQM.... etc excel in developing agri-business operations for capturing a higher percentage of global markets. These concepts facilitate us an insight into the most advanced approach to structuring, analyzing and managing production and operations systems. World-class agri-business companies, large or small, are predisposed to have effective methods of tact because they have exceptional long-range strategic business planning systems in place. The long term strategic plan for WCM in agri-business represents the best thinking and analysis about a competitive success in the global economy. Figure 1 illustrates the different types of WCBM concepts to be informational in character. This section goes in brief, regarding the WCBM concepts and its application in agri-business sector.

I. TOTAL QUALITY MANAGEMENT

Total Quality Management, (TQM), can be defined as the process of integration of all activities, functions and processes within an organisation in order to achieve continuous

FEATURES OF WORLD CLASS BUSINESS MANAGEMENT

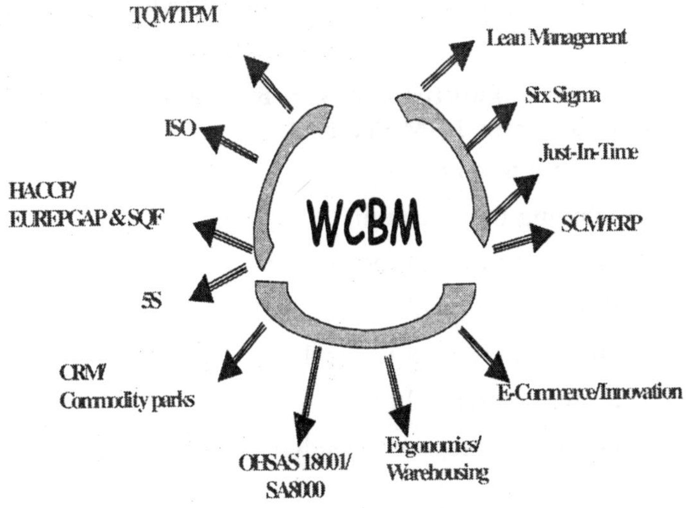

Fig. 1. Pictorial System of World Class Business Management Concepts

improvement in cost, quality, function and delivery of goods and services for customer delight'. Goal of TQM is customer delight, by means of continuous improvement. TQM occurs when as entire organizational culture becomes focused on quality and customer delight through an integrated system of processes, tools, techniques and training. The broad means of TQM are:

TOTAL: All Human Beings/ Resources

QUALITY: Consistency / Improvement (Consistency is inbuilt thing in Quality)

MANAGEMENT: Systems, Procedure, Policy, Practice, Statement, Etc.,

TQM a total organizational approach for meeting and exceeding customer expectations, involving all 'HR' to continuously improve the organisations' product, processes and services."

World of Work : Futuristic in Agri-Business in a Changing Scenario TQM Perspective

1. Control to empower
2. Training to education
3. From activities to result
4. Proactive to productive
5. From supervision to coaching
6. From hierarchical to flat
7. From storekeepers to leaders

TQM Tools

1. Policy Formulation
2. Error Deduction Vs. Prevention Strategy through Kaizen
3. Zero Defect (Quality is 100%)
4. Quality Circle at Grassroots Level: HD-TQM perspective, for Decision Making.
5. Quality Function Deployment (QFD)
6. Above Customer Expectations (ACE)

World class companies have stopped depending on inspection to catch defects; rather they are concentrating every organizational effort on doing everything right, the first time. They are striving to find and fix their quality problems, not to have inspection programs aimed at catching defects while sloppy production methods continue. And world class companies employ JIT manufacturing, product standardization, automated equipment, and preventive maintenance not just to reduce costs but also for their impact on quality and customer service.

World class companies are committing tremendous resources to put in place total quality management (TQM) programs aimed at continuous quality improvement. Birla group obtained an ISO certification, MTR and Real Good chicken have got HACCP certification. Total Quality Management (TQM) programs often includes these elements:

- Top management commitment and involvement
- Customer involvement
- Design products for quality
- Design production processes for quality
- Control production processes for quality
- Develop supplier partnership
- Customer service, distribution and installation
- Build teams of empowered workers
- Benchmarking and continuous improvement

2. TOTAL PRODUCTIVE MAINTENANCE (TPM)

The objective of TPM is much wider than just minimizing equipment lifespan. (Lifespan one means the time until the equipment gets obsolete.)

TPM Includes

1. Optimizing equipment effectiveness by elimination of all types of breakdown or failures, speed losses, defects and other wastes in operation.
2. Autonomous Maintenance by operators, which means the people who operate the machine, will look after

their machines by themselves. This would mean training and involvement of the operators. The idea is that the operating people would get to know their equipment even better so that they will be able to contribute not only in maintenance of the preventive and breakdown kind but also in the prevention of maintenance itself through their suggestions for improved designs of machines, processes, systems, materials and products.

3. Company wide involvement of all employees through small group activities which would support the above. Such participative management would enhance creative thinking and cross flow of information. Continuous improvement comes through such participative processes.

3. INTERNATIONAL ORGANISATION FOR STANDARDISATION (ISO)

Quality is clearly defined in ISO by its end results; the satisfaction of stated and implied needs. Quality management, the heart of business management today, consists of a customer-driven policy deployed throughout the activities of a company. The quality system provides a fundamental means to implement quality management. It links together the organization, the quality policy, people's responsibilities, the procedures, and the processes. Finally, total quality management is a management approach centered on quality and aiming at a company's long-term prosperity through customer and stakeholder delight as well as on the best results for the organization and society.

3.1. Introduction to ISO 9000 : 2000 (Quality Management System- QMS)

ISO standards address only the system that operates in the company and does not directly assess the quality of the product itself. ISO 9000 is often used to the entire family of ISO 9000 standards.

Standards of ISO 9000 : 2000

(A) ISO 9001 = Quality Management Systems = Requirements

(B) ISO 9004 = Quality Management Systems = Guidelines for Performance Improvements

(C) ISO 9000 = QMS = Fundamentals & Vocabulary (Definitions of Terms)

In View of Revision in ISO

- ISO 9002 & ISO 9003 of earlier version no longer exist, having been incorporated into ISO 9001 : 2000
- The benefit of ISO 9000: 2000 should bring through the TQM framework. Therefore, it is called *"Process Approach Quality Management (PAQM)" system.*

3.2 ISO :14000 (Environmental Management System–EMS)

Organizations concern to achieve and demonstrate sound environmental performance, impacts of environmental loss can tarnish reputable firms and costs associated with legal liabilities can be endless. ISO 14000 series of standards specify an internationally recognized system of environmental management system, which are illustrated below.

STANDARDS OF ISO 14000

ISO 14001	*Environmental Management Systems (Specification with guidance for use).*
ISO 14004	EMS – Guidelines on principles, systems and supporting techniques.
ISO 14010 ISO 14011 ISO 14012 1SO 14014 ISO 14015	Environmental Management Systems – Auditing
ISO 14031	*Environmental Performance Evaluation*
ISO 14020 ISO 14021 ISO 14022 ISO 14024	Environment labelling
ISO 14040 ISO 14041 ISO 14042 ISO 14043	Environment Life cycle assessment
ISO 14050	*Environment aspects in product standard guide.*

DIFFERENCE BETWEEN ISO-9001 & ISO-9004

Sl. No.	ISO-9001	ISO-9004
1.	Customer Requirement	Guidelines, fundamentals & vocabulary
2.	Ensure customer Satisfaction (i.e.,) product (or) service quality	Gives broad guidance on all aspects QMS
3.	Checklist for the statutory requirements	Technical manual

4. HAZARD ANALYSIS CRITICAL CONTROL POINT (HACCP)

The Concept

HACCP is an abbreviation for Hazard Analysis and

Critical Control Point. It is the most effective management system of maximizing product safety & quality and cost effective system. It targets system to critical areas of processing and reducing the risk of manufacturing and selling unsafe products. Critical control points are the steps in manufacture and value addition where control is essential to guarantee that potential hazards do not become manifest as actual hazards. A CCP is a location, a practice, a procedure or a process, which, if not controlled, could result in an unacceptable safety risk in commodity trade.

History and Development of HACCP

The HACCP system for managing food qualsafe concerns grew from two major developments. The first breakthrough was associated with W.E.Deming, whose theories of quality management are widely regarded as a major factor in turning around the quality of Japanese products in the 1950s. Dr. Deming and others developed total quality management (TQM) systems, which emphasized a total systems (pre & post harvest) approach to manufacturing that could improve the quality while lowering the costs "(Dhanakumar, 1999)".

The second major breakthrough was the development of the HACCP concept itself. The HACCP concept was pioneered in the 1960s by the Pillsbury Company, the United States Army and the United States National Aeronautics and Space Administration (NASA) as a collaborative development for the production of safe foods for the United States space programme. NASA wanted a "zero defects" programme to guarantee the safety of the foods that astronauts would consume in space. Pillsbury therefore introduced and adopted HACCP as the system that could provide the greatest safety while reducing dependence on end-product inspection and testing.

Principles of the HACCP System

The HACCP system consists of the following seven

principles, which outline how to establish, implement and maintain a HACCP plan for the operation in spice sector.

Principle 1

Conduct a hazard analysis. Prepare a list of steps in the process where significant hazards occur and describe the preventative measures.

Principle 2

Determine the Critical Control Points (CCPs) in the process.

Principle 3

Establish Critical Limit(s) for preventative measures associated with each identified CCP.

Principle 4

Establish CCP monitoring requirements. Establish procedures from the results of monitoring to adjust the process and maintain control.

Principle 5

Establish corrective actions to be taken when monitoring indicates a deviation from an established critical limit.

Principle 6

Establish procedures for verification to confirm that the HACCP system is working effectively.

Principle 7

Establish documentation concerning all procedures and records appropriate to these principles and their application. Diagram 2, represents a logical sequence for the application of HACCP in agri-business.

(*Source:* FAO, Training Manual, 1998)

DIAGRAM 2. LOGIC SEQUENCE FOR APPLICATION OF HACCP

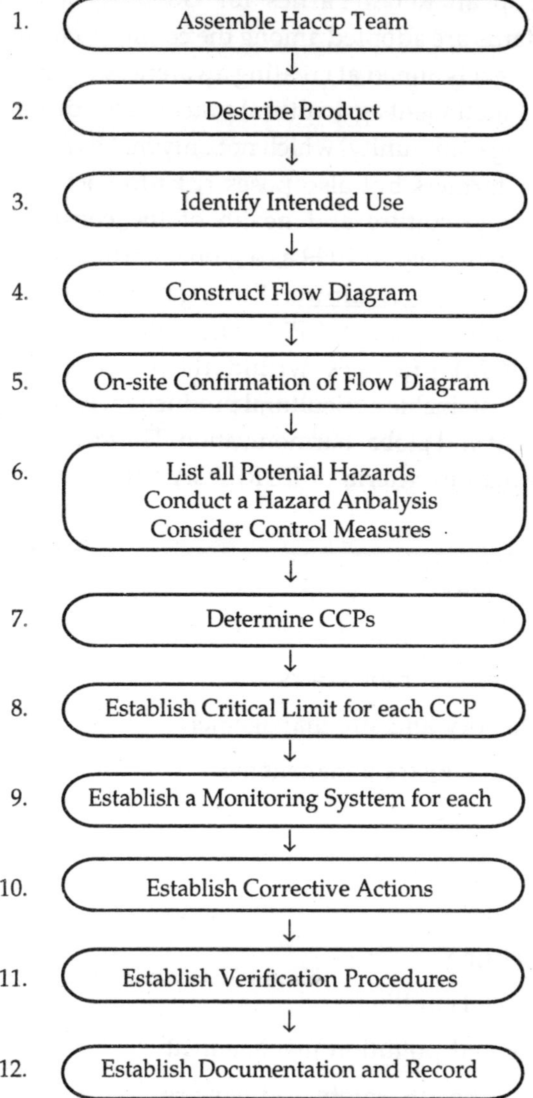

Source: FAO: FQSS, 1998.

5. EUREPGAP

Eurepgap (European Retail Parties for Good Agriculture Practices) standards are adopted among the commercial farms in India. The project is aimed at creating awareness regarding the harmful and inefficient agricultural practices followed by the Indian farming community, which not only makes farming unprofitable for farmers but also poses risks to sustainable development in agriculture and health of the consumers. Eurepgap was established in 1999 as a global partnership for safe and sustainable agriculture. Eurepgap incorporates Integrated Pest Management (IPM) and Integrated Crop Management (ICM) practices within the framework of commercial and sustainable agricultural production, with long-term improvement and global harmonization. Thirteen control points and complaints criteria of EUREPGAP are illustrated in the box.

1. Traceability
2. Record keeping and internal self-inspection
3. Varieties and root stocks
4. Site history and site management
5. Soil and substrate management
6. Fertilizer use
7. Irrigation/fertigation
8. Crop protection
9. Harvesting
10. Produce Handling
11. Waste and pollution management
12. Worker health, safety and welfare
13. Environmental issues

6. SAFE QUALITY FOOD (SQF)

The SQF mission is to provide leadership and services to deliver a fully integrated HACCP quality management system that can be applied at all links in the food supply chain. It is based upon a HACCP quality management approach. The system is unique as it focuses on the benefits to both, industry and the consumer. Improved safety and quality can aid both product marketability and profitability of food products. The international food community considers the SQF system as one of the best food safety management systems available for food supply chain, as a value chain.

7. 5S FOR HOUSE KEEPING

It's a participatory programme for effective approach to improve our work environment and total quality. It becomes a base for continuous improvement in the organization.

5S in Japanese Language and its Meaning

1. SEIRI
2. SEITON
3. SEISO
4. SEIKTSU
5. SHITSUKE

SEIRI

Sortout unnecessary items in the workplace and discard them.

SEITON

Arrange necessary items in good order they can be easily picked up for use.

SEISO

Clean your workplace completely so that there is no dust on floor, machine or equipment.

SEIKETSU

Maintain high standards of housekeeping and workplace organization at all times.

SHITSUKE

Train people to follow good housekeeping disciplines autonomously.

Examples of Slogans of 5S

Never make a mesh

Never spill

Never allow untidiness

Clean immediately if anything becomes dirty

Rewrite when writing become illegible

If anything peels off, stick it back on.

Time must be available for 5S

Abide by established rules.

Execute immediately.

8. CUSTOMER RELATIONSHIP MANAGEMENT (CRM)

CRM stands for Customer Relationship Management. It is a strategy used to learn more about customers' needs and behaviours in order to develop stronger relationships with them. A good customer relationship is at the heart of agri business success. There are many technological components to CRM, but thinking about CRM in primarily technological terms is a mistake. The more useful way to think about CRM in agri business is as a process that will help bring together lots of pieces of information about customers, marketing effectiveness, responsiveness and to continuously strengthen the network of the mutual benefit to the producers and buyers. The formation process of CRM refers to a process of developing a co-operative and collaborative relationship between the buyers and sellers. It also refers to all the organizational activities towards creating and maintaining a customer. The focus is now on maintaining the value equation, where customer delight & profits for clients and organization are on both sides of the equation.

Goal of CRM

The idea of CRM is that it helps agri-business to use technology and human resources to gain insight into the behaviour of customers and the value of those customers. If it works as hoped, a business can:

1. Provide better customer service
2. Make service more efficient
3. Sell products more effectively
4. Simplify marketing and sales processes
5. Discover new customers
6. Increase customer revenues

A Customer-Focused Culture

Adapting a customer-focused approach as Agri-Business Led Extension (A-BLES) requires a cultural change. Extension is often viewed as a department that supports all of the other functions of a society. Unless the entire organisation is committed to viewing its systems from the customers' perspective, extension will continuously be asked to support projects that meet the short-sighted goals of internal departments. As Chief Extension Officer (CEO), a key part of responsibility is to make sure that the entire organisation understands the value of our new CRM systems and extension-led business model for agriculture.

The onus is on management to lead by example and push for a customer focus on every project. If a proposed plan isn't right for our customers send the extension teams back to the customers to come up with a solution that will work for customers which will reward us in the long run. Customer satisfaction in extension service is no longer good enough to survive today's competitive market place. What is need is customer delight, being an organization of TQM.

9. COMMODITY PARKS

The Commodity Park has also seen selected as the nodal agency to implement a scheme to develop clusters. As part of this initiative, the park is expected to become a resource hub for agri-based industries in the area and will facilitate their growth. Another venture to be established in the park is a testing and certification laboratory for the commodity industry. This facility will be set up in partnership with the commodity board's and the common facilities service center and is expected to be especially useful to units in the park. The commodity park, which occupies as area of a little over 25-100 acres, involved as initial investment and offers occupants access to infrastructure required for commodity-based industrial units. Common facilities available at the park include a water supply system, power supply system, an effluent treatment plant, business centers, telephone exchange, guest houses, convention centres, library, ETU etc..

10. OHSAS 18001

What is OHSAS 18001 ?

OHSAS is an international occupational health and safety management system specification. It comprises two parts, 18001 and 18002 and embraces BS8800 and a number of other publications.

OHSAS 18001 has been developed to be compatible with the ISO 9001 (Quality) and ISO 14001 (Environmental) management systems standards, in order to facilitate the integration of quality, environmental and occupational health and safety management systems by the organizations.

The (OHSAS) specification gives requirements for an occupational health and safety (OH&S) management system, to enable an organization to control its OH&S risks and improve its performance. The standard is highly relevant to owners of process, premises or constructions in which employee exposure to occupational hazards, injury, risks or fatality can be reasonably anticipated by the practices or work-taking place.

The OHSAS 18001 system is geared towards reducing and preventing accidents and accident-related loss of lives, time and resources. The emphasis is placed on practices being pro-active and preventive by the identification of hazards and the evaluation and control of work related risks.

Benefits of OHSAS 18001:1999

Traditional occupation health and safety management usually meant reacting to work related incidents rather than planning for the control of work related risks that compose OHSAS 18001. Other costs facing organisations include but are not limited to, investigation time, wages paid for lost time, training replacements, extra supervisory time, clerical time, decreased output of injured worker upon return and the loss of business and goodwill.

OHSAS 18001 is the sound solution to the ever increasing challenge facings most organization due to high injury and illness, lost work days, increasing occupational health and safety regulations, large citations/penalties, rising worker's compensation costs, costly medical claims, worker retention and employee satisfaction.

Bottom line improvements for organizations that have a registered OH&S management system include efficient organizational discipline. Employee awareness and satisfaction, recognition by insurers, lower workers' compensation and medical costs, and increased control of regulatory issues.

Real world operating experience shows workers' compensation claims to be spiraling upward. In an global perspective, workers compensation increases by as much as 20% from last year. Surveys predict that more than one third of all workers' compensation throughout the United States will increase by between 11% - 20% by the end of this year. Other factors for the increase include claims as a result of the regulation such as OSHAS; increase of worker benefits and the leveling of managed care, ability to save money for insurers and employers.

Organisations that have been the pioneers in attaining OHSAS 18001 already reported the benefit of increased operational benefits, reduction in lost work days, fewer accidents and medical claims, recognition by insurers and improved worker' retention and satisfaction. These organisations report the process of attained registration through the NSAI approach has improved internal and external communication of the organization occupational health and safety commitment. Employees have responded favourably to registrated organisation's overt commitment to continued health and safety improvements.

Occupational Health and Safety will be a principal consideration for decision making and will be guided by the legal obligations and responsibilities, which are honoured and achieved by the compliant organisations.

OHSAS's Standards

The scope of the standard contains the following:

- OHS management system requirements
- OHS policy
- Planning

- Implementation and operations
- Monitoring and audit
- OHS management reviews

The standard is highly relevant to owners of process, premises or constructions in which employee exposure to occupational hazards, injury, risks or fatality can be responsibly anticipated by the practices or work-taking place. The standard is currently under review and subject to re-issue later this year to fully harmonize with ISO 9001:2000 by way of clauses references and content.

There are six (6) primary sections that classify the requirements in OHSAS 18001. Within these six sections of the standard are the specific requirements that an organization must apply to implement an OHSAS. The standard tracks very closely with the ISO 14001 standard and is designed to integrate with both the ISO 9001 and ISO 14001 management systems. Many sub-clauses are very similar, such as management review, document control, and corrective and preventive action. For further details refer to: ILO-OSH 2001 (International Labour Organization), Guidelines on occupational safety and health management systems and the OHSAS 18001 system is geared towards reducing and preventing accidents and accident-related loss of lives, time and resources.

Applicability

OHSAS 18001 can be applied to any type of business, organisation or industry that wishes to manage its risks for Health & Safety in the work place. The importance of managing Occupational Health and Safety is recognised by all interested parties – employers, employees, customers, suppliers, insurers, shareholders, the community, contractors, and regulatory agencies. OHSAS 18001:1999 is an Occupation Health and

Safety Assessment Series (OHSAS) for occupational health and safety (OH&S) management systems to enable an organisation to control OH&S risks and to improve performance. OHSAS 18001:1999 was released in April 1999. OHSAS 18002:2000 is the Occupational Health and Safety Management Systems-Guidelines for the implementation of OHSAS 18001. The specification takes a structured approach to OH&S management. The emphasis is placed on practices being pro-active and preventive by the identification of hazards and the evaluation and control of work related risks.

11. SOCIAL ACCOUNTABILITY (SA 8000)

In response to the inconsistencies among workplace codes of conduct, CEPAA (Council on Economic Priorities Accreditation Agency) developed a standard for workplace conditions and a system for independently verifying factories' compliance. The standard, Social Accountability 8000, and its verification system draw from established business strategies for ensuring quality (such as those used by the international standards organization for ISO 9000) and add several elements that international human rights experts have identified as essential to social auditing.

Social Accountability is an effort to provide standards that can be monitored by professional firms to declare individual factories or work sites "socially accountable", to that multinational firms can contract with them in the assurance that they have been declared acceptable.

The SA 8000 scheme is like to win some support among MNCs as being a consistent and relatively easily implementable approach. However, treating labour rights as a "quality control" issue similar to other ISO standards is unlikely to appease critics of corporate behaviour from the trade union and NGO communities. Unlike verification of the quality of a product, independent monitoring of codes requires the establishment of relationships of trust between monitors and workers, as shall be described in the issue section below.

Based on conventions of the International Labour Organizations and related international human rights instruments – including the Universal Declaration of Human Rights and the UN Convention on the Rights of the Child – SA 8000 is a common standard for companies seeking to guarantee the basic rights of workers.

SA 8000 provides a framework for the independent verification of the ethical production of all goods, made in companies of any size, anywhere in the world. It will provide a major opportunity for companies to demonstrate their commitment to best practice in the ethical manufacture and supply of goods they sell.

SA 8000 considers key issues such as child labour, compensation, discrimination, forced labour, working hours, health and safety, and freedom of association, disciplinary practices. It includes also a set of standards on the management system necessary for the successful implementation of SA 8000.

Many corporations are involved with the SA 8000 Corporate Involvement Program (CIP), which is designed to help businesses and other organizations to use the SA 8000 standard and verification system to assure human working conditions in their facilities and those of their suppliers.

How Companies can Implement SA 8000 ?

There are two options, certification to SA 8000 and involvement in the Corporate Involvement Program (CIP).

Certification to SA8000: Companies that operate production facilities can seek to have individual facilities certified to SA8000 through audits by one of the accredited certification bodies. Since the SA8000 system became fully operational in 1998, there are certified facilities in 30 countries on five continents and across 22 industries.

SA8000 Corporate Involvement Program: Companies that focus on selling goods or that combine production and selling can join the SA8000 Corporate Involvement Program. The CIP is a two-level program that helps companies evaluate SA8000, implement the standard, and report publicly on implementation progress,

- SA8000 Explorer (CIP Level One): Evaluate SA8000 as an ethical sourcing tool via., pilot audits.
- SA8000 Signatory (CIP Level Two):
- Implement SA8000 overtime in some or all of the supply chain through certification.
- Communicate implementation progress to stakeholders via SAI-verified public reporting.

SA8000 Criterias

Child labour is prohibited. Child labour means labour of children under 15 years old or according to the local laws if they are more restricted.

Forced labour is prohibited. Forced labour is defined as labour without remuneration. It is also not allowed to confiscate the worker's documents.

Health and Safety have to be guaranteed. The company has to maintain a health and safety management system.

Freedom of association and collective negotiations has to be guaranteed.

Discrimination is prohibited especially when it comes to admission, remuneration, and access to trainings, promotion and contract termination.

Disciplinary measures are prohibited. This includes corporal and verbal punishment and humiliation.

Working hours are not allowed to exceed 48 hours a week. On 7 working days one day off has to be given.

Salary has to cover costs of habitation, clothes and alimentation, as well as include an additional money on top of that.

Management systems have to guarantee the concordance and effectiveness of the rules. Documentation, implementation, maintenance, communication and monitoring of the rules included in the standard should lead to an on-going improvement process.

An integration of ISO, OHSAS and SA 8000 within agri-business system improve the competitiveness of an organization through continuous improvement on its product, services, people, processes and environment. All of these programme themes collect input from internal and/or external customers as appropriate to meet its global demands.

12. ISO 22000

It is the integration of ISO 9000 and HACCP. ISO 22000 specifies requirements for a food safety management system in the food chain, where an organisation

- Need to demonstrate its ability to control food safety hazards in order to consistently provide safe end products that meet both the requirements agreed with the customer and those of applicable food safety regulations, and
- Aims to enhance customer satisfaction through the effective control of food safety hazards, including processes for updating the system.

ISO 22000 may apply to all types of organisations within the food chain ranging from feed producers, primary producer's through food manufacturers, transport and storage operators and subcontractors to retail and food service outlets- together with inter-related organisations such as producers of equipment, packaging material, cleaning agents, additives and ingredients.

Food safety is related to the presence of and levels of food-borne hazards in food at the point of consumption (intake by the consumer). As food safety hazards may be introduced at any stage of the food chain, adequate control throughout the food chain is essential. Thus, food safety is a joint responsibility that is principally assured through the combined efforts of all the parties participating in the food chain.

13. ISO 26000- FUTURE GUIDELINE ON SOCIAL RESPONSIBILITY

The innovation came with the new approach by ISO to ensure that the global standard will benefit from broad input by all those with a serious interest in social responsibility. This is being achieved by the balanced representation of six designated stakeholder categories: industry, government, labour, consumer, non governmental organizations and others, in addition to geographical and gender based balance.

14. ERGONOMICS

Ergonomics systems are being dealt with the narrow man-machine concept in military and health endeavor. Currently, it has contributed to the development of industrial workplace, information technology, architecture, farm machinery etc to develop improvement measures, which are necessary to bring a balance between techno-workload and human capacity. The aim is to improve health, safety, well being and efficiency of total production management. The interface between technology and society is critical to the field of ergonomics at the micro-level approach (Vanwonterghen, 2000). Ergonomics and its applications attempt to harmonize work and the working environment to raise productivity and work efficiency and promote individual well being through optimizing the effort of the worker or user. Much of the ergonomics research has been focussed in the industrial sector; little work of an ergonomics nature has been done in agri-plantation for generation of appropriate technology relevant to people factor. It is a neglected area, but it has considerable potential for improving the quality of life through agri-plantation technology.

The aim is to formulate the concept of "Agriergonomics" and to provide a description of its concept and principles for the generation of sustainable production and processing technology and to discuss their validity and usability in the context of their application in agri-plantation organizations (APOs) to delight customer. Particular consideration is given to the possibility of integrating the concept of agriergonomics, providing a bondage between peasants and scientists mechanism for taking into consideration the way in which different functional groups and cultures have learnt to adopt, adapt and cope in participatory R&D systems. An example of this would be to provide recognition of agriergonomics as a distinct specialty for scientist, peasant and technology (SPT) environment interface. There is ample scope for redesigning and re-engineering existing plantation R&D patterns with a view to improve comfort and efficiency of production technology (PT) towards total quality of human endeavor. Agriergonomics centered R&D approach to plantation sector may develop an integrated strategy aimed at the well being and sense of satisfaction of Peasantry Resource Management (PRM), Scientific Knowledge Management (SKM) and Estate Resource Management (ERM) within total quality dimensions. (Dhanakumar, 1999).

15. E-COMMERCE

E-commerce simply means business through electronics. E-commerce is the means of selling goods on the Internet, using web pages. This involves much the same processes as selling goods elsewhere, but in a digital format. Presentation, placement, display, stocking, selling and payment are all familiar concepts, e-commerce demands that all this be done on screen, and as an automated process.

Using CAD/CAM for designing products and introducing products into production. The cost and time required to design and introduce products are greatly reduced.

Some of the Application of CAD/CAM in Agriculture

Marketing Advisor: Determine marketing alternative and optimal strategies. Input datas like information on storage, price level, price trends suggest different marketing options.

GOSSYM: Recommends daily management decision based on weather data, soil parameter, soil fertility levels. Eg., Prevention strategies for possible disease occurrence due to temperature, rainfall etc.

SUBERMAX: Help storage managers. Storage recommendation based on crop quality and environment E.g., Dehumidification based on relative humidity

FINDS: Farm level intelligent disease support system determine optimal machinery management practices.

Adopting ERP systems/SAP: To help automate various business processes for financial accounting and reduction in cost of production.

Improving computerized production control system to better plan and track customer orders, thus providing enchanced customer service, reduced costs, and improved flexibility.

16. BRANDING

At its most basic level, a brand is a unique identity. It is a shorthand way to business thinks about what you do, produce, serve, and sell. A well conceived and developed, a brand is a vibrant picture held in consumers' minds. Well-executed brands are worth millions, even billions of dollars, in sales and shareholder value. Brands stand out like beacons of light in a sea with high-quality products and services offered to meet consumer-expression needs, as consumers choose brands in great part to tell the world and themselves who they are. Branding is a central element of marketing strategies. The consumer believes, ' the only way I can be who I am is to have specific products or services'. A powerful brand, therefore, creates a must- have quasi monopoly for itself.

17. SUPPLY CHAIN MANAGEMENT (SCM)

World class companies see supply chain management as a key element in capturing increased shares of world markets. They have given the executives in charge expanded and new responsibilities. These supply chain managers' plan and control all the activities related to materials that move from suppliers, through the production processes and to customers.

Forming partnership with suppliers to quickly produce products of near – perfect quality precisely when needed and with little inventory. Providing suppliers with information about when customer orders are needed and training them in quality control and manufacturing techniques are becoming more common. Suppliers are selected and developed with a long-term view towards improving product quality, fast deliveries, and responsiveness to customers' needs. The success of SCM is depends upon the efficiency of vendor.

Vendor rating is highly relevant for selecting right supplier. The performance appraisal of the vendor is termed as vendor rating. The vendor rating for supply of agricultural inputs to the commodity producers' society for determination to its members.

The following criteria can be assessed based on

- Delivery time
- Quality of product
- Competitiveness of the price
- Other factors such as to meet emergency order, readiness of new design etc.

For example.

A) Commodity producers' society gives weigtage in the following pattern.

Delivery on time ————40%

Quality ————————30%

Price and performance —30%

Total———100%

B) vendors' performance

- 15 deliveries on time out of 20 order
- given an average of 10% rejects
- delivered the items at the performance index of Rs. 90/-

Rating of vendor is calculated as follows.

0.40*15/20*100 = 0.40*0.75*100 = 30 points

0.30*90/100*100 = 0.30*0.9*100 = 27 points

0.30*90/100*100 = 0.3*0.9*100 = 27 points

Total————84 points

Total rating of 84 points has been calculated for the above

case. The performance of vendor rate may vary depending upon life of agribusiness companies.

Although price is important, being able to deliver enough materials when needed, producing materials of exceptional quality, and being trustworthy and cooperative are even most important. Long-term, multiyear contracts are used to guarantee suppliers security and to provide incentives for developing trust and co-operation.

18. ENTERPRISE RESOURCE PLANNING (ERP)

ERP systems consists of many software modules that can be separately purchased to help manage many different activities in different functional areas of a business. For example, SAP's R/3 software, the largest selling ERP software, offers modules for sales and distribution, financial controlling, fixed assets management, human resources, work flow, industry solution, materials management, plant maintenance, and project systems. ERP systems require a major commitment and investment , often require companies to modify some of their processes to accommodate the software, and can take many years to implement. ERP for agri-business unit is an asset for the performance measure and total resource management.

19. JUST IN TIME (JIT)

Defined as:

The coordination of the movement of completed work from an upstream operation to the start of work at the successive downstream operation

JIT in Production

Emphasis is producing exactly what is needed and conveying it to where it is needed precisely when required. In nutshell, it is a system of production, based on the philosophy of total elimination of waste that seeks the utmost in rationality in the way we make things.

Four Principles of JIT

Streamline manufacturing operations

Control for total quality

Leverage with workers' creativity

Integrate JIT with supplier & customer partnership

Elements of JIT

- Smooth flow of work (the ultimate goal)
- Elimination of waste
- Continuous improvement
- Eliminating anything that does not add value
- Simple systems that are easy to manage
- Use of product layouts to minimize moving materials and parts
- Quality at the source
- Poka-yoke* – fail safe tools and methods
- Preventative maintenance
- Good housekeeping
- Set-up time reduction
- Cross-trained employees
- A pull system

* Foolproofing or Paka-yoke (make human error impossible)

Kanban Production Control System

Kanban

Card or other device that communicates demand for work or materials from the preceding station. Kanban is the Japanese word meaning "signal" or "visible record". Paperless production control system. Authority to pull, or produce comes from a downstream process.

Single Card' Kanban System

No inventory item is allowed to move without authorization by a move card.Each bin (product) contains a fixed quantity of inventory (no more or no less). Each bin carries a Kanban card. After finishing the task, the Kanban card is removed and place in a move card box. If all bins at a station contain fixed inventory, the operation stops until another card is received

Double Card' Kanban System

First kind of conveyance Kanban authorizes the transference of materials from a supplying work centre to a using work centre. Second card (Production Kanban) authorizes the production of materials to replace from existing unit

20. SIX SIGMA (6 SIXMA)

Six Sigma is a *customer focussed continuous improvement strategy* and discipline that minimizes defects and variation towards an achievement level of 3 defects/per million opportunities in our product design, production, service and administrative processes. ***Sigma*** A term used in statistics to represent standard deviation, an indicator of the degree of variation in a set of measurements or a process. ***Six sigma*** A statistical concept that measures a process in terms of defects – at the six sigma level, there are only 3.4 defects per million opportunities. Six sigma is also a philosophy of management that focuses on eliminating defects.

Six Themes of Six Sigma:

1. Genuine Focus on the Customer

Understanding the reality of the customer

Customer focus become top priority

"Sigma" improvement developed based on customer satisfaction and value

2. Data and Fact-Driven Management

Concept of management by fact rather than opinions and assumptions

Six sigma measures key variable for better performance

3. Process are where the Action is

Makes manager to master in process dimension as a way to build competitive advantage in delivering value to customer

4. Proactive Management

A proactive means acting in advance of events rather than reacting to it (e.g., HACCP)

5. Boundaryless Collaboration

To break down barriers and improve team work up, down and across organization

6. Drive for Perfection

Aim for perfection and yet also tolerate failure

Six Sigma Roles

Champion: A business leader who provides overall strategic direction for a Six Sigma project team. This individual serves as a laison between management and the project team; facilitates the acquisition of resources and support for the project.

Master Black Belts: Quality leaders responsible for strategy, training, mentoring and deployment of Six Sigma.

Black Belts: Six Sigma experts who work projects across the business.

Green Belts: Fully-trained individuals who work projects in their job.

21. LEAN MANAGEMENT

Lean production, manufacturing, service and management is termed as "LEAN" because it used less of every resources compared with mass production (i.e.), half the human effort in field & factory; half the manufacturing space, half the investment in tools; half the extension hours (cycle time of service) to make value added in extension service. Also, it requires keeping far less than half the needed inventory on site, results in many fewer defects, and produces a greater and ever growing variety of services.

Lean based procedure, set its rights explicitly on perfection: continuously declining costs, zero defects, zero inventories and endless services. According to Norman Bodek (1996), lean management is about operating the most efficient and effective organization possible, with least cost and zero waste. It is an approach that requires companies to make smart use of their resources i.e., technology, equipment and above all, the knowledge and skills of their people. Lean means no fat -no waste, but adopts the zero-waste.

Why Lean?

A Lean Service in extension is based on the concept that service can and should be driven by real customer demand. Instead of working what you hope to serve, Lean Service can do what your customer wants... with shorter lead times. Instead of pushing, it's pulled there through a system that's set up to quickly respond to customer demand.

Understanding Concept of Extension Service & Integrating LEAN

Goal of lean is to virtually eliminate wait time or inefficiency of work time.

Question is "How fast is fast" and "How slow is slow" in extension service. First, we need to understand the concept of total lead time and value added time with reference to extension service.

A. ***Total lead time*** - How long the process or service takes from start to end.

B. ***Value added time*** - Work that a customer would recognize as necessary to create a product or service.

Total cycle efficiency = Value added time/Total lead time.

The fundamental driver behind eliminating waste is *"true service efficiency"*, a matter of doing work using the best method known, waste removal and management. The focus on waste (or Muda in Japanese) was pioneered by Taiichi Ohno. He demonstrated seven fundamental form of waste which are summarized below:

Overproduction – the making of too much, too early or just in case.

Waiting—where materials or information are waiting to produce to the next process. They are not moving or having value added

Transporting—where materials (or information) are being transported into, out of or around the factory. Transport cannot be fully eliminated, but the aim is to minimize it.

Inappropriate processing—using machinery or equipment which is inappropriate in terms of 'capacity' to perform an operation.

Unnecessary inventory —which ties up capital and space and prevents identification of problems

Defects—defined in terms of product defects, rework defects, scrap defects or service defects.

Unnecessary motion— the ergonomics of the work place.

Source: Shingo, 1989.

Lastly, an appropriate framework on lean reflection in extension requires a Delta Zero mindset, a willingness to rethink the results desired as well as the factors required to achieve best extension service. Lean enterprise owe their success in part to maintaining zero waste free, but also because they expect the unexpected and meet each new challenge with moves unexpected by customers and competitors through the power of delta zero. The term delta zero refers to the union of 2 concepts; *delta,* the Greek letter symbolizing incremental change, and *zero,* the Arabic numeral symbolizing, void. Essentially, Delta Zero refers to the paradox or learning. All learning, personal as well as organizational, which takes place within a normal and accepted paradigm extension service.

22. WORLD CLASS OPERATION FOR INNOVATION IN AGRI-BUSINESS:

Product Design

- Getting products to market faster by using simultaneous engineering, new computer technologies, and autonomous new product development teams.
- Designing products for ease of production and for quality so that production systems can be used as weapons to compute in global markets and improving product design with continuous programs aimed at steady small improvements.

PRODUCT DESIGN FLOW CHART

Developing New Products

Recognizing new product opportunity

↓

Technical and economic feasibility studies

↓

Prototype design (should exhibit the basic form, fit and function of the final product)

↓

Performance testing of prototype design

↓

Market sensing and evaluation

↓

Economic evaluation of the prototype design

↓

If satisfactory, enters to the next stage

↓

Production design

↓

Market performance and economic evaluation of production model

↓

Continual modification of production model

Forecasting

Refining forecasting efforts so that the capabilities of production processes actually fit the needs of markets.

Forecasting use past data to determine future events (an objective forecast). Reduce the uncertainties faced by a business. World-class agri business units refine forecasting efforts by reducing forecasting error so that capabilities of production process actually fits the needs of the markets. Examples of forecasting errors.

Period	*Demand t*	*Forecast t*	*Error*	*(Error)²*	*% Error* = $\frac{Error}{Demand} \times 100$
Jan	30	25	+ 5	25	16.7
Feb	25	30	- 5	25	- 16.7
March	20	25	- 5	100	- 16.7
April	20	25	+ 5	25	+ 16.7
May	25	23	- 2	4	- 8
June	20	22	- 2	4	- 8

Forecasting error = 82.8/6 = 13.8%

Location and Layout

World-class companies recognize that long-range capacity decisions and facility location decisions are among the most important of their strategic decisions. Capital investment in production facilities is enormous, and the ability of production to be used as a competitive weapon in capturing world markets hangs in the balance. Capacity planning covers such long periods of time that fundamental changes can occur in the economy, consumer preferences, technology, demographics, and government regulations. Such planning is therefore subject to great uncertainty and risk.

Facility location decisions at world class companies increasingly involve a worldwide search for sites. National boundaries present less of an obstacle than in the past. A multitude of factors is considered in location decisions, and the importance of these factors varies with type of facility. The type of facility from input sector to food sector- has its own set of factors that must be carefully matched with those provided by potential site locations. The incentives offered by the government communities under consideration are important to the eventual choice of location. The eventual choice of facility location will involve the need to simultaneous consider many economic and qualitative factors.

Factor rating was commonly used to choose appropriate location and layout by considering different required factors. For example how site of Mallur Food Park was chosen in comparison with alternatives is given below.

Factor Ratings of Food Park for Location Alternatives

Factor	*Factor rating (5 point scale)*	*Location rating (10 point scale)*		
		Mallur	*chickballabur*	*Tumkur*
Accessibility to Airport and rail transportation	4	8 (32)	5 (20)	4 (16)
Agri R&D facilities	4	8 (32)	8 (32)	5 (20)
Availability of 2 MW electricity	5	8 (40)	6 (30)	6 (30)
Availability of 2.5 MLD of water	5	8 (40)	6 (30)	6 (30)
Availability of fruits and vegetables	4	8 (32)	7 (28)	5 (20)
Proximity to customers	3	7 (21)	7 (21)	5 (15)
		197	161	131

Key to World Class Management

Incremental and continuous improvements are necessary, but not sufficient, for becoming world class, which additionally looks for rapid, leap –frogging quantum- jumps in agri-business performance. The four key world class measures are given below:

Customer Delight

It measures customer's – perceived quality and value. In the scale of 0-100 per cent, an average of 80 per cent is 'good', 90 per cent is 'better' and 100 per cent is 'best'. The higher it is, the more is the customer delight, and so are customer loyalty and retention.

Inventory Turnover

This figure as cost of sales/on-hand 'Work in Process', reflects costly wastes, delays, scrap, rework, etc. Inventory turn of 25-30 times a year is 'good'; 50-60 'better' and 80-100 'best'.

Quality

Defined in terms of defective parts per million (ppm), 200 ppm is 'good'; 100 ppm is 'better'; 4 ppm (Six sigma) is 'best'. (Cf. 1 per cent = 10,000 ppm). The cost of quality gets several times reduced on achieving 200 ppm and less.

Process Cycle Efficiency

It's value-adding time as a percentage of total time taken (also known as the value added ratio). Here, 10 per cent is 'good', 30 per cent is 'better' and 50 per cent is the 'best'.

Hundreds of enterprises are already moving towards World class; thousands of others will do well to make extraordinarily bold goals and 'get going' to win the productivity race in order to become world class over a few years.

Conclusion

Agri business is moving towards more on customer focus and customer delight. Customer expects high quality, accuracy, branded and certified products for their consumption. WTO has given opportunity to our agribusiness units to export and promote their products globally. The competitive business environment of most agri-business industries has been influenced or even restructured by the two key forces of globalization and technological advancement. Considering these factors, there is a need for world class business concepts both at the domestic and global production systems of Agri business sectors to train their work force for effective implementation of WCBM concepts at field, processing and marketing levels.

REFERENCES

1. Buffa, S.E. (1994). Modern Production/Operations Management. John Wiley & Sons. Toranto.
2. Dhanakumar, V.G., (1999). New Techniques for Plantation Management: TQM Perspective. The Pnater's Chronicle. February 1999, pp. 87-93.
3. Dhanakumar, V.G., (2004). Production and Operations Management. Teaching Manual—MBA, IIPM, Bangalore.
4. Gaither, N and Frazier, G (2002). Operations Management. Thomson Asia Pvt. Ltd., Singapore.
5. Garten E.J., (2000). World View: Global Strategy for the New Economy. A Harvard Review Business Book, Boston.
6. Morton, E.T., (1999). Production Operations Management. South West College Publishing, Cincinnati.

5

Supply Chain for Agribusiness Management

Supply chain life cycle processes in agribusiness comprising physical inputs, information, financial and knowledge flows whose purpose is to satisfy end-user requirements with products and services from multiple linked suppliers. The supply chain is made up of *processes*. These cover a broad range including sourcing, manufacturing, transporting and selling physical products. Today, added value in the form of intellectual capital is vital to marketing profitable goods and services. The supply chain system in agribusiness should support the satisfaction of end-user requirements. These requirements give rise to the fundamental reason for the supply chain in the first place. The supply chain is not limited in terms of flow direction. Many consider supply chains only interms of flow from suppliers to end-users. For the physical process, this is largely true. But supply chain design cannot ignore backward flows for product returns, rebates, incentive payments and so forth.

Definitions of SCM

Supply Chain, encompasses all activities associated with the flow and transformation of goods from raw materials stage, through end users, as well as the associated information flows. Whereas, the term **Supply chain management** is the integration of supply chain activities through improved supply chain relationship to achieve and attain sustainable competitive advantage. **Total supply chain management,** is an organizational concept whose primary objective is to proactively manage the two way movement and co-ordination of goods, services and information from raw materials end user. In case of materials **management,** as part of SCM focuses on the co-ordination of goods, services and information from suppliers through operations and it is a subset of total supply chain management.

Evolution of Supply Chain (Evolutionary Stages)

In the 70's, the concept of SCM primarily focused on the integration of warehousing and transportation within corporate sector. In the 80's, the focus of SCM shifted to the reengineering of cost-structures. In the 90's, the focus of SCM has been shifted from reducing cost to improving customer service. The snapshot of SCM evaluation is given below.

1970's

- Manufacturing handled in isolation
- Integration of warehousing and transportation within the firm

1980's

- Integrating operations within the organization like procurement, manufacturing, distribution etc.
- Re-engineering of cost structure

1990's

- Linking of external partners like suppliers, vendors, distributors and customers
- From reducing costs to improve customer service

Supply Chain Strategy for Agribusiness

Supply chain, as a strategy in agribusiness will have a major impact on creating value for an organization and its partners. Based on collaborative strategy, demand flow strategy and customer service level strategy, an effective supply chain strategy may be formulated to meet the needs of the market and integrate them with technology to generate the highest level of customer satisfaction, while delivering the highest value to shareholders.

Close collaboration among supply chain partners can align the parties and then enhance the value of the network's combined activities. By collaborating with suppliers and manufacturers will derive benefits in key activities and capacity planning. Fig. 1 to 3, 3A and 3B illustrates a model SCM for fruits & vegetables, tea and agrochemical respectively. The collaborative opportunities between manufacturers and customers (such as wholesale-distributors and retailers) center on demand planning, inventory replenishment and consumer requirements are met efficiently. In order to make a best choice of tools, agribusiness organization must understand the capacity of SCM tools and their interrelationships & the degree of integration between the models (Refer Fig. 4, phase 1 to 3 of conceptual models).

Reverse Supply Chain

An organization's supply chain is not limited to delivering products to the end-consumers and it conforms to the defective products that are returned by the consumers' back to the organization.

The reuse of products and materials (e.g., rubber waste) is a common phenomenon, companies have long ignored this part of the supply chain, known as reverse supply chain or backward supply chain (Refer Fig. 5). A common example of reverse supply chain in food sector is the soft drinks bottles pickup and delivery system, where soft drink bottles are returned and reused repeatedly. Achieving visibility across a supply chain means not only being able to track the performance of a supplier, but also that of your suppliers' suppliers as well.

Necessity of Reverse Supply Chain

The foremost reason behind companies giving importance to reverse supply chain is that it reduces operating costs by reusing products or components of agribusiness activities. Companies have started realizing the importance of reusing products or components; as a result, reverse supply chains are becoming essential part of business. In some cases, companies are forced to set up reverse supply chains because of environmental regulations.

For many large manufacturing and technology companies, after market services form a significant portion of their revenue. Also, providing timely and efficient service has become a key competitive differentiator in many industries. "Better management of the reverse supply chain translates into higher customer service and consequently, higher customer satisfaction; and industries and the enterprises within them are realizing that management of the reverse supply chain is a revenue opportunity".

As an example, agri-business companies and good sector have been successful in fine-tuning their traditional supply chains, they need to make change in their existing supply chain management systems to implement reverse supply chain management systems. Opined Mike Nardella, "companies need to make a major paradigm change. No longer can companies accumulate returns in the back of the warehouse or stores and ignore the issue of returns". The first step in any successful reverse supply chain management system is to define the rules of reverse supply chain system. Karen Peterson views, "the first and most important activity is to actually understand where the reverse supply chain will contribute profits".

Reverse Supply Chain vs. Forward Supply Chain

Reverse supply chains differ from forward supply chains in information flow, physical distribution flow and cash flow. To manage reverse supply chain, companies need sophisticated information systems. Some of the technology involved in reverse supply chain is similar while in some areas the technology used differs from that of traditional use of supply chain. According to Glenn Mauney. "Depending on the volumes and complexity of the returned goods flow, there is some information capture specialization and processing efficiencies in returned goods processing that requires some unique systems". Technology in reverse supply chain such as real-time inventory tracking system (bar codes and sensors) is similar to that used in the forward supply chain.

The two types of SCM as illustrated below describe its importance and applicability in agribusiness sector.

1. ***Push-based SCM***: Push-based SCM is also known as traditional approach to SCM. In this approach to SCM, materials and products are flowing from supplier to consumer, via production and distributor unit.
2. ***Pull-based SCM***: Pull-based SCM is known as modern approach to SCM. It is also known as demand supply network. In this approach, the actual consumption pulls distribution, which in turn pulls production, in turn pulling material supply.

Global experience with various companies shows that pull-based SCM is better than push-based SCM. Experience shows 20-50% improvement in overall working capital, capacity utilization, cost of goods and customer service with 'pull-based' approach when compared to 'push-based' approach in addition to a 50-100% improvement in time to market and a 3-15% increase in market share.

For example, establishing a brand image in rubber sector with help of RPS would facilitate an effective functioning of pull based SCM system and intern to attain its sustainability in global/domestic market. Concept of traditional vs. customized SCM is illustrated in Fig. 6.

Quality in Supply Chain Management

A successful SCM requires the recognition of quality in SCM. Food quality and safety within the food chain is becoming an ever-increasing important feature for consumers. To stay competitive in the market of food grains, commodity, fruit and vegetables, the food providers need to create safe produce with perceived quality. To meet the changing demands for quality, availability, cost appearance and service the actors in the supply chain need to play a major role. A retailer is not capable of meeting the demand without cooperation with suppliers, wholesalers, growers, plant and seed suppliers and breeders. Servicing these consumer need requires an integration of safety and of quality handling throughout the entire supply chain cycle in agri-business sector.

There are five major quality defect occur in SCM, the first of those is the "product defect" i.e., defects in goods produced that are not caught by in-line or end-of-line inspection and are therefore passed on to customers. The second type is termed as service defect, where problem given to customer are not directly related to the goods themselves, but the results of the accompanying level of service (e.g., inappropriate delivery). In other words, defects, which the customers experience, are not concerned with production faults. The third defect is internal scrap i.e., the defects produced in a company that have been caught by in-line or end-of-line inspection. Fourth and fifth defects are lack of reverse cycle of supply chain (i.e.) from consumer to supplier back flow of information and materials within the system and the final defect on critical dimension of supply chain is hazards (i.e.) biological, physical & chemical related safety aspects of food chain. The quality defect approach in SCM has clear advantages in identifying where defects are occurring and hence in identifying problems, inefficiencies and wasted efforts in SCM process.

It is necessary to map intercompany and intracompany value adding processors in SCM cycle. The difference between the traditional supply (or) quality in SCM and the value stream is that the former includes the complete activities of all the companies involved, whereas the latter refers only to the specific parts of the firms that actually add value of quality to the specific product or service.

SQF for Food Chain

The Safe Quality Food (SQF) Quality System is an internationally known scheme for third party certification that can be relied upon by the whole food industry. The system consists of the SQF 1000^{CM} Quality Code and SQF 2000^{CM} Quality Code. Successful certification under either the SQF 1000^{CM} or the SQF 2000^{CM} schemes enables the product to display one of two SQF marks. The two SQF marks can demonstrate that the food is safe and meets the level of quality demanded by customers and can be used at all stages of the food chain, in any country. The SQF 1000^{CM} Code is a HACCP based supplier assurance code based on HACCP methodology. It is ideal for primary producers who supply food that requires further processing before consumption. This code suit fruit and vegetable producers who supply to different processing units/export. SQF 2000^{CM} Code is a rigorous HACCP quality management system. It can be used by all businesses within the food supply chain and can meet the growing demands of consumers for assurance of food safety and quality. It is designed to support industry or company branded products and encapsulates National Advisory Committee for Microbiological Criteria for Foods (NACMCF) and CODEX-HACCP Principles and Guidelines.

The Safe Quality Food (SQF) scheme is rigorous, flexible and complements government programmes and industry initiatives. SQF certification can provide benefits to all the following elements in the food supply chain. For food suppliers, it is a way to prove a demonstrable concern for quality product & safety, which can increase its attractiveness to global retailers, and to increase product demand. Food companies who ensure that their suppliers become SQF certified will be able to purchase foods of assured safe and quality from across the globe. The SQF certification can be used for all types of suppliers within the food chain. Access to an assured supply of safe, quality food, easily recognizable by the SQF mark placed on the packaging can provide consumers with an easy way to help protect their safety (Krishnan 2003). Between 1998 and 2002, the emphasis of SCM strategy gradually changed from chain optimization (reducing post-harvest losses, shrinkage, handling costs) to integral chain care (HACCP, good agricultural practices & certification).

Conclusion

SCM in agribusiness is the systematic effect to provide integrated service management to the supply chain in order to meet customers need and expectations. Initially, supply chain in agri-business is seen as a single inter-dependent process and as isolated functions controlled by independent units. In order to work effectively, a coordinated effort and a request for planning between customers and agribusiness organizations of chain is necessary.

This primary condition needed for the development of supply chain management, effort is to realize that the SCM is a part of agribusiness system, which means recognizing the interdependencies between the customers of the system interms of operations, goals and creating an integrated supply chain which benefit all the members of the system. It is important to get certification for SCM of concern firms. The particulars related to certification and agencies are appended in Table No.1 below:

TABLE 1

Certification and its Agencies for Agri-business

(A) Purpose of certification:

- Authenticate and specific of its supply chain and production. E.g., Electronic product made in Japan
- To demonstrate reliability to customers, public bodies or consumers. E.g., Electronic goods from Japan are more durable
- To meet a demand for specific levels of identity. E.g., Darjeeling tea, Coorg coffee
- To control the supply of specific raw material in order to capture a premium for "value –added" products. E.g., Kancheepuram silk sarees.
- Certification was conducted by the GeneScan Group or its partners.

(B) Agency Norms

- The resulting GeneScan certificate is valid for one year.
- The certificate is issued after a successful main audit.
- Follow-up audit is required to maintain certification status.
- Cost of consultation and certification are strongly dependent on the specific program and supply chain.

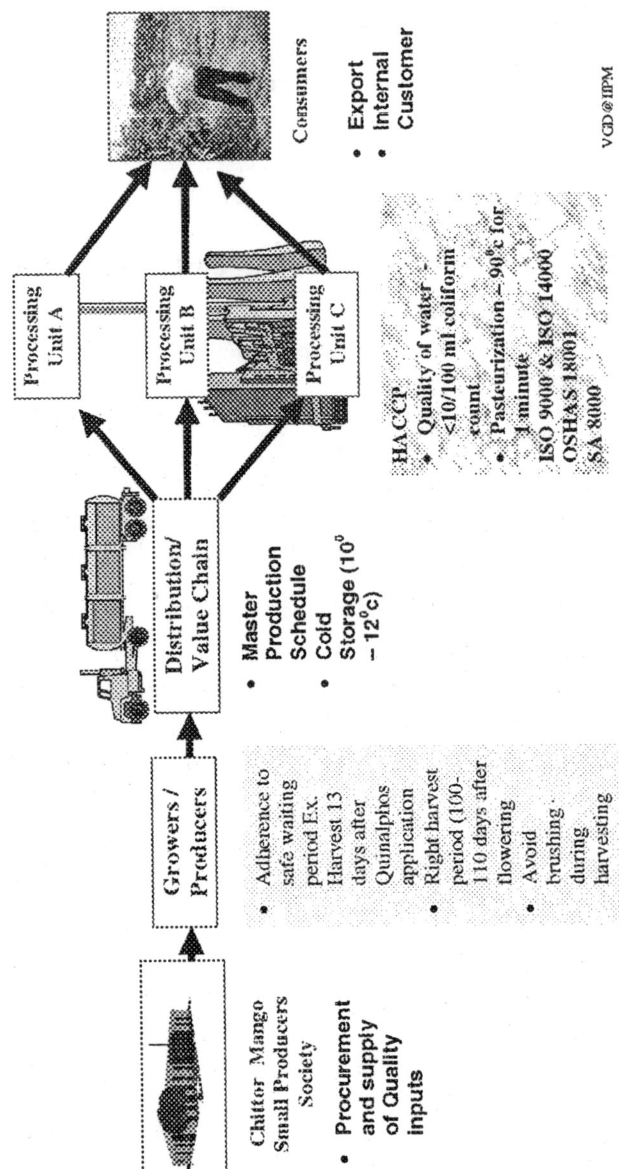

Fig. 1. Supply Chain Model with Value for Mango Processing in Chittor

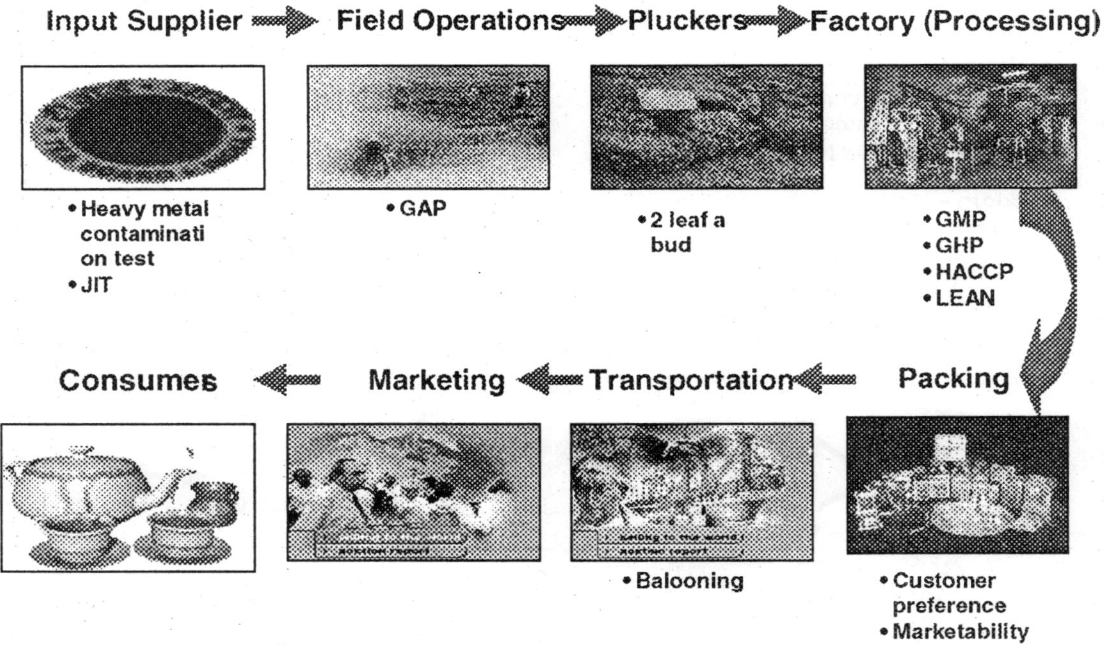

Fig. 2. Supply Chain Management in Plantations (Tea)

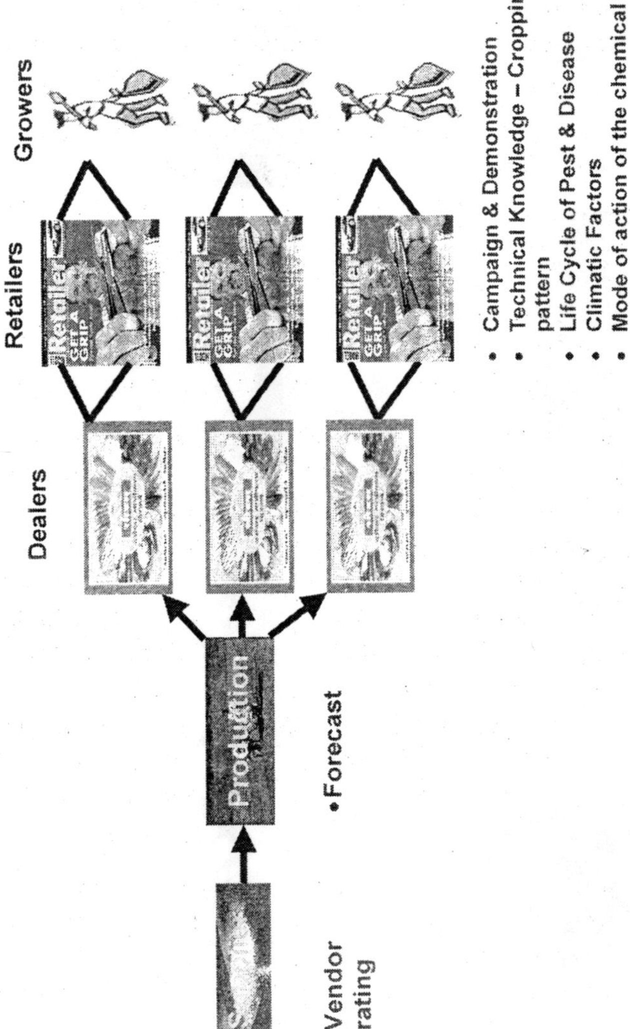

Fig. 3. Supply Chain Model for Agri-Chemical Sector

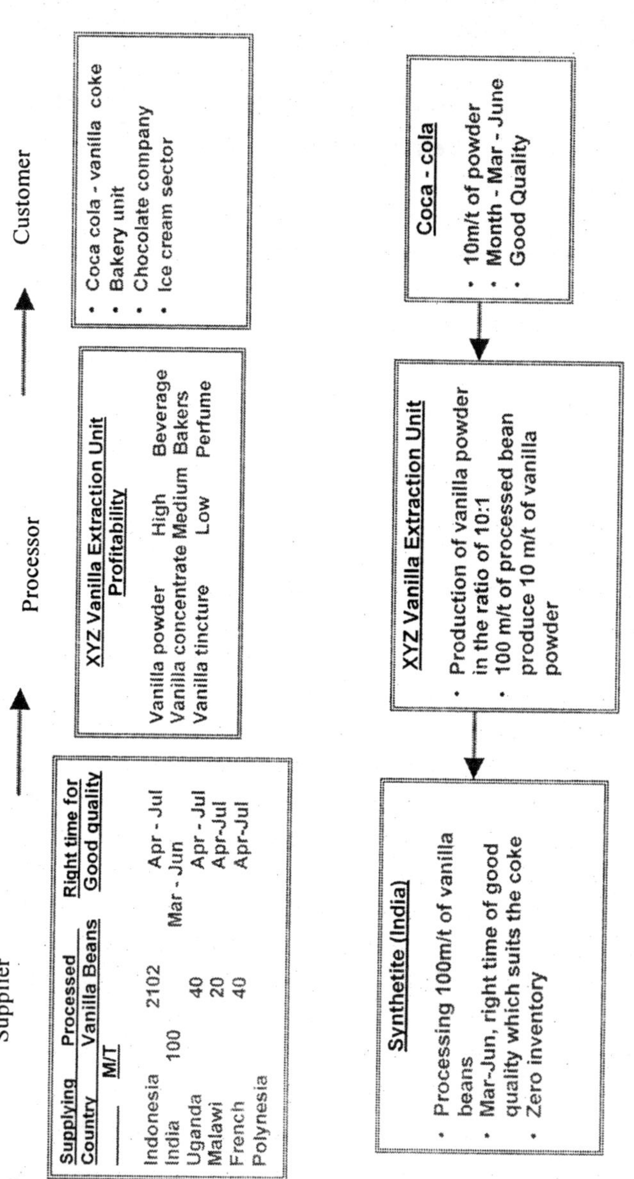

Fig. 3A. SCM for Vanilla Coke

Supplier	Cost	Quality	Accuracy
Synthetite (Indian curer)	**Stable**	**Good**	**High**
Indonesia	**Higher**	**Medium**	**Medium**
Uganda **Malawai** **French**	**Very high**	**Low**	**Low**

Fig. 3B. SCM Strategy for Procurement of Vanilla.

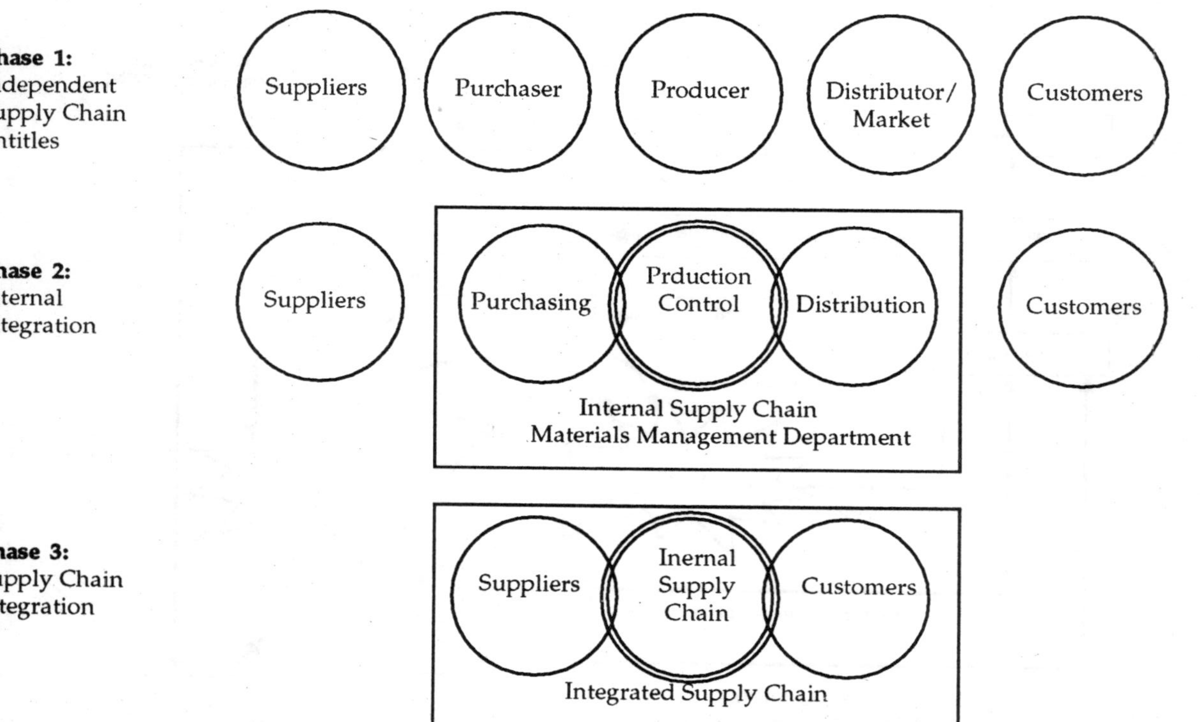

Fig. 4. Conceptual Supply Chain Models

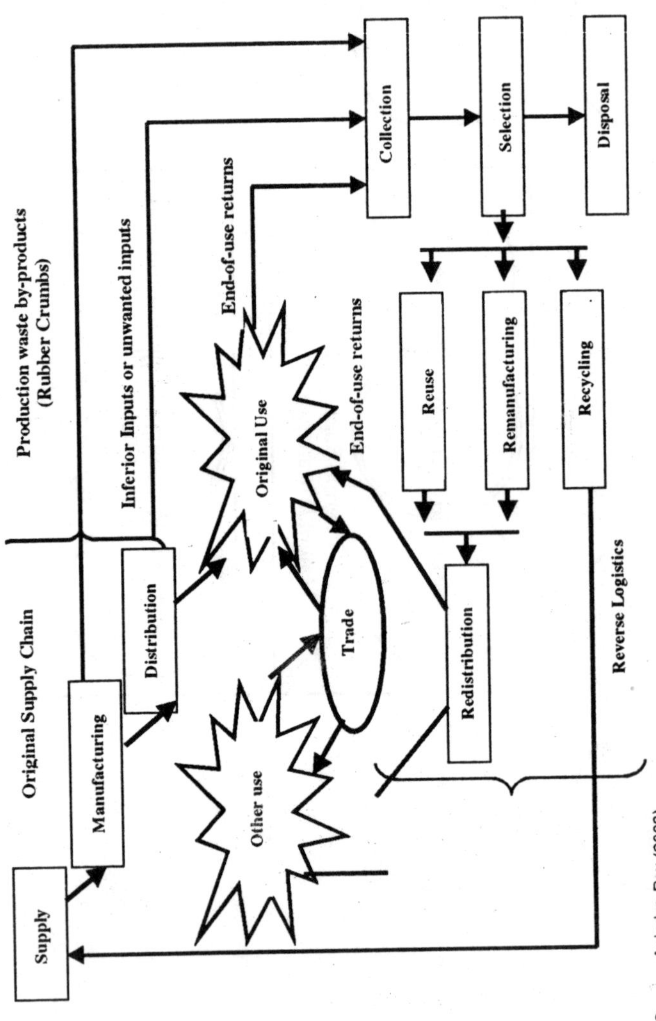

Source: Anindya Roy (2003).
Model has been modified to suit agribusiness system

Fig. 5. Reverse Supply Chain for Agribusiness

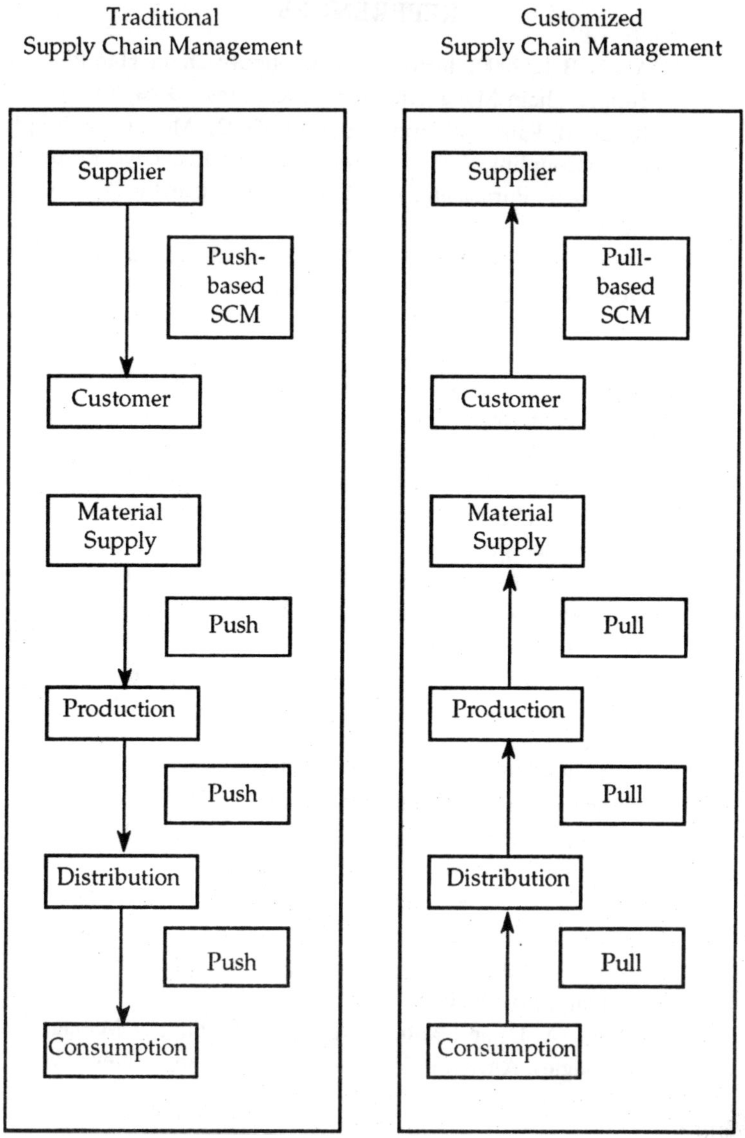

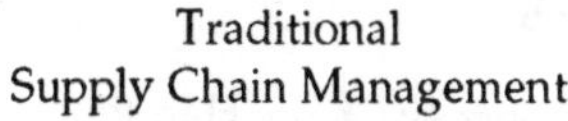

Fig. 6. Traditional Vs customized SCM models

REFERENCES

1. Ayers, B. J. (2000). Introduction to Supply Chain. Handbook of Supply Chain Management, St. Lucie Press, Boca, Raton.
2. Barut, M. Fairst, W. and Kanet, J.J. (2002). Measuring Supply Chain Coupling: An Information System Perspective. European Journal of Purchasing and Supply Management. Vol. 8, pp. 161-171.
3. Carale, and Rajani, L. R. (2002). Supply Chain Management. A New Paradigm for Customer Centric Organization, Supply Management in the Twenty-first Century. Macmillan India Limited, New Delhi.
4. Charles X. Wang (2002). A General Framework of Supply Chain Contract Models. Supply Chain Management: An International Journal. Vol. 7(5), pp. 302-310.
5. Dhanakumar, V.G, (2004). Quality in Supply Chain Management. The Case of Fruits & Vegetables Chain. Management Perception. Vol.VI. No.l.pp.54-60.
6. Dutta, D. (2003). Measure Your Supply Chain Performance. Effective Executive. January, pp. 41-44.
7. Huchzermier, A. lyer, A and Frecheit, J. (2002). The Supply Chain Impact of Smart Customers in a Promotional Environment. Manufacturing and Service Operations Management. Pp. 228-240.
8. Peleg, B. (2003). Supply Chain Collaboration and Standardization. Effective Executive. January, pp. 25-28.
9. Prasad, R. K. and Sahay, S. (2003). Supply Chain Management. Effective Executive, pp. 19-24.
10. Roy, A. (2003). How Efficient is Your Reverse Supply Chain ? Effective Executive. January, Pp.52-55.
11. Sethi, S. (2003). The Intelligent Supply Chains. Effective Executive. January, pp. 49-50.
12. Riggs, A. D. and Robbins, L. S. (1998). Supply Management Strategies. American Management Association, New York.

6

Business of Diversification and Profitability as Competitive Advantage

INTRODUCTION

Diversification is the theme common to agri business development and the need for diversification is a sign of managing rigid economic bases and management of risk. As an investor in stocks and shares, manages his portfolio to maximize returns and minimizes losses. In this respect, diversification is an ongoing process, which, anticipates and embraces change subject to ongoing review and refinement has no end. It follows that if we were to fail to contemplate risk in agri-business and thus fail to embrace change then we would falter. In practice, diversification is a partnership between the public sector, which seeks to create the conditions for sustainable growth, and the private sector, which is acknowledged as the primary driver of economic growth. It is the effectiveness of these partner arrangements that will determine the success of our endeavours. The fear of diverting land from food grains to horticulture or livestock production seems unfounded, since such diversification has occurred in rain-fed, hilly and coastal regions, and has benefited the land-less and marginal farmers. Diversification is a primary means by which many individuals reduce risk. Diversification is widely understood as a form of self-insurance in which people exchange some foregone expected earnings for reduced income variability achieved by selecting a portfolio of assets and activities that have low or negative correlation of income. Links between agri-business diversify goals and its management tact would be a good business goals. It should be included in the mandatory management policy framework of agri business. Asset, activity and income diversification lie at the heart of livelihood strategies as a cause and consequence of change.

Diversification within food grains (millets, legumes beside cereals) and between food grains, and horticulture (fruits and vegetables) and livestock products is essential for both national and household food nutrition security. If planned properly, it can benefit the agri business value both nutritionally and economically. The micro level determinants of diversification are mirrored at more aggregate levels. From the "push factor perspective, diversification is driven by limited risk bearing capacity in the presence of incomplete or weak financial systems that create strong incentives to select a portfolio of activities in order to stabilize income flows and consumption., by constraints in labour, land, markets, and climatic uncertainty. From the "pull factor perspective," local engines of growth such as commercial agriculture or proximity to an urban area create opportunities for income diversification in production and expenditure-linkage activities. The extent of literature on diversification lacks common definitions or well established conventions on the collection or classification of data on the use of indicators to capture observed diversification behaviors. This lack of standard approaches impedes effective comparative analysis and too often leads to mistaken inference.

The first issue relates to the variable(s) of interest in the study of diversification is behaviour. Individuals own assets, some of which (non-productive assets, such as human capital, land, livestock) generate "earned" income only indirectly through their allocation to activities such as farming, weaving or commerce. The most basic classification of activities follows the sectoral distinctions of national accounting systems: primary (agriculture, mining, and other extractive), secondary (manufacturing), and tertiary (services). This leads directly to the distinction between "agricultural" or "farm" income (derived from the production or gathering of unprocessed crops or livestock or forest or fish products from natural resources) and "nonagricultural" or "nonfarm" income (all other sources of income, including from processing, transport of trading of unprocessed agricultural, forest and fish products). The sectoral farm/nonfarm assignment concerns only the nature of the product and the types of factors used in the production process. It does not matter where the activity takes place (in the domicile, on the farm premises, in town, abroad), at what scale (in huge factory or by a single person), with what technology, or whether the participant earns profit or labour income (wages or salary) from the activity.

The Causal Origins of Diversification

The literature already shows that nonfarm earnings account for a considerable share of farm household income in rural areas. Most of the papers in this special issue confirm widespread reliance on nonfarm income sources by farm households. The first logical question is: why do households diversify? Farm household diversification into nonfarm activities emerges naturally from diminishing or time-varying returns to labour or land ,from market failures (e.g., for credit) or frictions (e.g., for mobility or entry into high return niches), from *ex ante* risk management, and from *ex post* coping with adverse shocks. Where returns to productive assets vary across time (e.g., land, labour or livestock across dry and wet seasons) or among individuals within a household or households within a community, data aggregated across time, individuals, or households will exhibit diverse assets, activities and incomes even if there is complete Ricardian specialization according to comparative advantage. Such aggregation likely accounts for a substantial proportion of the diversification reported in empirical studies.

Horizontal Approach

The commonly understood mechanisms are the addition of more crops to the existing cropping systems, which is the broadening of the base of the system. This method of horizontal diversification has special significance under small-holder production systems and has been responsible for production increases due to high cropping intensities.

Vertical Approach

The other types is vertical crop diversification, which reflects the extent and stage of industrialization of the crops with practicing of enterprises like agro-forestry, dry land horticulture, medicinal and aromatic plants, other economic shrubs and livestock. It has to be noted that crop diversification takes into account for economic returns from different crops, and is different to the concept of multiple cropping. Both types of diversification will be essential to improve crop yields and income generation at local, regional and national levels.

Crop diversification development approach can be classified into *viz.*,(I) 'land based approach' and (ii) 'water based approach. In 'land based' approach, area (land) identification is the primary focus and all supporting development such as water resources infrastructure is secondary. Conversely, 'water based' approach focuses on the availability or ease of water resources development as primary consideration and area / land in the vicinity subsequently developed.

Crop diversification essentially means moving away from a single crop to a number of crops. Such a move towards crop diversification helps in (a) fuller and better use of available

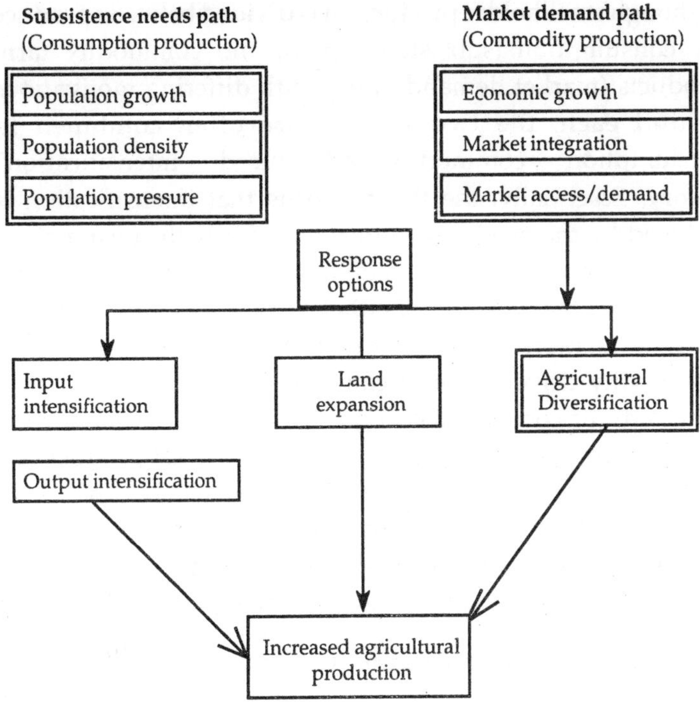

Fig. 1. Pathways from intensification and diversification.

land, labour, water and other resources; (b) reducing risks arising out of crop failures, yield losses and market failures , and (c) realizing quicker or regular returns to the farmer. However, these advantages of diversification are not with out costs to an individual farmer. Crop diversification demands higher level of managerial input from the farmer. More number of small surpluses creates difficulties in efficient handling and marketing of the produce. Further, it becomes prohibitive to acquire specialized and more efficient tools and equipments under diversified farming situations.

Fig 1. shows the two main pathways to 'improved well being' via agricultural input and output intensification.

Although smallholder production is divided between produce for consumption (subsistence path) and commodity farm products (market demand path), with differing motivations behind each, the two strands are often combined in consumption – commodity or "induced – intensification" theory. Essentially, the theory posits that intensification is induced by the need to produce food for both consumption and the market. "The overwhelming majority of smallholders throughout the world are neither pure subsistence nor pure market farmers". The composite of consumption and commodity driven intensification is a strong rationale, but they did not consider the degree of diversification, nor the extent of commercialization aside from 'market production'. Some of the factors influencing induced intensification include limited food reserves, climatic or environmental constraints, technological advantage/disadvantage, marketing opportunities/isolation, economic policies and civil unrest.

Application of Diversification in Commodity Sector (e.g. coffee)

This section presents a comprehensive framework for diversification and its fundamental strategy to resolve coffee crisis across businesses. Coffee prices reached their lowest levels in 30 years, and have risen only slightly with the ICO composite indicator price at 52.89 US cents/lb. According to the International Coffee Organization (ICO), in almost all coffee producing countries, such prices are unable to cover production costs and have led to serious social and economic problems, including increased poverty, indebtedness and abandonment of coffee farms. The crisis facing the coffee industry has been symptomised by massive over production, collapsing prices, deteriorating coffee quality, disease and above all the growing inequality in the coffee value chain. At the farmer level, price volatility has affected livelihoods of the farmers to the extent that they no longer have reliable source income, purchasing power and sustain their livelihoods. The overall negative effect is food insecurity leading to economic and social disorder in the various coffee households. The ICO and the World Bank ended a round table to share the burden of the present coffee crisis while also urging the industry representatives to discuss alternatives such as diversification, quality, added value and market development. The principal outcome of the meeting is to recommend potential diversification in coffee-producing countries.

Strategic Focus Through Diversification

Regions with a high concentration of "marginal" coffee producers are in-crisis and must diversify their economies with help of mixed farming. Diversification effort is not a matter of switching individual farmers or farmer groups from one crop to another. Rather, it involves introducing new "high-value" enterprises in crisis regions or helping existing farming system to work towards alternative sources of employment and income. Possible examples of high potential enterprises are: fruits & vegetables; ornamental plants, vanilla, cattle, medicinal & aromatic plants, eco-tourism, etc. It appears that few diversification efforts exist in coffee system because there is a concern that diversification products will be abandoned if coffee prices rise and there is a preconception that there are no viable diversification alternatives.

According to the United Nation's Food and Agricultural Organization (FAO, 1996), food security is achieved "when all people, at all times, have physical and economical access to enough safe and nutritive food to fulfill their dietary needs and alimentary preferences to lead an active and healthy life". To provide food security, food availability, an access must be guaranteed. Food security program empowered small farmers by helping them discover the potential production to feed their families and generate income. The definition of sustainability as the UN commission on Environment and

Development defined it as: "development that meets the needs of the present without compromising the ability of future generations to meet their own needs".

Methodology

This study was descriptive, exploratory and analytical in nature and relayed on qualitative and quantitative data. A number of researchers have commitment on the advantages of combining quantitative and qualitative methods (triangulations) in mixed farming. Both qualitative and quantitative data were used because in using the grounded theory approach "there is no fundamental clash between the purposes and capacities of qualitative or quantitative methods of data". An exploratory approach was considered necessary because of the scant literature on overall assessment of MFS.

Dindigul district in Tamil Nadu was selected for the study and datas were collected during the year 2003-04. The agripreneurs of coffee, coconut, chilli based mixed farming from thirty villages were selected for the study. From the villages selected, seventy-five agripreneurs each for coconut, chilli, coffee were represented with a total population of 225. In the study, commission agents, contractors, village leaders and traders were represented. The study focussed on the strategic policy orientation on a broad holistic dimensions of decision making process, MFS institutional support, group effectiveness, market orientation, quality of decision, WTO led extension, gender domain, supply chain management, risk management in agri-business, diversification in competitiveness, optimization of natural resources and leadership. However, this paper focuses only on the analytical aspect of the mixed farming in coffee and its diversification with reference to crisis management.

Results and Discussions

The important issue in mixed farming is selection of

appropriate technology or crop combination suited to coffee based MFS. In the first instance, technology or mixed farming pattern choice must be in a manner, which will maximize the net income that farmers perceive. In otherwords, the technology chosen must allow the farmers to make as much as money as possible. Sustainable coffee is more than a series of techniques, which balance among agronomic, management, environment, economic and social optimums.

The study result illustrated in Table 1 indicates the operational cost and net return on coffee based mixed farming under crisis situation. It indicates that farmers obtained a least net profit of Rs.5590/ac from coffee as compared with the income of lab lab at the rate of Rs. 32,500/season. Under the crisis scenario as indicated above, diversification in coffee in favour of more competitive and high value commodities is reckoned and important strategy to overcome emerging challenges. If carried out apparently in coffee system, diversification can be used as a tool to assignment of farm income, generating employment, resolve food insecurity, etc.

TABLE 1

Operational Cost and Net Return of Coffee based Mixed Farming

Sl. No.	*Crop combinations*	*Operational cost (Rs)*	*Gross Return (Rs)*	*Net Return (Rs)*
1.	Coffee	18110	23700	5590
2.	Orange	15200	34000	18800
3.	Banana	17700	52000	34300
4.	Pepper	16500	80000	63500
5.	Beans	12050	18000	5950
6.	Lab Lab	20000	52500	32500

Table 2 further elaborates the potential of coffee based MFS in generating employment opportunity within the family and at the village level. For example, a quantum of labour usage in coffee system reveals that introduction of sixth component of mixed farming fetched an annual higher labour requirement of 1520 mandays as compared with other combination. Data suggest that higher the combination of mixed farming, better in generation of employment opportunities.

TABLE 2

Employment Potential Under Different Crop Combination

Sl. No.	*Coffee based Mixed Farming*	*Annual labour requirements (Number of mandays)*
1.	Coffee + Orange	218
2.	Coffee + Orange + Chow Chow	395
3.	Coffee + Orange + Banana	273
4.	Coffee + Orange + Pepper + Chow Chow	485
5.	Coffee + Orange + Banana + Pepper + Beans	531
6.	Coffee + Orange + Cardamom + Pepper + Beans + Lab Lab	1520
7.	Coffee + Orange + Banana + Cardamom	605
8.	Coffee + Orange + Banana + Beans	464
9.	Coffee + Orange + Banana + Lab Lab	1217

Note: Perennial and annual crops are standardized at an annual (or) for year, other than annual crop like seasonal crops are standardized at per season.

If coffee based MFS capitalize on profitable growth opportunities in its present situation, there is no urgency to pursue diversification. But, when growth opportunities in coffee sector diminishing, diversification is usually the most viable option for reviving the coffee business.

As part of the decision to diversify, farmer can diversify plantation into closely related crops or into totally unrelated crops within the acceptable quantum of diversification. It can expand into agribusiness and leverage existing competencies and capabilities where same resource strands are key success factors and valuable competitive assets. It can pursue opportunities to get into other product markets where its present technological know how can be applied and possible in competitive advantage. It can diversify towards small extent or to a large extent. It can move into one or two large new mixed cropping or a greater number of crops in smaller areas.

Levels of Diversification

Diversified firms vary accordingly to their level of diversification and the connections between and among their businesses. Figure 2 lists and defines five categories of businesses according to increased level of diversification and availability of resources. Table 3, illustrates its level and types of diversification for 3 MFS. Highly diversified firms, which have no relationships, are called unrelated diversified firms. Related diversification is a strategy through which the firm

Low Levels of Diversification		
Single business:	More than 95% of revenue comes from a single business	A
Double business:	Between 70% and 95% of revenue comes from a single business	A, B
Moderate to High Levels of Diversification		
Related constrained:	Less than 70% of revenue comes from the dominant business, and all businesses share product, technological, and distribution linkages.	A, B, C
Related linked (mixed related and unrelated):	Less than 70% of revenue comes from the dominant business, and there are only limited links between businesses	A, B, C
Very High Levels of Diversification		
Unrelated:	Less then 70% of revenue comes from the dominant business, and there no common links between businesses.	A, B, C

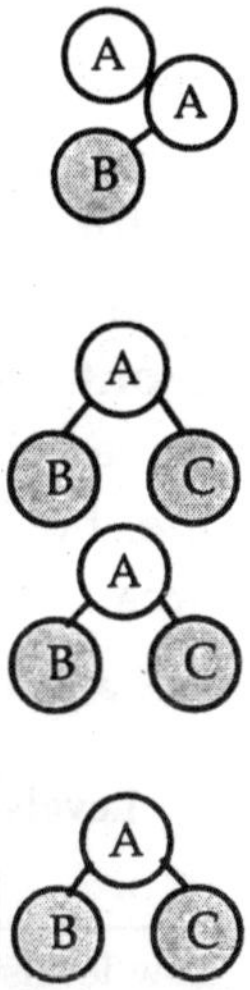

Source: Adapted from R.P. Rumelt, 1974, Strategy, structure and Economic Performance (Boston: Harvard Business School)

Fig. 2. Levels and Types of Diversification

intents to build upon or extend its existing resources capabilities, and core competencies in the pursue of strategic competitiveness.

A sound understanding of the pattern of coffee based diversification and the constraints it faces would help in crafting appropriate policies regarding institutional arrangements and creation of adequate infrastructure, which could benefit a large mass of small and marginal holder in MFS. The proposed study is an attempt to identify the optimum percentage of diversification in coffee sector. Within MFS, however, diversification is considered as a shift of resources from one crop (or livestock) to a target mix of crops and livestock. Keeping in view the varying nature of risks and expected returns from each crop/livestock leads to optimum portfolio of income in MFS.

Diversification in coffee sector is gradually picking momentum in favour of high value crops and livestock activities to assign incomes rather than a coping strategy to many risk and uncertainty. However, the nature of diversification differs across regions due to wide heterogeneity in agro ecological factor and socio-economic condition. Therefore, it would be interesting to delineate key areas where diversification is profitable. In Table 3, Levels and types of diversification for three Mixed farming System section is attempted to unfold the above features and diagonized the diversification in study area.

TABLE 3

Levels and Types of Diversification for three Mixed Farming System

Low levels of diversification	Type of Enterprises		
Single business More than 75% income	Coffee	Chilli	Coconut

from single crop			
Double business: 70-90 % income from single business	Coffee+orange Or Coffee+banana	Chilli + onion Or Chilli+beetroot	Coconut + Gherkin Or Coconut+ maize
Moderate to high levels of diversification			
Related constrained: 70% of income from main crop and remaining from related crops	Coffee+orange+ pepper	Chilli+beetroot+ beans	Coconut+ gooseberry+ maize
Related linked(mixed related and unrelated)	Coffee+orange+ vegetables	Chilli+onion+ dairy	Coconut+ sericulture + cow and goat
Very high levels of diversification			
Unrelated: Less than 70% income from main crop	—	Chilli+onion+ beans+Tobacco + foddergrass+ Dairy and goat	Coconut + beans+citrus+ cow and goat

Table 4 illustrates nine different components of mixed farming structure, out of which item number nine exemplify the combination. The above combination had shown a definite improvement in income. The cost benefit ratio of 1:2.61 indicates a profit of 260 per cent. The primary reason for taking up the combinations were due to significant income from banana and short duration bean.

TABLE 4

Coffee based MFS Structure and Cost Benefit Ratios

Sl. No.	*Combinations*	*B:C Ratio*
1.	Coffee + Orange + Chow Chow	1:1.27
2.	Coffee + Orange	1:1.58
3.	Coffee + Orange + Banana + Lab Lab	1:1.80
4.	Coffee + Orange + Banana + Cardamom	1:1.88
5.	Coffee + Orange + Cardamom + Pepper + Beans + Lab Lab	1:1.98

6.	Coffee + Orange + Banana + Beans	1:2.09
7.	Coffee + Orange + Banana	1:2.28
8.	Coffee + Orange + Pepper + Chow Chow	1:2.55
9.	Coffee + Orange + Banana + Pepper + Beans	1:2.61

The finding of the study also reveals that mixed farming sector should gradually diversify its farming with short duration high value commodities, vegetables, livestock, non-farming entrepreneurs activities, value addition, process based unit, etc to minimize the risk. Production of vegetables and livestock products has increased remarkably high income due to awareness & prediction skill on market demand. According to the finding, diversification in favour of varied enterprises was more pronounced as a successful parameter, than very high diversification in single enterprises under crisis situation.

An analysis of linear programming was taken to predict optimum income opportunities in coffee MFS. The study also brought out findings related to possibility of optimum income within the available resources. Linear programming is a more systematic and accurate method of determining mathematically the optimum combination of enterprises or inputs so as to maximize the income or minimize the cost with in the limit of available resources. LP results for Coffee based MFS comprises of three group of farmers viz., marginal (3.14 acres), small (7.3 acres) and medium (23.9 acres) which are classified based on land holdings as indicated in the parenthesis. The data reveals that existing and proposed optimum number of plants per unit area to optimize overall profitability in MFS varied from Rs.66, 665 to Rs.1, 40,177 for the category of marginal and small farmers respectively.

TABLE 5

Optimization of Coffee Based MFA

Categories	*Existing Income*	*Optimal Income*	*Optimal Allocation*
Marginal farmer without vegetables	59,062	66,665.80	Increase- no. of coffee, banana, pepper plants Decrease- no. of orange and cardamom plants
Small farmer with vegetables	1,01,940	1,40,177	Increase- marginal increase of jack Decrease- no. of banana plants Additional inclusion- beans
Small farmer without vegetables	94,990.50	1,38,689	Increase- no. of jack tress Decrease- no. of banana and lemon
Medium farmer with vegetables	4,93,285.50	7,22,169	Increase-two fold of pepper Nil-Chow chow Decrease-two fold of cardamom Additional inclusion-bean
Medium farmer without vegetables	4,29,877	6,70,954	Increase-two fold the no. of pepper vines Decrease- no. of cardamom plants

To sum up, coffee based MFAs are classified into five different categories for optimization through LP consolidated results are given in Table 5.

In case of marginal MFA category, LP predicts that increase in number of coffee plants, banana suckers and pepper vines are of good option for optimization. Further, the optimal solution suggests that number of orange and cardamom plants to be reduced.

The optimal solution for small MFAs growing vegetables along with coffee will have to increase marginally number of jack trees, with reduction of appreciable number of banana suckers and cultivation of beans are recommended to fetch Rs.1.40 lakhs/unit area (Refer Table No. 5 &6). Under the category of small MFAs, those not cultivating vegetables, it is recommended that the optimal plan of marginal increases in number of jack trees and decreases in number of banana and lemon plants. In a nutshell, the optimization revealed that small farmers are recommended to include beans in their farming system.

The optimum plan for medium farmers growing vegetables indicates that there should be two fold increase in number of pepper vines and area under beans. The optimization also suggested that 40% of cardamom plants are to be decreased. The medium farmer without vegetable cultivation in their fields are recommended to increase the number of pepper vines two fold and the number of cardamom plants reduced drastically (Refer Table No.7&8). The subtle observation of the optimization reveals that increase in number of pepper vines, decrease in number of cardamom plants and additional inclusion of beans would form an optimal plan for medium farmers.

The optimal solution indicates that medium farmers are expected to get more optimal income (Rs.6.7 to 7.2 lakhs) than marginal (Rs.60,000 to 66,665) and small farmers (Rs.1.3 to Rs. 1.4 lakhs) due additional income gained from vegetables.

The complexity of coffee based MFS system and intensified competition has been forced the coffee growers to predict crisis management in coffee. The result on hierarchical regression coefficient strongly suggests that risk bearing ability of coffee growers contributes as the only significant variable for the diversification of coffee based MFS. Furthermore, inorder to assess strategic risk management in coffee, the concept of break even analysis has chosen to predict risk related to coffee based diversification. The major factors such as effects of price and sensitivity of yield per acre contributed as a risk management tool in coffee based farming. The study also suggests that productivity of plant per acre is a crucial

TABLE 7

Normative Plan for Coffee based Medium Farmer without Vegetables

(No. of plants/unit area)

Sl.	Crops	Area (acre)	Existing number of plants	Optimal number plants
1.	Coffee (Arabia)	7.17	6453	6453
2.	Orange	5.07	761	760
3.	Banana	4.64	882	875
4.	Pepper	3.10	248	629
5.	Lemon	2.50	162	187
6.	Cardamom	1.50	900	500
7.	Chow Chow	-	-	-
8.	Beans	-	-	-
	Net income in Rs.	23.98	4,29,877	6,70,954

TABLE 8

Normative Plan for Coffee based Medium Farmer with Vegetables

(No. of plants/unit area)

Sl.	Crops	Area (acre)	Existing number of plants	Optimal number plants
1.	Coffee (Arabia)	7.17	6453	6453
2.	Orange	5.07	761	760
3.	Banana	4.64	882	875
4.	Pepper	3.10	248	630
5.	Lemon	2.50	162	187
6.	Cardamom	1.50	900	500
7.	Chow Chow	1.59	-	-
8.	Beans	2.00	-	3.50
	Net income in Rs.	27.48	4,93,285.50	7,22,169

TABLE 6

Diversification Activities and Necessary Capitals Requirements

	Natural capital	*Physical capital*	*Economic/ financial capital*	*Human capital*	*Social capital*	*Key institutions*
Trader/commi ssion agent		Transport vehicle	Investment in stock	Labour	Trading networks	Markets,transport agencies,household labour arrangements
Unskilled wage labour (on daily basis): food for work, agricultural labour, painting, porter, sand collection, state farm labourer.				labour	Networks to seek employment	Markets, farmers association, household labour arrangements
Cultivator	land	Animal power (or)tractor	labour	Networks to	KVK, banks land enable access to	KVK, banks
Herder		livestock				Land tenure, livestock accessing institutions
Artisanship: potter, blacksmith	Materials for tranformation		Tools	Labour skills	Membership of particular caste	Caste

Formally employed: teacher, health worker , vet, NGO worker, local agent of party, woreda council member, maid, guard			Investment in skills or education	Skill or education	Networks for entry to occupation	NGO; labour market
Handicrafts: carpender, spinning, basket making, roof thatching, mat making	Materials for transform ation, often CPRs		Tools	Labour skills	Networks to for entry access to CPRs	Natural resource tenure institutions
Forest products: charcoal, wood, grass, lumber	Materials for transformation			Labour	Network to enable access to CPRs	Natural resource tenure institutions

tool to manage risk in the current price fall scenario of coffee based system.

Conclusion

Sustainable mixed farming in coffee requires the balancing of variety of goals. This means that often no single goal can be maximized, since such optimization might totally preclude the achievement of one of the other goals of sustainability. For this reason, trans-disciplinary team containing advocates of various goals, with ability to negotiate, prioritize, provide an important input into Sustainable Mixed Farming Business and Management (SMFB/M) is warranted. Further coffee growers' participation on this team is particularly crucial, because sustainable coffee means that the farmer shifts from a user of technology to producer of technology and monitor of its impact.

To compliment and improve upon early gains in coffee system, agronomic research for small farmers should focus on optimization with respect to different types (Refer Figure no.2) of diversification under the crisis situation. Enhancing growth of small farmers in achieving more equitable income among coffee growers are paramount objectives of sustainable mixed farming business and management. Most agronomist agree that sustainable mixed farming business and management (SMFB/M) is interdisciplinary and farmer oriented, with the system approach to agronomic research.

SMFB/M presents a systematic methodology for changing mixed farming systems, including changing the actions of farmers, researchers and extension personnel. It has a tradition of involving interdisciplinary teams in its implementation. Key changes in team formulation and dynamics would be needed for SMFB/M to function as a major mechanism for generating and implementing more sustainable coffee systems. Broadening the composition and mandate of the trans-disciplinary teams would be one mechanism for such change. To enhance the process of diversification in agri business, we need to take series of measures to reform grassroots structural framework and multi-dimensional system approach. Table 6, illustrates the details related to diversification activities and their related inputs, as part of diversification. For example, if a cultivar wants to diversify his profession as a trader (or) commission agents he/she need to equip the features given under the column of trader in Table 6.

REFERENCES

1. Barrelt, B.C., Rearden,T and Webb,P. Non farm Income Diversification and Household Livelihood Srategies in Rural Africa: Concepts, Dynamics and Policy Implication. pp 1-24
2. Carswell, G. (2003). Diversification in southern Ethiopia. Institute of Development studies, pp 3-12.
3. Dhanakumar, V. G. (1999). An Analysis on the Decision Making Process and Organization Effectiveness. Journal of Rural Development. Vol. 18. No. 1, pp. 65-81.
4. Dhanakumar, V. G. (2004). An Analysis on the Decision Making Processes and Its Impact on Mixed Farming in Agri-Plantation Sector. ICAR Project- Annual Report, Indian Institute of Plantation Management, Bangalore.
5. Turner, B.L, II and Ali, A.M.S. (1996). Induced Intensification: Agricultural change in Bangladesh with implication for Malthus and Borerup. Proceedings of the national Academy of sciences 93: 14984-91.

7

Venture Technology: Nano-Technology, Hurdle Technology and Gene-Tech Perspectives

Venture is often referred to a risky start-up or enterprise company with optimal capital and resources made available to firms and small businesses for exceptional growth potential. Most venture capital money comes from an organized group of wealthy investors. Venture Capital is an investment company that invests its shareholders' money in startups and other risky, but potentially very profitable ventures. Every established business was once a start-up, successful start-up has had an innovation around which the growth had been built. The innovation could have been in the area of product/service, raw material discovery, new market discovery, new technology, distribution, promotion, service of business model etc.

Large corporations with financial resources has a deep knowledge base in disciplined management processes, have talent pool, brand image, customer (Hippel, 1977) and supplier franchise, distribution network and other tangible and intangible assets which can leverage into new businesses but they didn't venture into new agri-businesses significantly. On the other hand, small businesses with creative ideas and newly developed technologies, flexibility to operate and quickly learn from failures are emerged as a challenging company. But, they are very close to the customer groups and have customer knowledge, but lack disciplined management processes, brand image and limited or missing financial and talent pool. This section aims to deliberate the details related to different available venture technologies and its relevance to agri-business sector with appropriate examples.

A. NANOTECHNOLOGY

Nanotechnology can best be considered as a 'catch-all' description of activities at the level of atoms and molecules that have applications in the real world. A nanometre is a billionth of a metre, that is, about 1/80,000 of the diameter of a human hair, or 10 times the diameter of a hydrogen atom. In agriculture, where once we had crossbred individual animals or plants, biotechnology enabled us to manipulate the genes themselves. Now nanotechnology takes us to an even smaller scale to the level of the atom, the building block of everything that exists. The implications of nanotechnology are huge. By manipulating and exploiting the structure of materials at the atomic level, it becomes possible to engineer a new material with entirely new properties never before identified in nature. Nano particles are already introduced to Sunscreen Lotions and food package sector. Nano technology may eliminate farming and ranching while making Nanofoods through air we breathe. Nano based molecular manufacturing may shut down existing mining and mineral operations. Nano based storable solar energy will reduce ash, hydrocarbon, carbon-di-oxide emission and oil spills in near future.

Different Types of Nano Particles

Coarse - diameter less than 10 micron

Fine - Average diameter less than 2.5 micron

Ultrafine - (Average diameter less than one micron)

One micron (m) is one millionth of a metre and 1000 nanometers (nm)

Nano Vision

Nano technologies have the potential to produce plentiful consumer goods with much lower input of materials and much less production of waste, thus reducing carbon dioxide build up and reducing global warming. They also have the potential to reduce waste, converting it to natural materials which do not threaten live.

Nano Food Products

Novel products are tailored to taste buds of each consumer. For example, Nano particles in a clear, tasteless drink activated with domestic microwave to produce whatever tastes the consumer desire and/or perceive. Personal food products with nano-particles that recognize an individual nutritional or health profile (allergies or nutritional deficiencies). Food packaging those changes colours and alerts the consumer when the food inside starts to spoil.

Nano Motors

Building motors on a molecular state. University of California created the world's smallest electrical device. (One hundred million of which could fit on the end of a pin). Rural India use diesel engines but they don't have way to set the timing for operation. Little Nano controller sensor device is worked out in India to watch the flywheel movement to monitor fuel flow, on & off the system automatically.

Agriculture Development Through Nano-Technology

Nano-sensors sprinkled on crops or soil monitor temperature, water, salinity, nitrogen and disease. Nano particles are used as chemical delivery system for pesticides. Bioactive Nano particles that bind with bacteria in industrially farmed poultry meat, aimed to reduce their ability to infect humans through microorganisms (eg. Salmonella).

Nano Technology in Medical/Health Sector

Artificial red blood cell able to deliver 236 times more oxygen to tissues than natural red blood cells. Glucose sensor implanted into diabetic patients to control blood sugar level. Nano capsule gel to deliver drugs into the eyes through soft contact lenses. Nano particle drugs delivered through the skin at high velocity. For example, L'oreal incorporated nano capsules containing Vitamin E deep into the consumer skin. The new venture enterprises are working to identify agro-based nano particles for bio-pharmaceutical industry.

Nano Discoveries

Nano sensors - Detect gas leakage in chemical plants and refineries, its cost is 10 times lesser than conventional gas detection. **Nano filters** - Physical filters with nanometer scale pores can remove 100% of bacteria, viruses and even prions. **Molecular nanobots** - disassemble toxic waste and dispose it safely. Molecular recycling & bio-mimicry - mimicking natural processes to produce synthetic materials that break down more easily in nature. Averting catastrophe - Nanobots are developed to detect and dissolve asteroid to prevent natural disaster like earthquakes.

B. IRRADIATION

Food irradiation is a process of exposing foods, either prepackaged or in bulk to very high-energy, invisible light waves (radiation) such as gamma rays, X-rays or electron beams to prevent spoilage and contamination. Small Irradiation dose modify properties of the food, such as sprouting and ripening and higher doses can alter molecules in microorganisms. CODEX accepted food irradiation as a safe and effective technology. Immunocom promised that people benefit from food irradiation due to reduction in bacteria. Nearly, 40 countries approved > 100 food items for food irradiation because food irradiation is a means of safety and security. Irradiation should be used as approved by the competent food safety authorities for disease-causing germs. The dose for food irradiation for different foods are given in Table No. 1.

TABLE 1

Irradiation D Values for Food-borne Microorganisms Irradiable Foods

Food	*Dose*
Meat	4.5 kGy
Poultry	1.5- 3 kGy
Grains	0.2 – 0.5 kGy
Fruits & Vegetables	1 kGy

kGy - kilogray

Non-Irradiable Foods

Oysters and other raw shell fish

Eggs

Food Irradiation Process

Facilities for Food Irradiation are similar to sterilizing medical equipment. Radiation source (Cobalt-60) is contained in slender pencil like stainless casing. Package food travels in pallets on a conveyor and exposed to the radiation source. **Radicidation** - ionizing radiation to reduce non-spore forming pathogenic bacteria. **Radurization** - to enhance keeping quality. **Radappertization** - to reduce activities of microorganisms (except viruses).

Absorbed Dose

Food Irradiation process termed as absorbed dose.

Measured in units of Kilogray (KGY)

1 Gray = Energy absorption of one joule/kg.

The Killing effect of irradiation on microbes is measured in D values.

D value is the amount of irradiation needed to kill 90% of the organisms. Eg.0.3 Kilo Grays to kill 90% of E-coli.

Examples on the Success of Irradiated Food

Camembert cheeses and Mechanically debone poultry meat is commercialized as Irradiated Food in France. Irradiated henham (2 kg Gy) fetched more prices than non-irradiated food. In Bangladesh, irradiated dried fish fetched higher price than fish fumigated with pesticides (Eg.DDT). Irradiated frog legs met strict microbial specification in France for the past 10 years.

C. HURDLE TECHNOLOGY

The demand by consumers for high quality foods having 'fresh' or 'natural' characteristics, that require a minimum amount of preparation led to the development of ready-to-eat and convenience foods that are preserved using mild technologies. The main preservation technique is refrigeration, but because of the difficulty in maintaining sufficiently low temperatures throughout the production, distribution and storage chain, additional barriers (or 'hurdles') are required to control the growth of spoilage or pathogenic micro-organisms. The concept of combining several factors to preserve foods had been developed by Leistner (1995) and others into the Hurdle effect (each factor is a hurdle that micro-organisms must overcome). This in turn had led to the application of Hurdle Technology, where an understanding of the complex interactions of temperature, water activity, pH, chemical preservatives, etc. is used to design a series of hurdles that ensure microbiological safety of processed foods. The hurdles are also used to improve the quality of foods and the economic properties (for example, the weight of water that can be added to a food, consistent with its microbial stability). To be successful, the hurdles must take into account the initial numbers and types of micro-organisms that are likely to be present in the food. The hurdles that are selected should be 'high enough' so that the anticipated numbers of these micro-organisms cannot overcome them. However, the same hurdles that satisfactorily preserve a food when it is properly prepared are overcome by a larger initial population of micro-organisms, for example, if raw materials are not adequately cleaned. In this example, the main hurdles are low water activity and chemical preservatives in the product, with storage temperature, pH and redox potential having a smaller effect. Blanching* vegetables or fruits has a similar effect in reducing initial numbers of micro-organisms before freezing or drying. If the same hurdles are used with a different product that is richer in nutrients that can support microbial growth, again the hurdles may be inadequate to preserve it and a different combination may be needed or the height of the hurdles increased. It should be noted that although the hurdles are represented as a sequence, in practice the different factors may operate simultaneously, synergistically or sequentially.

The combination of hurdle technology and HACCP in process design is described by Leistner (1994). By combining hurdles, the intensity of individual preservation techniques can be kept comparatively low to minimise loss of product quality, while overall high impact on controlling microbial growth in food chain.

D. Gene Technology

At present Biotechnology offers two per cent of the global market share and it will increase by 10 per cent of the global market share. It is anticipated that agri biotech will occupy 15 per cent of the Indian biotech sector within five years period. Biotechnology techniques offer a more versatile and precise method of introducing one or more genes into a plant

---

* Blanching refers to take the color out of, and make white.

from unrelated organism. It is a genetic modification tool used to customize plants with special qualities that can allow farmers to grow crops that are more nutritious, more resistant to pest and disease and high productive. In the future, new crop plants may be source of valued medicines, biochemical, and chemicals feed stocks and specialty 'niche' crops. Breakthrough of Biotechnology components are given below:

Malaria Proof Mosquitoes : GM mosquito for reduced capacity to transmit malaria

Potato for Cancer: Transgenic potatoes for protection against *Human Papiloma* (HP) virus

Silkworm Spins Skin: GM silkworms for skin and wound dressing

Bald Chicken breed : Featherless skin for easy consumption

Blood from Tobacco plants: Transgenic tobacco plants to produce drugs, vaccines and blood compounds

Application of Bio-tech in Food Sector

- Reduced Allergencity : Decrease or eliminate allergentic protein Eg. Rice
- Medical Benefits: Eg. Plants are used to produce edible vaccines. Tobacco plants are used to produce therapeutic vaccine
- Healthy Farm Animals: Feed with lower level of phytate to reduce P, N and odour from animal waste. For example, corn is nutritionally more dense and easier for the animals to digest.
- Environmental benefits: Minimization of chemical usage. Eg. Herbicide - tolerant soybeans reduced farm input costs by 3 to 6 %.

- Tomato with an antisense gene requires less energy to process into tomato paste
- Level of major rice allergen has been reduced by using biotechnology

Plants are used to produce edible vaccines and to increase the production of medical products

Biotechnology in Marketing

- Israel increased its export of watermelon by 50 times more by producing box shaped watermelons with help of gene technology.
- Flander, Belgium have developed designer-potatoes with the shape of customer choice of same size, shape and quality.

Bio-tech in Agriculture

- Genetically Modified plants
- Hybrid seeds
- Tissue culture
- Bio-pesticide & Bio-fertilizer
- Bio-informatics and Genomics
- Nanotechnology

Genetically Modified Organism

Organisms in which the genetic material (DNA) has been altered in a way that does not occur naturally

Genetically Modified Food/Plants

Selected (individual) genes to be transferred from one plant to another, also between non-related species

GM Crops Currently in the Market

- Insect resistance

- Virus resistance
- Herbicidal tolerance

Process of Gene-Transfer

A. Insect resistance

Bacterium

(*Bacillus thurengiensis*-BT)

↓

Gene for toxin production

↓

Incorporating into the food plant for resistance

B. Virus resistance

Viruses which cause disease

↓

Gene from such viruses

↓

Incorporating into the food plant resistance

C. Herbicide tolerance

Bacteria

↓

Gene for resistance to some herbicide

↓

Incorporate into the food plant resistance

Are GM Foods Safe?

- Different GM organism include different genes in different ways
- Individual GM foods and safety should be assessed on case-by-case basis
- GM foods currently available on international market have passed risk assessments
- Not likely to present risks for human health

- No effects on human health have been shown as result of consumption
- Continuous use of risk assessment based on codex principles is essential

(a) Bio-Pharming

Exploring the ability of plants to make medically important protein

- Manufacture of therapeutic compounds at lower cost and in greater amounts

  Eg., GM corn protein used in swine vaccines

Importance of Bio-Pharming

At present, drugs are produced from bacterial culture & fermentation process. Fermentation facilities incur huge capital & construction costs. Alternatively, "Plant-made Pharmaceuticals" (PMPs) are produced by Genetically Modified Products (GMP) to produce specific compounds, especially proteins and this is comparatively cheaper than the bacterial culture.

Crops considered for Pharmaceutical Production

- Alfalfa
- Potato
- Safflower
- Soybean
- Sugarcane
- Tomato

Plant Parts that produce Pharmaceuticals

Seed—Common production and storage of engineered product

Leaves—Alfalfa & tobacco

Tubers—Potato

Bio-informatics

"Study of information content and information flow in biological systems and process".

Maintaining and operating a unique database and knowledge base.

Bio-informatics Process

Bio-Data (plant based)

↓

Bio-information

↓

Bio-knowledge

↓

Drugs Development

Importance of Bio-informatics

- Future pharmaceutical discoveries will stem from biological discoveries
- Pressure to reduce costs and speed up the drug discovery cycles, provide a strong demand for software and information based technology in bioinformatics
- Data oriented research environment in which collaboration of molecular biology, chemist and computer scientists is essential
- Change from specialist niche tool to essential corporate technology
- Laboratory based tool to integrated corporate infrastructure

FUTURE TRANSGENIC PRODUCTS

Crops	*Purpose*
Tomato	Slow ripening salt tolerant
Golden rice	Addition of Vit .A in rice for vision impairment, diarrhea, respiratory diseases & measles
Canola	Enhancing Vit .A content
Banana	Production of edible vaccines
Coffee and tea	Decaffination

Product	*Genetic change*	*advantage*
Canola oil	No transfats	Alternative oil for baking, frying snack food
Cotton	BT Cotton	Bollworm reduction and reduced use of pesticide
Milk Production	Chymogen	Milk to produce cheese
Peanut/ Groundnut	High Oleic acid	Longer life for nuts, candy and peanut butter
Sunflower	High Oleic acid	Temperature stability
Tomatoes	Increase Pectin	Firm longer and tomato paste

CONCLUSION

While consumer expectation on gene products have increased over the years, the availability of venture technology to deliver and promise inherent in most of the brands in the business has seldom kept up. Infact, venture technology has delighted the customers towards felt needs and enhanced their purchasing power. The implication of venture technology for production, marketing, value addition and packaging are performed well. The venture technology such as irradiation, hurdle technology, gene technology will deliver consistently the product through brand names needed for the long-term success of the company and well being of the consumer. The operational concept of venture technology should be integrated as strategic approach in agribusiness sector.

REFERENCE

1. Hippel, Ericvon, "Successful and Failing Internal Corporate Ventures: An Emperical Analysis", Industrial Marketing Management, volume 6 (1977), pp. 163-174.
2. http://www.learnthat.com/define/view.asp? id = 342
3. W.M. Urbain, *Food Irradiation*, Academic Press, New York, 1986.
4. J.F. Deihl, Will irradiation enhance or reduce food safety. Food Policy 18(2): 143-151 (1993).
5. Entrepreneurship and Nanotechnology Symposium 2004.
6. Letourneau, K.D. and Burrows, E.B. (2001). Genetically modified Organisms. RS Press, Baco Raton.
7. Thomas, J. (2005). Promosing the World, or Costing the Earth? Ecologist Asia. Vol. 12, No. 1, pp. 48-54.

8

Contract Farming as a Tool for Corporate Agriculture

Contract farming is a forward contract between the Corporate Agri-business Circles (Processing Units) and farmer producers to make available a specified quantity and quality produce at a particular price on a future specified period/point of time. Contract farming ensures the uniform distribution of raw materials and integrated supply chain. Contract farming based agreements can be made based on market specification, resource providing and operations management. Market specification contracts are pre harvest agreements that bind the firm and grower to a particular set of conditions like specified price, quality and timing. Resource providing contracts, supply crop inputs in exchange for a marketing agreements and production management contracts bind the farmer to follow a particular production method or input regime.

No Contract farming venture should be initiated unless some basic preconditions are met. The following sections illustrate the podium of contract farming under the headings of profitability, the physical & social environments and government support.

STAKE HOLDERS

1. The Sponsor

Must have identified a market for the planned production.

Must be sure that such a market can be supplied profitably on a long-term basis

2. The Farmer

Must find potential returns more attractive than return from alternative activities and must find the level of risk acceptable. Must have potential returns demonstrated on the basis of realistic yield estimates

3.Physical and Social Environment

The physical environment must be suitable in general, and in particular for the product to be produced. Utilities and communications must be suitable for both farming, e.g., feeder roads, and for agro-processing, e.g., water and electricity. Land availability and tenure – contracted farmers require unrestricted access to the land, they farm. Input availability-sources of inputs need to be assured. Social considerations - cultural attitudes and practices should not conflict with farmers' obligations under the contract and managers must develop a full understanding of local practices.

4. Government Support

The Enabling and Regulatory Role

Suitable laws of contract and other laws are required as well as an efficient legal system. Governments need to be aware of the possible unintended consequences of regulations and should avoid the tendency to over-regulate. Governments should provide services such as research and sometimes, extension.

The Developmental Role

Governments should take steps to bring together agribusiness and suitable stakeholders as indicated below:

Stakeholders of Contract Farming (CF)

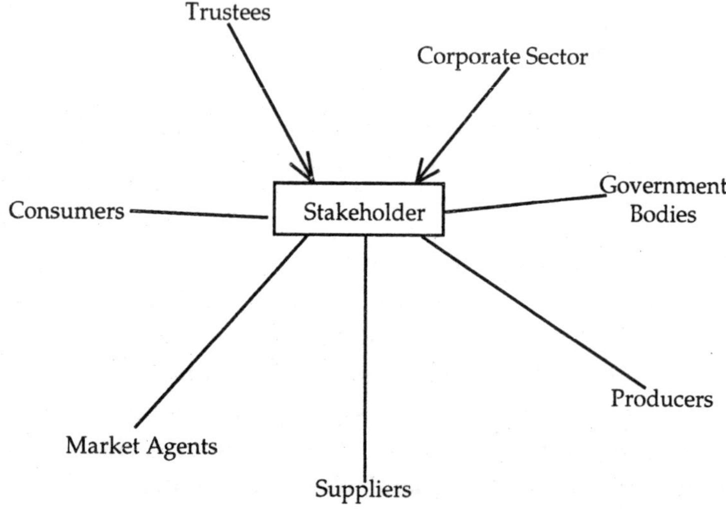

Role of Stakeholders in Contract Farming

Coalition building

Institution building

Developing "Council" for local operations based on the need

Material Management "SCM" perspective

Advisory Team from Corporate Headquarters and Farm Representative (or) Local Bodies

(a) Farm Management (Operations)

(b) Input Management

(c) Procurement/Price

(d) Quality Management

(e) Value addition

(f) Contracting Contractor of Contractors (CCC)

Assurance to Insurance and Pay & Buy-back.

LEAN Strategies

Government regulations (tax, levies, legal etc.)

Farm Risk Management

Consultancy and Management

5. Most Required Technical Guidance for Contract Farming

- Varieties (Disease resistant, pest resistant varieties)
- Growing season (Sowing and harvesting period)
- Integrated Pest Management
- Quality Management Practices (or) systems

Corporate Contract Farming : Steps for the Formation of Contract Farming

Corporate Decision (Crops, varieties)

- Supplier to

1. Own use
2. Other Company
3. Mass Farming

↓

Identification of Areas (State/District)

- Existing Cropping areas (or)New Cropping areas

Formation of Self Help Groups/Institution Building

(Sourcing (or) Resourcing of Farmer)

Formation of a Body (or) Committee

(State & Central Government Organization, Farm Business Service Centre, Banks & Insurance Companies)

↓

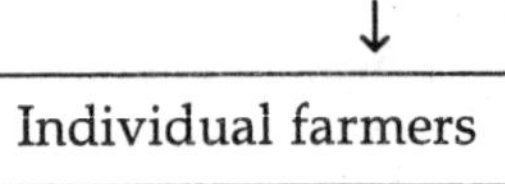
Individual farmers

- Crop loan and insurance
- Quality input supply
- Assured pay back
- Technical guidance
- Quality Systems (ISO)

Model Agreement Contents

1. *Parties to Agreement*
    - Contract farming sponsor- sole proprietor or partnership firm
    - Contract farming producers- includes agriculturist, farmers associations, self help groups, authorized tenants

2. *Description of Farm Land*
    - Acreage, location- land particulars as recorded with the revenue authority
    - Facilities available – availability of irrigation etc.
    - Nature, tenure, rights etc of contract farming production on the land

3. *Duration of Agreement*
    - Seasonal
    - Annual
    - Long term (3-5 years)

4. *Description of Farm Produce*
    - Agricultural produce with specific variety the buyer wants to produce

5. *Quantity Specification of the Farm Produce*
   - On volume basis
   - On area basis
   - Entire crop
   - Fixed quantity

6. *Quality Specifications of Commodity Contracted*
   - Size, weight, degree of maturity, packaging
   - Agency to decide quality, in case of dispute
   - Consequences of non-conformity with quality specification
   - Rejection
   - Reduction in price
   - Any other

7. *Crop Delivery Agreements*
   - At farm gate
   - At processing unit
   - At specified collection centers
   - Transportation arrangements

Organisational Models for Contract Farming

(a) *Centralized model:* The sponsor purchase crops from farmers for processing, and market the product. Quotas are distributed at the beginning of each growing season and quality is tightly controlled. This model is generally associated with tobacco, cotton, sugarcane, bananas, coffee, tea, cocoa and rubber crops.

(b) *Nucleus estate model:* The sponsor owns and manages a plantation usually close to a processing plant and introduces technology and management techniques to farmers (sometime called "satellite" growers). This model is mainly used for tree crops, but has also been applied to dairy production.

(c) *Multipartite Model:* This usually involves statutory bodies and private companies jointly participating with farmers. It is common in china where government departments, township committees and foreign companies have entered into contracts with villages and individual farmers.

(d) *Informal or Individual Developed Model:* Individual entrepreneurs or small companies make simple informal production contracts with farmers on a seasonal basis particularly for fresh vegetables and tropical fruits. Supermarkets frequently purchase fresh produce through individual developers.

(e) *Intermediary Model:* Formal subcontracting of crop production to intermediaries is common in Southeast Asia. In Thailand, large food processing companies purchase crops from individual 'collectors' or farmer committees, who make there own informal arrangements with farmers.

Different Contract Farming Models operating in Dindigul region: (ICAR-IIPM Project)

At present two types of contract models are exist in this region.

1. Centralized Model

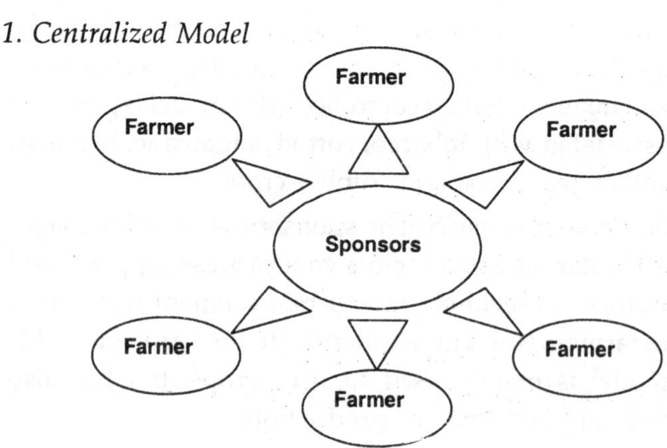

The sponsor purchases crops from farmers for processing, and markets the product. Eg. *Jasmine, milk, poultry.*

2. Intermediary Model

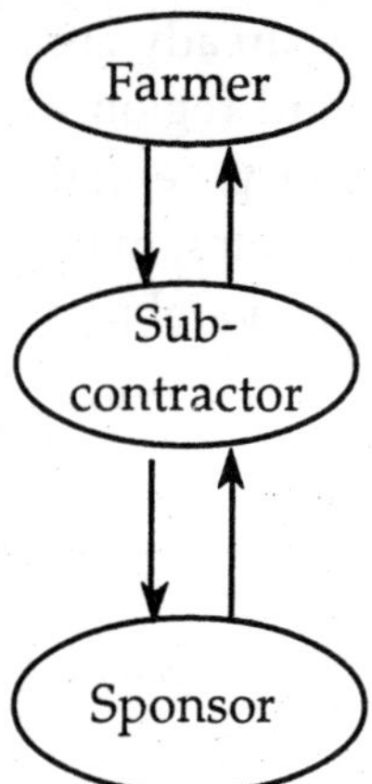

Formal sub-contracting – "collectors" on behalf of any company make their own informal arrangements with farmers. Eg. *Maize, Cotton, Medicinal Plants.*

Proposed Contract Farming Model for Dindigul Region

1. Bio-fuel (Jatropha) based contract farming had been suggested for diversification in Dindigul region. Since commercial plantation of Jatropha is new to the farmers and still market potential is not clear, *Nucleus Estate Model* of contract farming can be followed by the sponsor company as illustrated below:

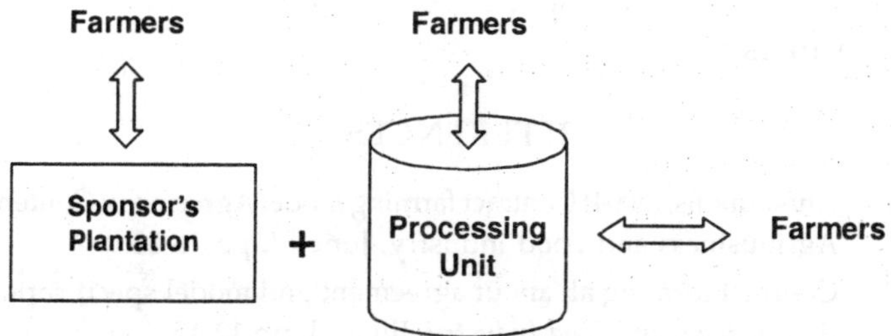

According to this model, the sponsor owns and manages a plantation, usually close to processing plant and introduces technology and management techniques to farmers.

2. Government has already approved Nilakkottai Food Park and Dindigul region as SEZ. Our study also identified a lot of potential for food processing in tomato, cut vegetables, mango pulping unit etc. For this, Multipartite model as give below can be used:

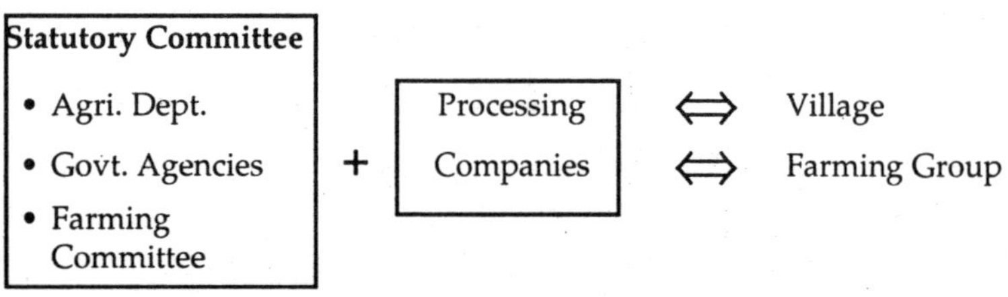

Conclusion

India is the largest producer of raw materials but least in processed foods. Currently many food-processing industries have entered into agri business sector. These agribusiness units need consistent quality raw materials for effective supply chain process. Since they need large raw materials, contract farming served as a source to the farmers for their supply. Different regions and crops warrants varied models of contract farming. Agri business units should select appropriate payment procedure and legal aspects before entering into contract with farmers.

REFERENCES

1. Annoymous, (2004) Contract farming model Agreement: Contents Agribusiness and Food industry, June Id. pp 16-18.
2. Contract farming all about agreement and model specification. *Agribusiness and Food Industry*, June Id. pp 12-15.

3. Dhanakumar, V.G., (2004). *"An Analysis of Decision Making Process and its Impact on Mixed Farming in Agri Plantation Business Sector".* ICAR Report. IIPM, Bangalore.
4. Rajagopal, (2001). *Agribusiness and Enterprenuership.* Anmol Publications Pvt. Ltd., New Delhi.
5. Ricketts, C and Rawlins, O. (2001). *Introduction to Agribusiness.* Delmar. Thomson Learning. United States.

9

Global Standards for Agribusiness

INTRODUCTION

Access to good quality, safety and nutritious food is considered as a basic right of the people. Consumption of unsafe, contaminated food leads to food-borne diseases, which cause considerable morbidity and mortality. Agri-business and plantation processing industry is widely recognized as a "sunrise industry" in India having a huge potential for uplifting agri-business economy creation of large scale manufacturing and food chain facilities. India has enormous growth potential from its current status of being the world's second largest food producer to the world's number one producer. However, there are several bottlenecks that need to overcome for achieving such position. It is very important that processed food available is safe and hygiene and free from contamination, intoxication and adulteration.

The establishment of the World Trade Organization paved the way for several multilateral agreements on trade which include agreements on the application of Sanitary and Phytosanitary (SPS) measures and on Technical Barriers to Trade (TBT). These agreements encourage countries to adopt international standards. In its pursuance of harmonization, the SPS agreement specifically mentions the Codex Alimentarius Standards as the international standard and guideline. Within the context of the TBT agreement, the Codex

Alimentarius Commission has been recognized as an international standardizing body.

Therefore, food regulations, programmes and standards have become a sensitive subject in the regulation of the quality of the food products. Quality being the first consideration for the Consumer acceptance, which in turn is linked with recognized national and international standards, reflecting the national and international markets which are essential for the manufacturer to be able to design, produce and market products embracing the Consumer's needs of quality features and using upto date technologies. Compliance with these standards is ensured through the use of regulatory standards and quality assurance systems.

FOOD REGULATIONS, STANDARDS & GUIDELINES

In the food and agriculture sector of India there are number of organizations responsible for the formulation of Standards and monitoring their quality. These can be generally classified in two systems as under.

A. Compulsory Legislation

1. Prevention of Food Adulteration Act 1954

The most important compulsory legislation in our country in the area of Food Products is the Prevention of Food Adulteration Act (PFA-1954). The PFA-1954 Act is the basic Statutory regulation is intended to protect the common Consumer against the supply of adulterated food products. The Prevention of Food Adulteration (PFA) rules prescribes the minimum requirements for many types and categories of food. The PFA rules were first introduced in 1955 and have been subsequently amended in 1968 and 1976.

The Act makes provision for prevention of adulteration of food products and lays down that no person shall manufacture for sale, store, distribute any adulterated or misbranded food products not conforming to the Standards laid down under the Rules. These Standards are of minimum quality and are intended to ensure safety in the consumption of these food products and safeguarding against harmful impurities, contamination and adulteration etc. Provisions of this act are mandatory and contravention to these rules leads to both fine and imprisonment.

The Central Committee for Food Standards (C.C.F.S.) and its various Subcommittees under the Directorate General of Health Services (D.G.H.S.), Ministry of Health and Family Welfare is responsible for operation and enforcement of the Act. Various interests concerned with Food Standards including consumer interests have representations in this Committee.

2. Essential Commodities Act 1954

A number of Control orders have been formulated under the provisions of the Essential Commodities Act. The main objectives of the Act are to regulate manufacture/production, Commerce/trading and distribution of the essential commodities including the food products.

Some of the important orders of the act are enumerated below: -

The Government of India promulgated the Fruit Products Order (FPO) in 1946, under the Defense of India Rules. In 1955, the order was revised. The FPO lays down minimum standards of sanitation and hygiene to be followed in the factories.

(i) The Fruit Products Order (F.P.O.-1955) The fruits products order regulates manufacture and distribution of fruits and vegetable products, sweetened/aerated waters, ready to serve beverages, synthetic syrups, vinegar etc. The objective of the order is mainly to regulate, ensure the quality and hygiene of these products as per Standards laid down under the order.

The objective of PFA and FPO standards is to obtain a minimum level of quality for food, consistent with the minimum quality attainable under Indian conditions by the majority of farmers, processor, traders and distribution agencies.

(ii) Solvent Extracted Oils, De-oiled Meal and Edible Flour Control Order, Vegetable Oil Products Order, Meat and Meat Products Control Order. These regulatory orders control the manufacture/production and distribution of the products enumerated - the objective being to ensure the quality and hygiene of these products as per various standards laid down in the order. Meat Food Products order is operated by the Directorate of Marketing and Inspection.

B. Voluntary Standards

Two bodies mainly organize the Voluntary Certification Systems in the food products in India. The Bureau of Indian Standards (B.I.S.) is looking after the processed foods and their raw materials, while the Directorate of Marketing and Inspection AGMARK is looking after the standardization of various raw and finished agricultural produce.

1. Bureau of Indian Standards (B.I.S.)

The main functions of the Bureau of Indian Standards are formulation of Indian standards for food and food products and their implementation by promotion and through voluntary and third party certification systems. These standards in general cover raw materials permitted and their quality parameters, hygienic conditions of manufacturing and product safety with respect of microbial Contamination.

B.I.S. maintains and gives recognition to various laboratories for the purpose of standardization and quality control. The B.I.S. Standard mark on the food products certifies that the product complies with a particular Indian Standard Specification and also guarantees that the manufacturer operates a quality assurance/control scheme in the production on a continued basis.

The Certification Scheme is basically voluntary but for some products of mass consumption affecting the health and safety of the consumer is brought under Compulsory/ Mandatory B.I.S. certification marking under various Act/ Rules and Notification of Government of India. Under BIS many of the standards are laid down based upon ISO standards, which is a worldwide federation of National Standard Bodies.

2. Directorate of Marketing and Inspection (D.M.I.)

Directorate of Marketing and Inspection formulates grade Standards known as "AGMARK" with relevant quality definitions and grade designation marks in respect of various agricultural, horticulture, live stock, dairy and forest products. The quality of the product is assessed and determined with reference to various factors like different areas of production, variety, shape, weight, colour, moisture, fat content and other relevant chemical and physical parameters.

AGMARK grades are statutory grades expressed through AGMARK label/replica. These are framed under the provisions of the Agriculture Produce Grading and Marking Act and the General Grading and Marking Rules (1986 and 1988). Grading under the provision of this Act is voluntary but penalties for contravening the rules include fine, cancellation of manufacturing/production license as well as imprisonment.

3. Eco-Mark

The Ministry of Environment and Forests has instituted on labeling of environment friendly products, on a national basis. With the consciousness of environment conservation growing day by day the adoption of ECO-MARK in different categories of food products will become necessary. The products will have to carry ECO-MARK a new standard certifying them environment friendly. The scheme provides to identifying, accreditation and labeling of consumer products which do least damage to the environment and also meet the quality standards/requirements of the relevant Indian Standard for the product.

Some of the food products identified under the ECO-MARK Certification are Tea, Coffee, Refined Vegetable oils, Vanaspati, Food Additives/Preservatives, Processed Fruits and Vegetable Products, Infant Foods and Beverages.

4. ISO Standards

With the increasing focus being given to the management of quality worldwide, the International Organization for Standardization (ISO) has introduced the quality system standards ISO 9000 series. These Standards provide guidelines and criteria for the formal control of products and services by the manufacturing company and assure the purchaser/ consumer a consistent acceptable standard of products and services. ISO Standards reflects a long term concepts and terminology, quality systems and supporting technologies.

5. Hazard Analysis and Critical Control Point (HACCP)

Hazard Analysis and Critical Control Point (HACCP) is an important quality assurance system. This system ensures that the products are safe and of good quality. The system is extremely desirable in view of the changing scenario in the International trade. The Ministry provides grant of 50% subject to a limit of Rs.10 lakhs towards the cost of implementing Total Quality Management (TQM) including HACCP and ISO-9000 certifications. This Ministry sponsors a one-day seminar and five-day training programme organized by APEDA in collaboration with NSF-International strategic Registration Limited, USA, which is the main authority for certifying HACCP-ISO 9000. HACCP is an important requirement for ensuring the quality of products from health and safety aspects and is crucial for exports.

(A). HAZOP for HACCP

Hazard & Operability (HAZOP) analysis is recognized as one of the most powerful computer tools for identifying potentially hazardous scenarios and for developing a course of action to minimize the risks. It may also be used to enhance process efficiency. The HAZOP method (short for Hazard and Operability) was firstly introduced by engineers from ICI Chemicals in UK, in midst 70s.

Although the HAZOP method is still the new to many commodity companies, it is rapidly becoming the preferred hazard analysis technique. It has been proven that HAZOP, if carried out by experienced personnel, results in the most comprehensive evaluation of a plant's safety and operability. Widely used is the package HAZOP-PC, developed by Prima Tech Inc., USA and Camden & Choley Group: www.camden.co.uk

(B). Safe Quality Food (SQF)

The SQF mission is to provide leadership and services to deliver a fully integrated HACCP quality management system that can be applied at all links in the food supply chain. It is based upon a HACCP quality management approach. The system is unique as it focuses on the benefits to both, industry and the consumer. Improved safety and quality can aid both product marketability and profitability of food products. The international food community considers the SQF system as one of the best food safety management systems available for food supply chain.

6. Social Obligation for Estate Sector

The standards such as Occupational Health and Safety

Assessment System 18001 (OHSAS) and Social Accountability 8000 (SA), Safe Quality Food 2000 (SQF), etc. are administered by estate sector to improve socio-economic, health and statutory requirements of the employees and workers. OHSAS 18001 is an international occupational health safety management system, which facilitates integration of quality environment, occupational health and safety of the organization. SA 8000 is a standard for work place conditions and a system for independently verifying organization compliance.

7. International Food Standards

International Food Regulation laws have substantial influence on the manufacturer. Adoption of Good Manufacturing Practices (GMP), Good Hygiene Practices (GHP) and HACCP helps food processing industries to maintain food quality and safety. The international "Codex Alimentarius" commission is the principal organization of a worldwide food standards programme, under the joint auspices of FAO and WHO, the two specialized agencies of the United Nations Organization.

General Principles of the Codex Alimentarius

The codex alimentarius is a collection of internationally adopted food standards presented in a uniform manner. These food standards aim to protecting consumers' health and ensuring fair practices in the food trade. Their publication is intended to guide and promote the elaboration and establishment of definitions and requirements for foods to assist in their harmonization and thus facilitate international trade.

The codex alimentarius is to include standards for all the principal foods, whether processed, semi-processed or raw, for distribution to the consumer. Materials for further processing into foods should be included to the extent necessary as defined. The codex alimentarius is to include provisions in respect of food hygiene, food additives, pesticide residues, contamination, and labeling and presentation methods of analysis and sampling. The WTO agreement on the application of SPS measures and TBT will be applicable to all members of WTO countries. The details of SPS & TBT and its relevance to estate sector are illustrated in ***Figure No. 1***.

The Codex contract Point in India is the Directorate General of Health Services (DGHS) in the Ministry of Health; however, the Ministry of Food Processing Industries is closely associated with the activities of Codex Alimentarius.

8. Export Inspection Council of India

The Export Inspection Council of India (EIC), the official certification body for exports, is developing standards for exports based mainly on Codex, but it also takes into account that an importing country may impose stiffer requirements. It has a regulatory basis in the form of the Export (Quality Control and Inspection) Act of 1963. The EIC was set up under this Act with statutory status to certify the quality of products for exports. All inspection agencies are gearing up to implement ISO 17020, "*General Criteria for the Operation of Various Types of Bodies Performing Inspection*", issued by the International Organization for Standardization (ISO), as well as the Codex "Guidelines for the Design, Operation, Assessment and Accreditation of Food Import and Export Inspection and Certification Systems".

The main system of export inspection and certification being followed in the Indian food sector is the Food Safety Management Systems-based Certification (FSMSC), which is founded on international standards including HACCP, Good Manufacturing Practices (GMP) and Good Hygiene Practices (GHP). All units approved by EIC necessarily have to implement HACCP/GMP/GHP at all stages of food production, in addition to meeting end-product requirements.

9. Eurepgap of the Federation of Indian Chambers of Commerce and Industry (FICCI)

FICCI launched EUREPGAP (European Retail Parties Good Agriculture Practices) standards among the commercial farmers in India. The project is aimed at creating awareness regarding the harmful and inefficient agricultural practices followed by the Indian farming community, which not only makes farming unprofitable for farmers but also poses risks to sustainable development in agriculture and health of the consumers. EUREPGAP was established in 1999 as a global partnership for safe and sustainable agriculture. EUREPGAP incorporates Integrated Pest Management (IPM) and Integrated Crop Management (ICM) practices within the framework of commercial and sustainable agricultural production, with long-term improvement and global harmonization.

By September 2001, a total of 118 companies and organizations had signed up for the EUREPGAP terms of reference. To ensure effective implementation, they have been structured to be certifiable by third party certification bodies accredited as per ISO/IEC Guide 65 issued by the International Electro-technical Commission based in Geneva.

10. International Federation of Organic Agriculture Movements (IFOAM)

Organic agriculture (biological or ecological) is a whole system approach based upon a set of process resulting in sustainable ecosystem, safe food, food nutrition, animal welfare and social justice. Organic production, therefore more than system of production that includes or excludes certain inputs. The IFOAM Basic Standards (IBS) provide a framework for certification bodies and standard-setting organizations worldwide to develop their own certification standards and cannot be used for certification on their own. Certification standards should take into account specific local conditions and provide more specific requirements than the IFOAM Basic Standards.

Producers and processors that sell organic products are expected to be certified by certification bodies, using standards that meet or exceed the requirements of the IBS. This requires a system of regular inspection and certification designed to ensure the credibility of organically certified products and build consumer trust. The IFOAM basic standards 2002 consist of eight principles under the section B of IFOAM.

Prerequisite Programmes (PRP) to Food Hygiene

As one traces the hygiene methods for the measurement of perceived food quality, it is important to keep in mind the distinction between the concepts of "degree of excellence" and "difference from a standard". The former refers to the initial quality of a food item, while the latter refers to changes or deviations from this initial or target quality. Conveying with these measurement concepts is the issue of who performs the judgements. Traditional estate approaches have assumed that product experts, not consumers, are best able to identify good quality. This has led to the establishment of expert grading standards as mentioned above for various commodities to index the degree of excellence of the product and to the use of expert panels to detect differences from pre-established standards of quality.

Prior to effectively implementing food hygiene programme, food business should already have in place various practices including ingredient and product specifications, staff training, cleaning and disinfectant regimes, hygienically designed facilities and be engaged in good hygiene practices (GHP). These collectively may be termed "prerequisite programmes (PRP)".

A number of hindrances to the effective implementation

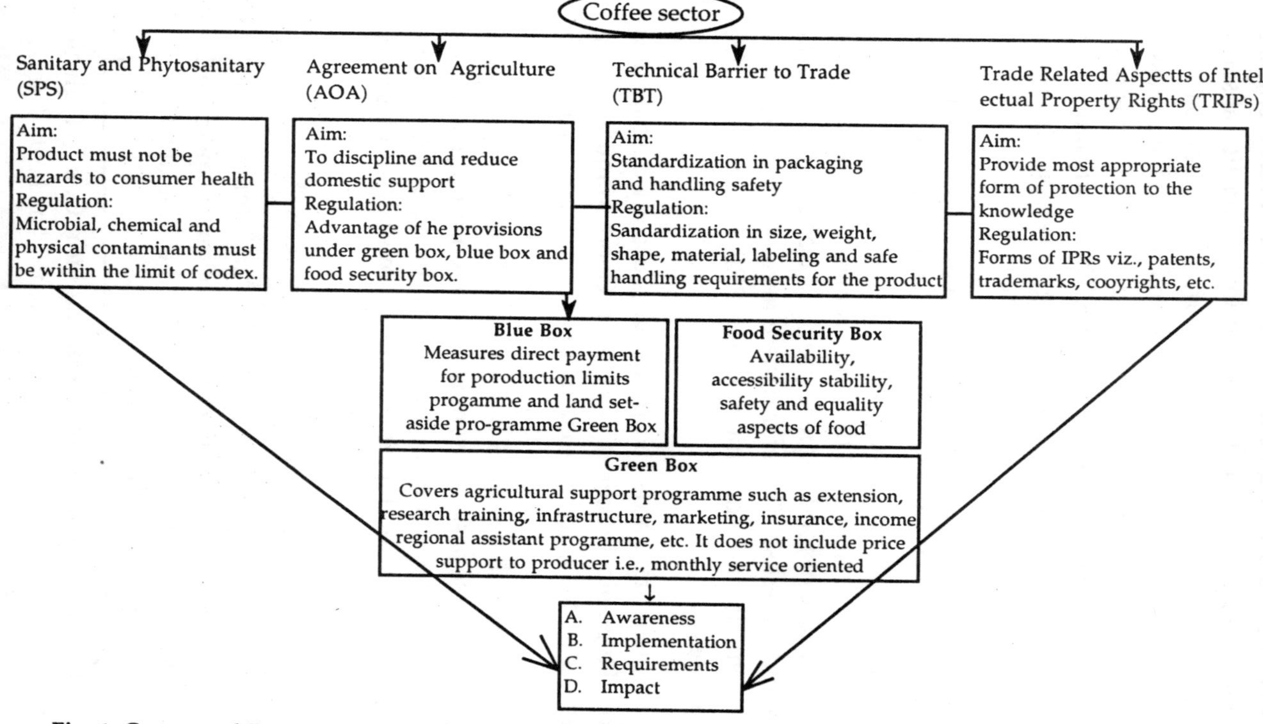

Fig. 1. Conceptual Framework to Understand WTO-SPS-AOA-TBT Agreements and Its Relevance in Coffee Sector

in small businesses (e.g., coffee estate) have been identified such as lack of expertise and perception of benefits, absence of legal requirements, as well as various attitude barriers and financial constraints. In addition, many small businesses believe that they must abandon existing control systems prior to implementing hygiene programme. These difficulties may be due to hygiene programme being developed from the perspective of large, as opposed to small, food companies.

This section presents data on the implementation of food hygiene and PRP by small coffee businesses, assessed in person on the premises. Despite the current legal requirement for food safety, majority of the food business managers claimed that their lack of food hygiene progress was due to a lack of time and expertise. Therefore, there needs to be a proactive enforcement and education about PRP for small coffee businesses.

Hygiene standards and procedures usually described as Good Hygienic Practices (GHP) or Good Manufacturing Practices (GMP), have been in place for many years and constituted an essential tool in traditional food control. These concepts are still essential in a modern food control system by providing the basic environmental and operating conditions for production of safe food and thus being a requisite or foundation for food hygiene in an overall food safety management program (Figure 2).

Good Manufacturing Practices (GMP)

Those procedures for a particular manufacturing operation which practitioners of, and experts in, that operation consider to be the best available using current knowledge.

There is no clear definition of the term Good Hygienic Practice (GHP). However, "food hygiene" has been defined by Codex (CAC, 2001) as "all conditions and measures necessary to ensure the safety and suitability of food at all states of the food chain" and GHP can therefore be regarded as:

Good Hygienic Practices (GHP)

All practices regarding the conditions and measures necessary to ensure the safety and suitability of food at all stages of the food chain.

Assurance of Site Quality

Issues related to implementation of recommended international code of practice for general principles of food hygiene within the norms of CAC/RCP1-1969, Rev 3 1997 and 1999, the following clauses are enforcing cleaning method and procedure with special reference to food sector in general.

3.4: Cleaning, maintenance and personal hygiene in primary production.

4.43: Cleaning

6.2: Cleaning programmes

6.12: Cleaning procedure and method and blind spots, etc. It is noted that R&D system have not issued a clear scientific guidelines and standards for cleaning and cleanability of coffee fermentation tank, as per the norms of CAC.

Methodologies for cleaning of fermentation tank are readily acceptable by the planter. It is recommended that based on codex clause, the coffee R&D unit may identify any one of the following methods with scientific data for cleaning of fermentation tank/unit. As stated above, alkaline cleaning is quite good option for sanitation of coffee fermentation tank. However, in-view of carbon dioxide venting the alkaline cleaning methods is not compatible. On the otherhand, acid cleaners are CO_2 compatible as there is no venting required.

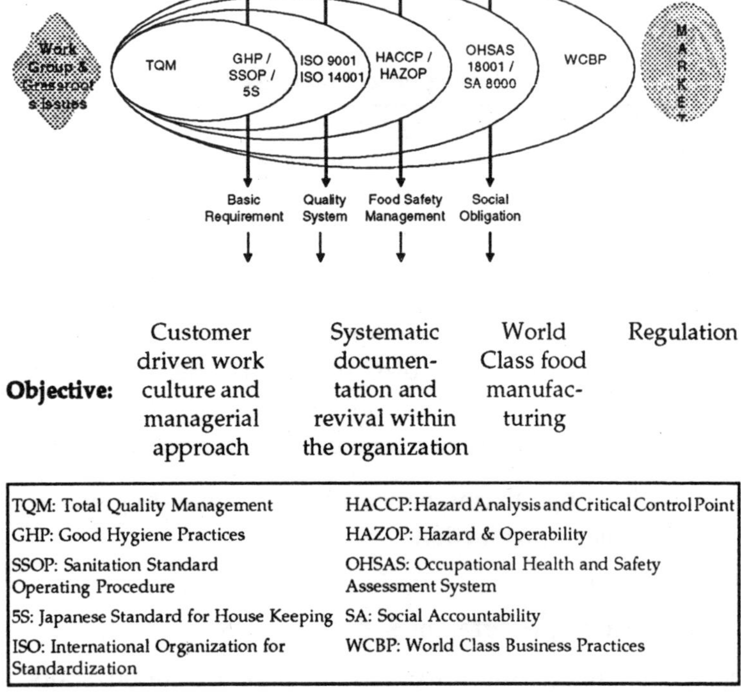

Fig. 2. Pre-requisites Steps for Sustainable Food Safety and Quality for Indian Agri-Plantation Business Sectors

Currently, acid detergent technology has been so advanced that can easily remove undesirable material.

Orica Chemnet, one of the leading suppliers in cleaning and sanitary confirms that Single Stage Cleaning (SSC) is better sanitation compared with alkaline or acid cleaning process methodologies for cleaning and cleanability standards within codex clause. Proven methods of cleaning should be dispensed for coffee to meet the norms of CAC. Moreover, a training cum workshop is required for R&D and Extension Units of Coffee Board to develop a scientific procedure for coffee hygiene to meet norms of CAC clause. Annex A illustrates examples of coffee hygiene connections, including an acceptable cleanability compared with an unacceptable one within the norms of hurdle technology.

As previously discussed, this type of clean and cleanability approach requires some degree of external input (i.e., training, guidelines, software, or auditing). A stratified approach, similar to the Dutch ABC system for unhygienic site, could be developed for the classification of potential coffee production supreme export quality sites, eg.,

A. *No coffee production* (strong evidence that use of site (e.g., fermentation tank or pulping unit) would result in production of hazardous coffee stuffs).

B. *Permission required* (evidence that one or more inputs to the site are a potential hazard to coffee production: Default classification).

C. *No restrictions* (all available evidence indicated that site is safe for coffee production. Only adherence to normal recommended coffee production practices required).

Designating 'B' as the default position would mean that all new sites automatically require external assessment before they can be used for food production. Furthermore, the classification of most coffee production sites as 'B' would make routine auditing and assessment compulsory activities for the majority of sites.

The 'B' category could be further stratified according to any restriction placed on coffee production.

B1. Site unsuitable for coffee production and no coffee production is allowed. This status is analogous to 'A' and site should be so designated such until contrary evidence is provided.

B2. Site suitable for coffee production although monitoring and special practices may be required in addition to normal recommended coffee production practices.

B3. Site suitable for coffee production although monitoring may be required in addition to normal recommended coffee production practices.

B4. Site suitable for coffee production, although special practices may be required in addition to normal recommended coffee production practices.

B5. Site suitable for coffee production with only adherence to recommended coffee production practices. This status is analogous to 'C' and site should be designated such until contrary evidence is provided.

This approach could be interpreted as HACCP, for e.g., production site has been identifies as a potential CCP.

Conclusion

"Codex" is a word frequently used in agri-business and plantation industry, by consumers and food regulators to denote a product, a process and people. But to understand its role in food legislation and trade, it is necessary to have a clear understanding of the meaning and clause of the words used and its operability.

Codex Alimentarius for Coffee (CAC) is a process of collection of food standards and presented in a unified, codified manner, together with associated materials such a codes of hygienic, good manufacturing and production practices through recognized codex methods of analysis and sampling. To support the codex clause and its operability, R&D units of coffee sector may work and advice based on Quality Index Method (QIM). The QIM for coffee hygiene parameters (CHP) should also be based on human sensory evaluation, which is scientific discipline to characteristics of food hygiene as perceived through the senses of sight, smell, touch, taste, attitudes of work force, motivation, etc. QIM for coffee should serve as a method that implies the transformation of grassroots plantation culture through scientific knowledge of the coffee in a consumer friendly solution that can be used by the traders and the consumers in common, which is both rare and desirable for the Sustainable Coffee Hygiene Management in India. A speedy and authoritative search for coffee safety and quality management and to simplify current fragmented legal system and the adoption of world standard programmes, an institutional reform such as establishment of "Coffee Park" is recognized.

Implications

In India, quality management with regard to food products is being enforced through various regulator mechanisms like PFA, AGMARK, CAC, FPO, EIC, etc. While efforts are being made to implement QMP viz., HACCP in the organized agri-business sector of the food industry, there is a need to implement it in the unorganized sector as it accounts for 70-80% of food produced and processed in India. Thus, in the context of globalization and post WTO era, codex committee on food hygiene proposed that "obstacle on the application of HACCP, particularly in small and less developed business (SLDB)" should be approached and tackled.

Majority of coffee producers in India being under unorganized, the primary production unit has no control and it is difficult to monitor coffee hygiene practices. Therefore, it is obvious that application of Coffee Hurdle Technology (CHT) system to be developed in the Indian context and would yield the desired results of improving the coffee hygiene and safety within HACCP norms.

The strategic approach for coffee based hurdle technology should be based on the delay and prevention of microbial growth using factors that most influence the growth or survival of micro organisms. These factors include processing, storage, temperature, water activities (a_w), pH, oxidation prediction potential, etc. The hurdle technology also illustrates that complex interaction of microbial stability of coffee and its association with the processes within system perspective should be addressed. It also recommends a package for high standard personnel hygiene, hand washing, safe handling, safety sign, safe transport, clean area, etc. The application of the synonymously called combined methods, combined processes, combination preservation, combination techniques and barrier technology is termed as "Hurdle Technology".

An improved understanding of the mechanisms underlying the effectiveness of the hurdle technology and QIM in coffee and the combination of coffee hygiene system is urgently required sustaining coffee sector. However, adequate extension education and R&D management programmes for coffee hygiene are in the subjects, needs to be undertaken with special reference to codex based coffee production and management.

ANNEX A

Examples of Proposed Hurdle Technology for Coffee Hygiene Management

According to CAC/RCP 1-1969, Rev 3 (1997), Amd (1999) clause no. 4.4.4. personnel hygiene facilities should be available to ensure that an appropriate degree of personal hygiene can be maintained and to avoid contaminating food. Where appropriate, facilities should include:

- Adequate means of hygienically washing and drying hands, including wash basins and a supply of hot and cold (or suitably temperature controlled) water
- Lavatories of appropriate hygienic design; and

- Adequate changing facilities for personnel. Such facilities should be suitably located and designated.

To understand and implement the clause 4.4.4.of CAC, persons involved in coffee processing must know scientifically on how and when to wash their hands using approved cleaning compounds. Figure 3 below shows codex based proper hand washing techniques. Similarly, coffee sector needs to develop a draft for food hygiene with special reference to cleaning of coffee processing unit, hand washing, flooring and related hygiene practices.

Source: FQ-CRC, Washington, DRC

Fig. 3. Proper Handwashing Technique for Coffee Sector

Food technologist suggests that the benefits of quality and safety are high with reference to well-coated and sealed flooring in food processing. Epotread, the two part, water based epoxy floor coating is really simple solution to manage everyday problems that occur in processing facilities. It is non-tainting, resistant to alkali and acids, strongly adhert, durable and easily cleaned floor coating. It is also water based coating and resist the raising damp.

According to FDA 1995, for its clause no. 7.2.4-maintenance of facilities for personnel hygiene suggest the following:

Wash basin taps must not be hand operated. Hand washing facilities must include the following:

- Liquid soap in a dispenser
- Hot water (40-43^{0}c)
- Disposable paper towels or air blowers
- Hand disinfection facilities

An example for common prerequisite hygiene programme is illustrated above, Coffee Board may establish a key sanitary and phytosanitary conditions within the norms of SSOP. The written package or documents for coffee hygiene management should explain a thorough sanitary concern, controls, in-plant procedures and monitoring requirement. This will demonstrate the commitment of Coffee Board of India to Codex, traders, buyers and inspectors to ensure that everyone from management to production workers understands the basis of SPS aspect of WTO for plantation and agri-business sector.

REFERENCES

1. Anonymous (2000). Application of Hazard Analysis and Critical Control Point for Improvement of Quality of Processed Foods. *ICMR Bulletin.* Vol. 30 No. 5.

2. Armand V. Cardello (1998). *Perception of Food Quality*. CRC Press, Washington, D.C., pp. 1-5.
3. CAC/RCP 1-1969, Rev 3 (1997), Amd (1999).
4. Dhanakumar, V.G. (2004). Safety Management for Fruits & Vegetables. *Journal of Agri Business & Food Industry*. Vol. 1, Issue 6, pp. 19-23.
5. Dhanakumar, V.G. (2004). Quality in Supply Chain Management: The Case of Fruits and Vegetables Chain. Working paper series of IIPM, Bangalore.
6. Dhanakumar, V.G. (2002). Biological Risk Management (Biosecurity) in Coffee : An HACCP Perspective: Part I & II. Indian Coffee. Vol. LXVII April 2003, pp. 14-17 & Vol. LXVIII No. 7, July 2003, pp. 18-21.
7. Dhanakumar, V.G. (2004). World Class Features of Food Park, Agri Export Zone and Agri Business Center in India. Working paper series of IIPM, Bangalore.
8. Elizabeth Walker *et. al.* (2003). Hazard Analysis Critical Control Point and Prerequisite Program Implementation in Small and Medium Size Food Businesses. Food Control 14 (2003), pp. 169-174.
9. http://www.codexindia.nic.in/bbip.htm
10. http://www.pfionline.com/regulations/regulations.html
11. http://www.pfionline.com/features/quality/qua1/qua1.html.
12. http://mofpi.nic.in/food&health/foodsafety/safety.htm
13. IFOAM Basic Standards. (2002). IFOAM Basic Standards for Organic Production and Processing. IFOAM General Assembly, Victoria, Canada, August 2002.
14. Jaime Jurado (2003). Hygienic Design, Installation, and Maintenance Standards for Draft Beer Dispense: German Progress and North America's Challenge. *MBAA TQ*. Vol. 40, No. 4, pp. 271-279.
15. Karl Ropkins (2003). Development of Hazard Analysis by Critical Control Points (HACCP) Procedures to Control Organic Chemical Hazards in the Agricultural Production of Raw Food Commodities. *Critical Reviews in Food Science and Nutrition*. Vol. 43 (3), pp. 287-316.
16. Krishnan, V.V. (2003). HACCP & SQF 2000[CM] Quality Code. *Journal of Beverage & Food World*, Vol. January 03, pp. 29-33.
17. Lt. Gen. Lal, H. (2003). Bridging the Gap. *Times Agriculture Journal*, Vol. 2 No. 5, pp. 47-48.

18. Mauricio Colosia (2004). Acid Cleaning : Your Futures to Greater Savings, Higher Productivity, Increased Safety, and a Better Environment. *MBAA TQ*. Vol. 41 No. 3, pp. 111-114.
19. Ramakrishna P.V. (1997). *Prevention of Food Adulteration Act,* Sixth Edition, S. Gogi and Company, Hyderabad.
20. Shashi Sareen (2003). *Food Safety in Food Security and Food Trade. Case Study: India Responds to International food Safety Requirements.* International Food Policy Research Institute, USA.
21. Vanisha Nambiar (2004). *Food Contamination and Safety,* Anmol Publications, New Delhi.

10

Warehousing and Packaging Technology

Warehousing is a part of a firm's and producer's organization that stores products at and between point of origin and point of consumption. Warehouses can be used to support manufacturing, to mix products from multiple production units to single customer and vice versa. Warehousing has traditionally used for storage of products (referred to as inventory) during all phases of the logistics process. Two basic types of inventories can be placed into storage: (1) raw materials, components, and parts (physical supply); and (2) finished goods (physical distribution). Also, there may be inventories of goods-in-process and materials to be disposed of or recycled, although in most firms these constitute only a small portion of total inventories. Warehouses can be used to support manufacturing, to mix products from multiple production facilities for shipment to a single customer, to breakbulk or subdivide a large shipment of product into many smaller shipments into a single higher-volume shipment. Warehousing is used increasingly as a "flow-through" point rather than a "holding" point, or even bypassed (E.g., scheduled deliveries direct to customers), as organizations increasingly substitute information for inventory, purchase smaller quantities, and use warehouses as "consolidation points" to receive purchased transportation rates and service levels.

Operational Aspects of Warehouse

Warehouse plays a vital role in the supply chain & service

between organization and its customers. Warehousing is expensive and it consumes 5% of the cost of sales of a company. With renewed emphasis on return-on-assets, minimizing the cost of warehousing has become an important issue in business operations. Issues related to warehouse operations in Rubber Sector as an example has been illustrated in Table No. A and B with respect to single operation and clustering of RPS (Rubber Produces Society) operations respectively.

TABLE A

Existing Warehousing Operations at RPS, Rubber Board

Receiving →	*Put-away/Storage →*	*Order Picking (Supply)*
• Collection • Maintenance of records • Straining of latex • DRC estimation • Inventory	• Large inventory • Stored in floor • Microbial contamination and quality deterioration • High relative humidity and temperature	• Supply in less quantity • More transportation cost

TABLE B

Proposed Warehousing Operations and Management for a Cluster of RPS

Receiving →	*Put-away/Storage →*	*Order Picking (Supply)*
• Direct supply • Cross-docking • Bulk ordering	• Single deep pallet rack • Relative humidity (75%) and temperature (35-37)	• Warehouse near to the market area

Receiving

Receiving is the first step for all the warehousing activities of RPS. If we don't receive products (eg., latex or sheet rubber) properly it will be difficult to handle it properly in storage, transportation and supply. If we allow damaged or inaccurate deliveries in the door, we are likely to supply inferior or inaccurate products out of the door. Eg., if latex received from customer is contaminated with dusts or foreign particles, sheets produced also may contain these particles. The world class warehouse operation in receiving principles minimize work content, mistakes and time. Some of the principles related to operational aspects of warehouse are as follows:

Direct Supply

For some materials, the best receiving is no receiving. In direct supply, RPS by pass warehouse completely and supply directly to the customers, i.e., to rubber company (or) processing unit. Natural Rubber (Latex) can be supplied in this pattern. Because the items (latex) not required to the warehouse they do not have to be unloaded, graded, checked, etc. Hence, all the labour, time and equipment normally consumed and all the mistakes and accidents that often occur in the warehouse are eliminated.

Cross-Docking

When material cannot be supplied direct, the next option may be cross docking. In cross docking, warehouses serve primarily as "distribution mixing centers". Product arrives in bulk and is immediately broken down and mixed in the proper range.

In Cross-docking

- *Loads are scheduled for delivery to the customers*
- *Out bound orders are transported immediately to their out bound dock*
- *Receiving stage or inspection is not required*
- *Product storage is not required*

In doing so, the traditional warehousing activities involving receiving, inspection, putaway, storage are eliminated and cost of operations is minimized.

Put-away and Storage – involves the physical movement into the warehouse for storage.

World-class principles for putaway are:

- *Direct Put-away*
- *Block Stacking*
- *Single-Deep Pallet Rack*

Direct Put-away

Put-away directly to primary or reserve locations. Goods were immediately stocked upon receipt as opposed to the delays and multiple handling that are characteristic of traditional receiving and put-away activities. Left to their own devices, most put-away locations that are easiest to locate nearest the floor. But this type of storage mechanism in the rubber leads to microbial contamination in rubber sheets.

Block Stacking

Block Stacking refers to unit loads stacked on top of each other and stored on the floor in storage lanes (blocks). Loads in a block should be retrieved under a last-in-first-out (LIFO). Block stacking is not a feasible storage method. As loads are removed from a storage lane, a space-loss phenomenon referred to as honey combing occurs with block stacking. Because only grades can be effectively stored in a lane, empty pallet spaces are created that cannot be utilized effectively until an entire lane is emptied. Therefore, in order to maintain high utilization of the available storage positions, the lane depth must be carefully determined.

Single-Deep Pallet Rack

Single-deep pallet racking is a simple construction, if metal uprights and cross-members provide immediate access to load stored. Unlike block stacking, where a pallet spaces is created by the removal of a load, a pallet opening available in single-deep racking. Also, because racking support the stackability and/or crushability of the loads do not limit every load, stacking height. The major advantage is full accessibility to all unit loads. Selective pallet rack might be considered the bench mark storage mode, against which other system may be compared for advantages and disadvantages

Order Picking/Supply

Order picking as the highest priority activity in the warehouse for productivity improvements. Renewed emphasis on quality improvements and customer service have forced warehouse managers to reexamine the order picking activity from the standpoint of minimizing product damage, reducing transaction times and further improving picking accuracy.

Issue Pack Optimization

By encouraging customers to order in full-pallet quantities or by creating quarter/half-pallet loads, much of counting and manual physical handling of cases can be avoided both in company warehouse and also in customer's warehouse. In similar fashion, by encouraging, customers to order in full-case quantities, much of the counting and extra packaging associated with loose case picking can be avoided.

Order Batching

By increasing the number of orders picked by an order picker during a picking tour, the travel time per pick can be reduced. For example, if order picker picks one order with two items while travelling 100 feet, the distance traveled per pick is 50 ft. If the picker picked two orders with four items. Single line orders are a natural group of orders to pick together. Single line orders can be batched by small zones in the warehouse to further reduce travel time.

Packaging

Packaging is an art, which determines the buying decision. Technically packaging is a system or method by which a product from the manufacturing point to the consumer reaches in safe and sound conditions at an affordable cost.

Packaging protects its brand names, slogans and packaging innovations with trademark & copyright. Eg., One package of cold brew blend displays (K) registration mark six times and (C) copyright notices one.

Functions of Packaging

Containment

This is the basic function of packaging.

Protection

This is often regarded as primary function of the package to protect its contents from outside environmental effects be they water, moisture, vapour, gases, odour, micro-organisms, dust, shocks, vibrations, compressive forces etc., and to protect the environment from the product.

Convenience

With the changing the life style and role of women, there is a demand for convenience in food i.e., eating snack type meals frequently but on the run rather than regular meals i.e., 'grazing'.

Communication

An old saying that a package must protect what it sells and sells what it protects. It may be old but it is still true. A package functions as a silent salesman. Marketing would fail, if the message were not communicated by the package.

> "Packaging labels send signals not just to consumers but to other companies proclaiming legally protected status."

New Packaging Trends

1. *Flexible Packaging*

- Food packaging
- Stand-up pouches
- Re-sealable zippers and sachets

2. *Aseptic Packaging*

- More suitable for fresh, processed and export foods
- Sterilization of the packaging material, equipment and sterile condition throughout the production operation

3. *Blow Moulded Industrial Packaging*

- Bottling at Coca-Cola & Pepsi

4. *Multi-layer Barrier PET Bottles*

- Suitable for beer, fruit juices, milk, tomato ketch-up, etc.
- Temperature resistance upto 90^0c and withstand sterilizing temperatures

The Factors that Will Dictate the Future Trends in Packaging are:

Eco-friendly, ease of recycling and reuse, tamper evident and pilfer proof, convenience in general for senior persons / kids, unit pack-dispensing ease, shelf-life as mentioned on the package, economy etc.

Bio-degradable Packaging for Food Industry

Cellulose based materials:

- Packaging of baked goods, processed meat, cheese and candies,
- High moisture barrier properties

Chetin/chitosan:

- Hardened composite structures of exoskeleton of insects
- Low oxygen permeability
- Anti-microbial properties

Casein:

- Isolated from milk by using carbon-dioxide under high pressure
- Used for packaging of meat

Importance and Development of Packaging in Tea: A case analysis

In case of Tea, during the first 3 months improvement in quality is essential and afterwards its deterioration is more unless proper precautions are taken to preserve quality of packaging. Changes during the storage leads to reduction of theaflavin and thearubigin and loss of flavour volatiles & flavanols.

Extent and Speed of Changes

Depends on extent of moisture content and Capacity to absorb odour.

Moisture Content

Less than 5 percent - temperature capacity to absorb odour stored for a year without quality loss.

Greater than 5 percent - tea become musty on storage.

Greater than 7 percent - suitable medium for microorganisms.

Capacity to Absorb Odour

- Tea absorbs odour of wood, paper, plastic, glue, etc.
- Tainted tea - cheesy, chesty, earthy, tinny smell.

(A) Bulk packaging of tea: -

Plywood chests:

- Popular container for packaging tea.
- Chests filled with tea confirm following quality test.

1. *End compression test:* To measure the ability of the fully packed chest to withstand heavy overhead loading.
2. *Progressive corner-drop test:* Measure the ability of the filled chest to withstand *rough handling.*

Short comings of plywood tea chests.

- Difficulty in obtaining plywood.
- Changing pattern of consumer preference.

Substitute bulk package :-

1. Corrugated fiberboard box.
2. Multi-wall paper sacks.
3. Poly- hessian sacking.

1. Corrugated Fiber Board Box (CFB)

Rigid enough for packing leaf grade tied without quality loss and in the box, there will not be any splinters in the tea.

CFB boxes handled in palletized form and expensive than plywood chests.

2. Multi-wall paper sack

Positive aspects

Correctly packed and handled, hardly any deterioration of quality, reduce the strain of forest resources and easily re-cycled and there disposal is cheaper and easier.

Negative aspects

Restricted to the brokens, fanning and dust grades.

3. Poly-hessian sacking

Jute sacks

Disagreeable odour, Colour of the jute bag is not attractive and shedding of fibers from the jute bags.

Jute sacks with Poly-hessian sacking

Lamination on the both sides of the hessian material.

(B) Retail packaging

1. Metal caddies
2. Paper board cartons
3. Flexible pouches
4. Sachets

1. *Metal caddies*

Metal container of cylindrical square or rectangular cross section, Filling of caddies of these shapes is easier and even the last bit of tea can be possessed out without difficulty.

2. *Paper board cartons*

Coated out board, coated chrome paper and duplex board and inner bag - HDPE (High-Density Polyethylene).

3. *Flexible pouches*

Pouches made of a wide variety of films and laminates Eg., PE + LDPE. Retail packaging of tea bags, instant tea and speciality.

Tea Bags

Chlorined bleached tissue paper replace by unbleached one because of carcinogenic offset. Tea bag has poorer shelf life (contents are either CTC or fanning and dust which absorb moisture).

Importance of Package

Primary vehicle for brand and slogans, customer perception creates brand equity and purchase loyalty. Appearance stimulates memories and emotions of purchaser and colour, imagery and slogans combine to facilitate customer allegiance. Package image determines success or failure.

Influence of Package Colour

Blue generates more sales (e.g., Liptons cold brew blend)

— Blue colour conveys positive emotions like security and relaxation.

— "Baby blue", "sky blue", "powder blue" and "ribbon egg blue" - friendly, safe, modestly charming images with an air of calm family life style.

Yellow & red packages

— Attract a shopper, helping the tea package to stand out from many other brands.

Packaging in Coffee

Coffee beans are usually packaged in new bags of woven natural materials (Eg. jute or sisal), which allow free air circulation. Coffee shipped in a sisal outer bag containing a plastic inner bag. This plastic inner bag is perforated. Woven plastic bags, as are occasionally used for transport have no effect on the quality of the coffee, provided that they are air-permeable.

The protective and ventilation measures conventionally taken in a general cargo ship do not generally apply to containers. Containers have increased handling speeds decisively. The constant increase in container ship tonnage has increasingly reduced the supply of space in conventional ships. Approximately 95 % of European coffee imports transported in containers changed over to containerized coffee transport.

Conclusion

Although warehousing is important in supply chain management and logistics, its systematic approach and order activities to agribusiness sector presentation process is required in profiling. In agribusiness product movements holding up efficiency and accuracy as the keys to success in warehousing operations. The process of selecting warehouse profiling, performance measures, storage and retrieved system, selection, order packing strategies, warehouse management systems etc and implementing a Warehouse Management System (WMS) alongwith Better Packaging System (BPS) can raise a warehouse to world class status in agribusiness sector. The WMS selection process for agribusiness with the decision to build or buy the system and the pros and cons are summarized in table 1. Bar codes, bar code scanners, symbologies etc., can serve as an automatic identification technologies for WMS.

TABLE 1

WMS Buy Vs Build Strategy: Agribusiness Perspective

Constraints	*Buy*	*Build*
Initial expense	Initial WMS expense is lower through large package suppliers because their development expense is leveraged against clients	
Maintenance expense		If the in-house staff is highly competent in WMS, then the in-house maintenance may be more timely and less expensive. Otherwise, a package supplier will be less expensive and perhaps the only feasible alternative.
Customization	The world's best warehouse management systems were all built in-house. Customization of world-class operating principles to unique industry settings is the key. If warehousing is a key to your competitiveness, customization is critical.	
Response to change		If the in-house staff is highly competent in WMS, then the in house changes will be more timely and less expensive. Otherwise package supplier will be less expensive and perhaps the only feasible alternative.
Influence of		If either case, the WMS design should be influenced by someone knowledgeable in world-class warehousing practices. Unfortunately, many WMS providers lack true warehousing expertise.

REFERENCES

1. Frazelle, H.E. 2002, *World Class Warehousing and Material Handling.* Tata McGraw-Hill Publishing Company Limited. New Delhi, pp 220.

2. Jain. K.N. 1999. Global Advances in Tea Science. Aravalli books International Pvt Ltd., New Delhi.
3. Mithra K.K. 1999. Development of Packaging in Tea. Global Advances in Tea Science. Aravalli books International Pvt Ltd., New Delhi, pp. 817 – 824.
4. Rohit Chawla. 2004. Packaging. Times Food Processing Journal, pp. 39-41.
5. Special coverage on Packaging. 2003. Times Food Processing Journal. August-Sept.

11

Technology for Concentrated and Condensed Products

India produces fruits like mango, banana, papaya, orange, mosumbi, guava, apple, pineapple, chikku, litchi etc. Despite such high levels of production in this sector, 30 per cent of the produce gets spoiled due to inadequate or improper post harvest handling, lack of adequate demand and processing facilities, and absence of linkages between the processors and marketers of fruits. This results in a national loss of about Rs.3000 crore every year. This industry sector receives a wide range of fruit and milk and processes them into final or intermediate products for human consumption. Processed products involve other unit operations such as crushing, centrifuging, evaporating, drying, blending and many other operations to provide diversity in product selection, add value and increase shelf life through pasteurization, sterilization by heat or other means.

Classification of Three Major Product Based on its Content

1. Drinks: Juice with Pulp content less than 40%
2. Nectars: Juice with Pulp content between 40% - 80%
3. Juices: Juice with Pulp content more than 80%

Procurement Techniques

Procurement of products must focus on the following terms (Tehno-procurement) than conventional methods. The characteristics of Product must follow the given aspect (s) based on the specific commodity. A list of norms and characteristics followed for procurement of fruit juice, pulp and concentrate are given below:

- pH
- Titrable Acidity
- Total Soluble solid
- Ascorbic Acid (2, 6 dichlorophenol indophenol method)
- Specific gravity
- Percentage of Air bubbles (which is the source of quick deterioration)
- Separation of squash solids (gives undesirable appearance
- Finish product – Example Mango squash content
- Juice - 25%; TSS - 45%; Acidity - 1.2 to 1.5%
- Presence of preservatives

  Sulphur dioxide – 350 parts million

  Sodium benyoate (1,000 part million)

Make sure that Puree is heated at 90°c for 1 minute and cool to 35°c before filling into container and frozen at 23°c. Use of Polyethylene container is a good source for preservation

Steps for Processed Tropical Fruits

Fruits and its products are sold in a variety of processed or semi-processed forms and product are groups based on the following three main aspects:

1. Canned Fruit
2. Fruit Juices/Pulp/Concentrates
3. Dried/Dehydrated Fruit

Fruit Processing Plant and Machinery

Machinery for processing of fruits and vegetables with latest technology.

Pulping / Milling / Slicing

Virtually all fruit and vegetables are required a suitable equipment for peeling, slicing, destoning, deseeding, etc. and manufactured to the highest specification in stainless steel and incorporating the latest operator protection and safety systems. A complete variety of cutting and pulping blades are used to produce an extensive selection of pulps, purees, chips, slices etc. Each unit can be individually installed or as part of a complete processing line.

Pasteurization Systems

For juices and pulps, both plate and tubular systems with heating and regeneration sections cope with the full range of product viscosities. The use of hot water as the heating media via steam or electric heating avoids scorching of product. All the above systems are designed to be Cleaned-in- Place (CIP). Full temperature, monitoring and flow control ensures optimum pasteurization processes.

Orange Juice Extraction

For the extraction of fresh orange juice without contamination from the peel oils. Complete modular units with capacities from 100 Kgs/ hr up to 8000 Kgs/hr is required. All systems integrally linked to intake and milling systems. Other citrus juice systems are available including essential oil recovery components. The important steps for the processing of citrus, grapes and mango are given in Fig. 1 to 3 respectively.

Jam and Puree Production

A variety of processing techniques are offered from simple open boiling pans to continuous automatic vacuum systems.

Specialist formulations, mixing, slicing and syrup incorporation options are available. Packaging of puree into jars, pots, tubs etc. complete with jar washing and coding systems.

Water Treatment

Complete incoming water and recycling treatment systems should be available, tailor made to specific site water analysis. Combined with continuous ongoing technical support and provision for specialist filter media, ensures hygiene and sterile water at all times, whatever the source.

Environmental Waste Processing

Increasingly, environmental issues are paramount and unit offers tailored systems for wastewater recovery and recycling, solids disposal, and drying/de-watering systems etc. to turn waste problems into income-generating solutions.

Units of Production and Marketing of Milk Products

- Sugam Dairy at Vadodara in Gujarat is the most modern plant of manufacture of traditional dairy products.
- Sugam Dairy markets shrikhand, gulabjamuns, pedas and lassi, apart from flavored milks.
- The Mother Dairy in Calcutta markets mishti doi and dahi in a similar fashion.
- Dairies in Punjab and Haryana market paneer and kalakand (also, lately, milk cake).
- Cooperative dairies in Tamilnadu, Andhra Pradesh and Karnataka sell makkham (butter), khoa, peda (a form of sweet meat) and kulfi.

India is the first largest milk producing country and milk surplus states in India are:

Uttar Pradesh

Punjab
Haryana
Rajasthan
Gujarat
Maharashtra
Andhra Pradesh
Karnataka
Tamil Nadu

Production of Milk Products

Infant milk food, malted food, Condensed milk & cheese	—	3.07 lakh tonnes/annum
Milk powder including infant Milk food	—	2.25 lakh tonnes
Cheese & condensed milk	—	5000 - 11000 tonnes

Biggest "companies" in the dairy business.

The Gujarat Cooperative Milk Marketing Federation (GCMMF).

The Kaira District Cooperative Milk Producers' Union Limited.

The Mehsana District Cooperative Milk Producers' Union.

Reverse Osmosis and Ultra Filtration Techniques

Reverse osmosis is based on pressure activated membrane separation techniques. Reverse osmosis operates at the pressure of 100-2000 lb/in^2 where as ultra filtration operates at 10-100 lb/in^2. Both these techniques remove 60 per cent of water from the milk.

Freeze Concentration

Freeze Concentration involves cooling of milk below the freezing point and removal of ice crystals. Possible to concentrate milk to 36-38 percent at a single stage and concentrated usually at the rate of 3:1.

Important Milk Products in the Market

1. Evaporated Milk
2. Condensed Milk e.g., Nestle & Amul

Fruit Juices

(a) Citrus

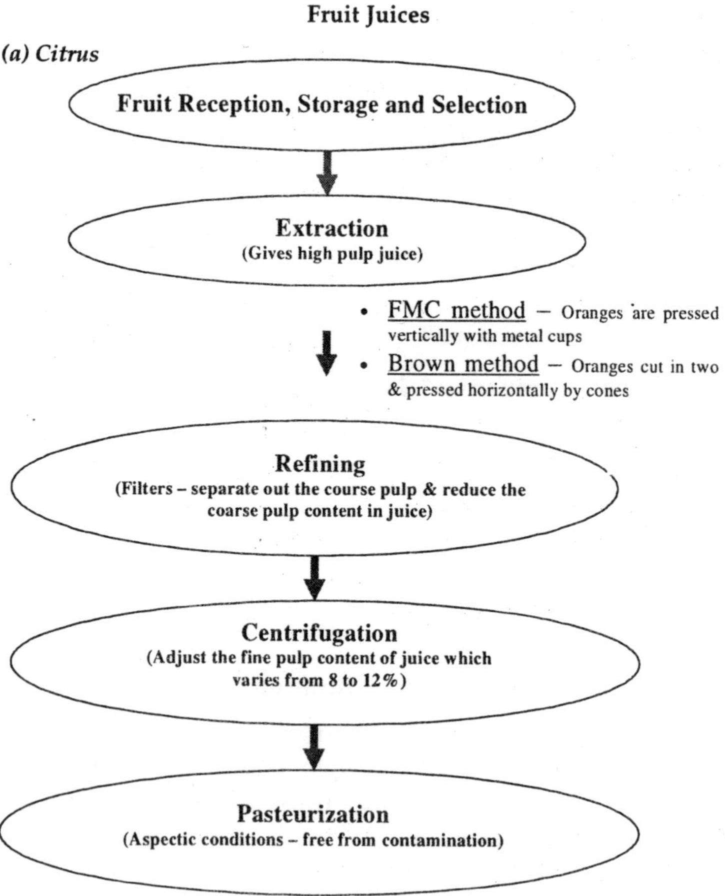

- Fairly at high temperature and short periods of time

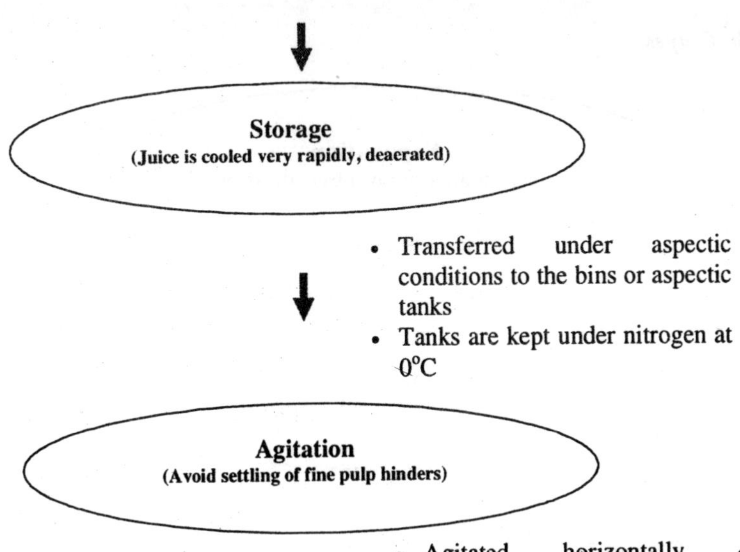

Fig. 1. Citrus Juice Manufacturing Process

(b) Grapes

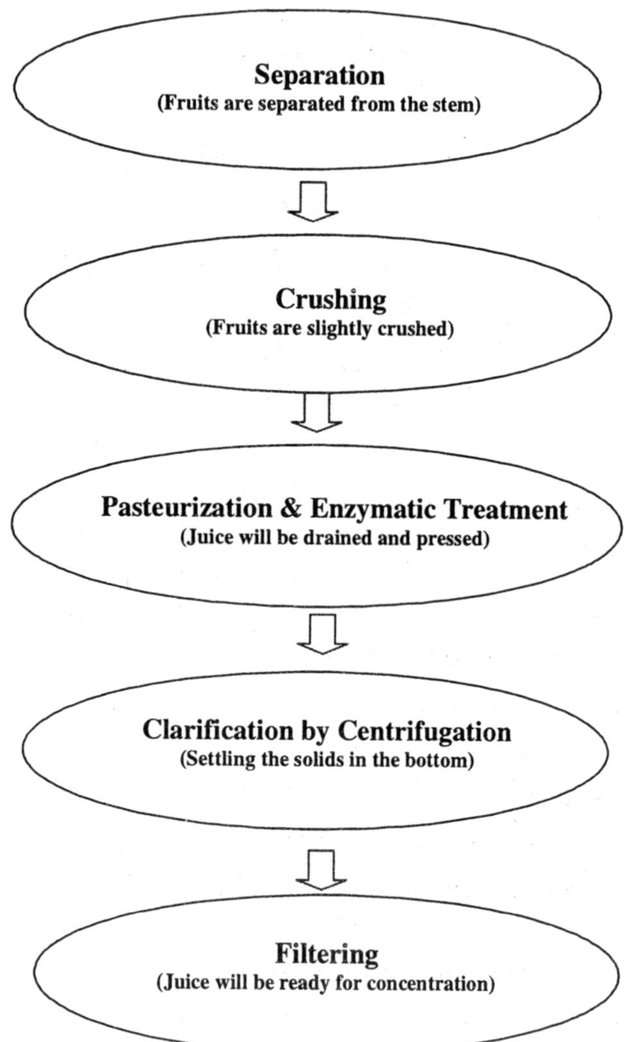

Fig. 2. Grape Juice Preparation

(c) Mango

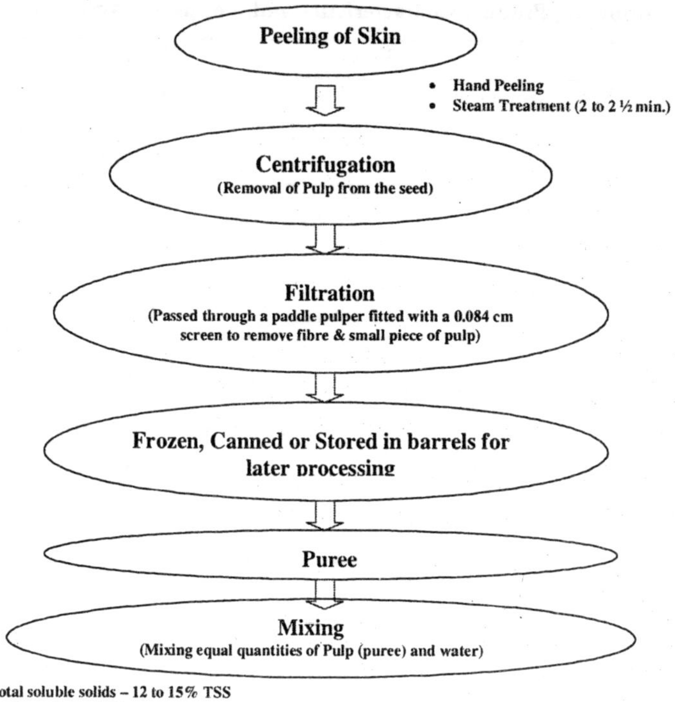

Fig. 3. Mango Juice Manufacturing Process

TABLE 1

In International Trade of Fruit Juices, Pulp & Concentrates, the Following Product Characteristics and Norms are Adhered

Product	*Brix*	*Main source*
Pineapple concentrate	60-65°	Thailand Phillippines Indonesia
Passion fruit (a) Juice (b) Concentrate	14-16° 50°	Ecuador Brazil Peru, Kenya
Mango (a) Pulp (b) Concentrate	13-18° 28-32°	India Peru, Ecuador
Guava (a) Puree (b) Concentrate	8-11° 20-25°	South Africa Malaysia, India
Papaya (a) Pulp (b) Concentrate	9-10° 21-25°	India, Peru, Brazil
Banana (a) Puree	20-24°	Ecuador Brazil Honduras India

Source: ITC (UNCTAD/WTO)

Conclusion

The agribusiness sector in India in the area of concentrated and condensed products remains competitive to the global market. The trend on the above sector need to focus more on storage and keeping quality to meet the requirement of the global consumer. For example, availability of milk are usable for a period of one to two days. Study reveals that consumer prefer such product availability to a extendable days such as 10-15 days with no added preservatives.

REFERENCES

1. Von Loesecke, W.H. 2001. Outlines of Food Technology. Agrobios (India). Jodhpur.
2. SBP. Hand Book of Food and Agro Based Industries. SBP consultants and Engineers Pvt Ltd.

12

Organic Agriculture: An HACCP Perspective

Introduction

"Organic farming is a philosophy of farming, but it doesn't guarantee a greater safety". "Organic" is a labeling term that denotes products that have been produced in accordance with organic standards throughout production, handling, processing and marketing stages, and certified by a duly constituted certification body or authority. The "organic" label is therefore a process claim rather than a product claim. It should not necessarily be interpreted to mean that the foods produced are healthier, safer, or "all natural". It simply means the product follows the defined standard of production and handling, although surveys indicate that consumers consider the "organic" label as an indication of purity and careful handling. "Organic" standard will not exempt producers and processors from compliance with general regulatory requirements, such as food safety regulations, pesticide registrations, general food and nutrition labeling rules, etc.

"Consumers need to understand that organic production does not mean pesticide-free and pathogen-free production," says IFT food science expert Carl Winter, the director of the Foodsafe Program at University of California at Davis. It is a requirement of the EU regulation that no claims may be made on the label or advertising material that suggests to the purchaser that the indication of organic production methods constitutes a guarantee of superior organoleptic, nutritional or salubrious quality. In its Report on Organic Farming the House of Commons Select Committee on Agriculture stated that "there is clearly a strong consumer demand for organic products but we are very conscious that the consumer may attribute benefits to organic products which cannot be sustained in the present state of scientific knowledge and which cannot legally be claimed by producers."

We have reservations about the claims made for organic and we believe that far more work needs to be done to establish a scientific basis for these claims. The scientific evidence indicates that health risks associated with disease-causing microorganisms are far greater than risks associated with pesticide residues, which are negligible. Organic food is a product of a farming system which avoids the use of man made fertilizer and pesticides instead relies mostly on animal & plant manure's, waste materials such as slurries, sewage & sludge, organic pesticides, etc. Use of animal waste, organic pesticides, needs to be properly managed to avoid food poisoning from foods.

For example, organic food materials are at a higher risk for E.coli. *(www.purefoods.org)* Some organic pesticides are as toxic, or even more toxic than many synthetic chemical pesticides. (www.hgi.clemson.edu). Certain organic pesticides have mammalian toxicities that are far higher than many synthetic pesticides. (www.cgfi.org). Gregori (2000) found that mycotoxins, are often carcinogenic and much more harmful than any pesticide. Jukes (1990) observed that organically grown produce (using natural pesticide like pyrethrins) contain more natural toxins than produce grown using conventional pest management. For example, apple juice from organically raised apples contains more patulin, a probable carcinogen, than conventionally raised apples. Organic foods have the potential for greater microbial contamination than just pesticide residues. It is therefore, important to consumer to understand the nature and process of organic farming than measuring the standard of product by labeling and standardization.

Review on Risk related to Organic

Copper sulfate used in organic farming is highly toxic to fish, known to cause liver disease in humans, and is a permanent soil contaminant. The Organic pesticide ryania is also very toxic to fish. Pyrethrum, a botanical nerve toxin used in organic farming is a "human carcinogen". Still other "natural" pesticides, such as the insecticide rotenone, may also pose human health. Also, some organic pesticides may be toxic to beneficial Insects, such as honey bees, if they are combined with other materials, such as combining pyrethrins with rotenone. The primary organic fungicides are sulfur and copper are mined from natural mineral ores. Both are toxic to a broad range of organisms and are long-term soil and environmental contaminants. (www.cgfi.org). Extoxnet FAQ.doc found that, Municipal sewage sludge used as fertilizers in rice crop caused human cadmium toxicity in Japan. Anonymous (1999) revealed that using only organic fertilizers contaminate the soil with level of cadmium, copper and lead. Use of biosolids from waste water treatment facilities (sludge) to produce food crops leads to contamination of food by heavy metal, toxic organic compounds (dioxin, PCB) and persistent microbial pathogen.

The bacteria E.coli 0157:H7, a deadly pathogen found in every cattle manure, which organic farmers use as a primary source of fertilizer. 0157:H7 afflicts an estimated 20,000 people in the United States, killing upto 500. (www.cgfi.org). IFST (2001) revealed that, the use of FYM as fertilizer, whether in organic or non-organic agriculture, gives rise to concerns about the possible contamination of agricultural produce with pathogens (especially E.coli 0157) and the possible contamination of ground and surface water. IFST (2001) also found, composting kills only vegetative pathogens, but will not destroy spore-formers such as *Clostridium perfringens* and even *Clostridium botulinum*. Gregori (2000) observed that animal manure is generally considered better for soil structure, but may have a high content of salts, and it may harbor toxic chemicals, viruses, harmful bacteria, insects, worms, or other pests. Dennis Avery, (1997) viewed that organic farming contains more E.coli than conventional produce. Fresh manure, particularly during summer months, has a high probability of carrying 0157 and other pathogens. Kudva et al. (1998) attribute some of the increase in food borne pathogens to the increased density of animals on farms and the development of quick methods for disposal of wastes, notably use of slurries versus traditional methods employing bedding and composting. COG, (2003) revealed that E. Coli 0157 survives much longer in manure products than in the live animals, and thus manure contaminated materials are suspected to be a reservoir of 0157 for reinfection of livestock. Anonymous (2002) found that, the bacteria E. Coli 0157:H7, a deadly pathogen found in every cattle herd, found in the manure which is the primary source of fertilizer in organic farming.

Quality and Safety (QUALSAFE) in Organic Practices

Best Agriculture, Manufacturing and Hygiene Practices (BAMHP) is an important process in organic farming within food safety regulations to organic food production. It is essential that all appropriate food safety procedures are established and monitored by the food scientists and technologists involved and diligently operated.

As indicated earlier, farmyard manure and other animal wastes (FYM) are widely used in organic agriculture, gives rise to concerns about the possible contamination of agricultural produce with pathogens (especially E.coli 0157). A more recent report titled " A Study on Farm Manure Applications to Agricultural Land and an assessment of the risks of Pathogen Transfer into the Food Chain" (Nicholson et. al. 2000) considers the risks associated with Campylobacter, E.coli, Salmonella, Listeria, Protozoa and viruses. Fresh manure, particularly during summer months, has a high probability of carrying 0157 and other pathogens. Composting, a key component of organic farming, is a pathogen reduction process. According to Soil Association Organic Standards, for FYM, a compost temperature of 60°C must be reached to facilitate the destruction of vegetative pathogens and that the compost heap be maintained for at least three months (an alternative regime is stacking for six months) as part of best agriculture practices.

Colueke (1991) found sewage carries E.coli 0157 and if sewage sludge or other forms of body wastes are composted, then complete destruction of pathogens is possible [if "Farm effluents is hold in tanks with proper aeration for appropriate lengths of time (1 to 3 months or as required) before being used as fertilizers]. Improperly incubated and/or stored slurry can serve as a vehicle for environmental spread and propagation of pathogens that may include E. coli 0157:H7". Composting and curing, aging of uncomposed manure and aeration of slurries are obviously important in order to reduce levels of 0157 in livestock. E. coli 0157 grows in wet feeds, but growth can be stopped by using mixed rations containing silage with high levels of certain acids: frequent cleaning and appropriate sanitation of water troughs can potentially prevent replication and/or long term maintenance of E.coli 0157 in sediments.

The food industry must ensure the quality and safety of their products through the implementation of quality assurance programmes, including food safety programmes based on the Hazard Analysis and Critical Control Point (HACCP) system and EUREPGAP, designed to ensure compliance with all relevant regulations. Need for food safety measures to be based on risk analysis following principles and procedures elaborated by relevant international organizations. International food safety standards and food hygiene requirements are equally valid for conventionally and organically produced food. Further research is required on pathogen survival in untreated manure, treatments to reduce pathogen levels in manure, and assessing the risk of cross-contamination of food crops from manure under varying conditions. Recent research suggests for example that some pathogens, such as the hepatitis A virus, have a higher thermal threshold than others. In addition, the time and temperature required to eliminate or reduce microbial hazards in manure or other organic materials may vary depending on regional climate and the specific management practices of an individual operation.

Guidelines for Organic Processes & Products

In 1999, the Codex Alimentarius Commission (CAC) adopted guidelines for the production, processing, labeling and marketing or organically produced foods. These regulations set out the principles of organic production at farm, preparation, storage, transport, labeling and marketing stages. The adoption of international guidelines is an important step in providing a unified approach to regulating the organic food sub-sector and thus the facilitation of trade in organic food. A common understanding of what is meant by "organic" as well as the existence of internationally-recognized guidelines (eg. HACCP) provide an important measure of consumer protection against deceptive and fraudulent practices.

It is important to realize, first of all that organic foods

must meet all quality and safety standards applied to conventionally produced foods. Specific regulations and guidelines for organically produced foods provide additional requirements arising from the fact that production methods are an intrinsic part of the identification and labeling of, and claim for, such products. In the regulation of organic foods, it is therefore necessary to establish mechanisms whereby assurance can be given that all relevant guidelines are adhered to in the production of these foods. This is achieved through a system of inspection and certification.

Inspection and certification is an intrinsic part of organic agricultural production. In fact, according to the EC and Codex guidelines, the use of terms inferring that organic production methods have been used are restricted to products derived from operators under the supervision of a certification body or authority and are subject to a regular inspection system meeting minimum requirements. Certification may be based, as appropriate, on a range of inspection activities covering the production and processing system and including auditing of quality assurance systems and examination of finished products.

It is through inspection and certification, therefore, that the consumer is assured that the essential elements constituting "organic" production are met and that foods labeled as "organic" are really what they claim to be. Growing consumer demand and expanding economic interests in organic production have led to increasing distances between producer and consumer: this highlights even further the importance of external control and certification procedures to ensure consumer protection. Governments are responsible for ensuring that organic inspection and certification systems within the country meet all relevant requirements of HACCP and Organic Standardization.

Organic Standardization: IFOAM

The advantages according to the certification agency are that it acts as a trust building system between farmers and customers, helps in authentication of the product, enables transparency and strengthens the position of the primary producer and helps in market promotion of product. The certification includes inspection at all stages of production and marketing. A number of organizations promoting the organic concept worldwide are (i) the International Federation of Organic Agriculture Movements (IFOAM) which has been in the forefront of promoting, monitoring and certifying organically farmed produce, (ii) the Soil Association Certification Limited (SAC) in UK, (iii) the United Kingdom Register of Organic Food Standards (UKROFS), (iv) the California Certified Organic Farmers (CCOF) in USA (v) ECOCERT International, (vi) SKAL, Zwolle, the Netherlands (vii) Institute for Market Ecology (IMO), Switzerland.

For example, the IFOAM Basic Standards provide a framework for certification bodies and standard-setting organizations worldwide to develop their own certification standards and cannot be used for certification on their own. Certification standards should take into account specific local conditions and provide more specific requirements than the IFOAM Basic Standards. Procedures and processors that sell organic products are expected to be certified by certification bodies, using standards that meet or exceed the requirements of the IFOAM Basic Standards (IBS). This requires a system of regular inspection and certification designed to ensure the credibility or organically certified products and build consumer trust.

The IBS and IFOAM Accreditation Criteria are used by the International Organic Accreditation Service (IOAS) in the accreditation process for certification bodies and standards setting organizations. The eight IFOAM Basic Standards are presented below as General Principles, Recommendations, and Basic Standards.

1. The Principal Aims of Organic Production and Processing
2. Organic Ecosystems
3. General Requirements for Crop Production and Animal Husbandry
4. Crop Production
5. Animal Husbandry
6. Processing and Handling
7. Labeling
8. Social Justice

In the principle 4, the focus is on avoiding contamination in organic farming within the aspects of HACCP to ensure that organic soil and food is protected from contamination. In case of risk, or reasonable suspicion of risk, that contamination may occur, the standard-setting organization should set limits for the maximum application levels of heavy metals and other pollutants. The standards should place emphasis on detection of contamination sources, improvement of the production system taking into account the procedures developed for HACCP, and the assessment of background contamination levels.

Future of Organic Farming

The government is launching a national project on organic farming to encourage

the production of chemical, biological & physical hazards-free food products in environment-friendly manner. A national institute of organic farming will be set up to undertake research and development activities for organic farming. A special thrust is proposed to market development, quality and safety regulation of organically produced products. The future of organic farming encompasses a range of practices, including the elimination of biological and physical hazards rather than concentrating only on agri-chemical free products and best agriculture management practices that unify the transparency in organic farming processes to the consumer. Ultimately, research should be expanded on consumer attitudes towards paying slightly higher prices for organic foods with HACCP certification, which will help policy makers and farmers make more informed choices to alternative farming.

Conclusion

In order to regulate food, it is necessary that objective parameters be to be established according to which regulatory decisions can be made for the sustainability of organic farming. It is important to realise the need and resulting growth of this sector are impeded in the absence of biological and physical hazards in organic farming processes. The food sector must ensure the quality and safety of their products through implementation of HACCP system, designed to ensure compliance with all relevant regulations. On a global basis, a rating of health risks arising from foods showed that risk due to food additives and pesticide residues are relatively minor as compared with microbiological and physically occurring toxins. Despite this static, however, the problem of food contamination by chemicals is perceived as an important public health concern, than biological toxin.

This chapter does not seek to make a value judgement on the right approach to organic farming. Rather, it presents a critical and transparent overview of issue that relates to safety and the authenticity of organic foods. These trends interact in different ways with the phenomenon of organic farming and organic foods.

REFERENCES

1. Anonymous (1999). *The Organic Food and Farming Report 1999,* Soil Association, p.27.
2. Avery, D. (1997), *Chemistry & Industry,* pp. 1014.
3. Colucke, C. G. (1991). When is compost safe? In the Biocycle Guide to the Art and Science of Composting. *J.G. Press.* Ch. 49, pp. 220-229.
4. Dhanakumar, V.G. (1985). *Organic Agriculture: Lab to Land Perspective.* Zonal Unit VIII. ICAR. Bangalore.
5. Dhanakumar, V.G. (2001). Total Quality Management in Tea Through Quality, Safety and Risk Management: An HACCP Perspective, *International Journal of Tea Science.* Vol.1 No.2 & 3 - 2001-2002.
6. Dhanakumar, V.G. (2002). Quality, Safety & Risk Management in Coconut: An HACCP Perspective. *Indian Coconut Journal.* June 2002, pp. 7-23.
7. Dhanakumar, V. G. (2002). Biological Risk Management (Biosecurity) in Coffee : An HACCP Perspective: Part I & II. *Indian Coffee.* Vol. LXVII April 2003, Pp. 14-17 & Vol. LXVIII No.7, July 2003, Pp.18-21.
8. Dhanakumar, V. G. (2003). HACCP for Chilli Safety Management. *Workshop Manual.* Vol. No.5 - 2003-2004.
9. Excute News Report (2000). Nutraceulise Announces New E.Coli 0157:H7 Inhibiting Bacteria
10. FAO. (2000). *Food Safety and Quality as Affected by Organic Farming.* Twenty Second Regional Conference for Europe, Porto, Portugal, 24-28, July.
11. Food – Extoxnet FAQ.doc
12. Hancock, D. B. (1998). What we have learned about E.Coli 0157:H7. Snowdon Lecture. CSIRO Australian Animal Health Laboratory.
13. http://www.cgfi.org/materials/articles/2002/Oct22
14. http://www.foodnews.org/questions.php
15. http:/www.ift.org
16. http://www.wholefoods.com/issues/ecoli.html
17. IFOAM Basic Standards (2002). IFOAM Basic Standards for Organic Production and Processing. IFOAM, General Assembly, Victoria, Canada.

18. Institute of Food Science and Technology. http://www.ifst.org/hottop24.html
19. Jukes, J. H. (1990). Organic apple juice no antidote for alar. *J. Am Dietetic Assoc.* 90 (3):371
20. Kudva, I.T., Blanch, K. and Horde, C.J. (1998). Analysis of Escherichia coli 0157:H7 survival in ovine or bovine manure and manure slurry. *Applied and Environmental Microbiology,* 64:3166-3179.
21. Nicholson F.A., Hutchison M.L, Smith K.A, Keevil C.W, Chambers B.J, and Moore, A (2000). *A Study on Farm Manure Applications to Agricultural Land and an Assessment of the Risks of Pathogen Transfer into the Food Chain.* MAFF.
22. Report on Organic Farming (2001).
23. Royal Commission on Environmental Pollution. *Sustainable Use of Soil,* 1996, HMSO, ISBN 0-10-131652-6.
24. Thomas R. DeGregori (2000). *Can Organic Agriculture Feed the World?*
25. Winter, C. (2002). *Organic Foods not Healthier than Conventional.* Institute of Food Sciences and Technology.

13

WTO Agreements (SPS – TBT – AOA - TRIPS) and its relevance to Agri- Business Sector

The next phase of agriculture growth is diversification and commercialization of agriculture. Apart from the Green Revolution, India has achieved revolutions in many other sub-sectors. There has been commendable progress in the fields of dairy, oilseeds, sugarcane and cotton. A record of over 69 million tones, India is the first largest producer of milk in the World. Milk production quadrupled from 17 million tonnes at independence to 69 million tonnes at present. This popularity is known as White Revolution. Fish production rose from 0.75 million tonnes to nearly 5 million tonnes during the last five decades, which is known as Blue Revolution. Another Revolution which is known as Yellow Revolution refers to production of oilseeds, which is has increased five times from 5 million tonnes to 25 million tonnes since independence. The production of Eggs recorded a quantum jump from less than 2 billion to 28 billion. Sugarcane production has risen five-fold from 57 million tonnes to 276 million tonnes. Cotton production has registered an increase from 3 million to 14 million bales. India is the largest producer of fruits in the world and second largest producer of vegetables.

The structure of WTO document and implications arising out of its agreements are presented in figure 1, which are likely to influence the Indian organization and its business.

The bold faced agreements shown in Fig. 2 such as SPS, AOA, TBT & TRIPS will also have an effect on agribusiness. This paper gives an idea on WTO and revolve around the issues arising out of these important agreement. In WTO terminology, subsidies in general are identified by 'boxes' with colours of traffic lights: - red (forbidden), green (permitted) and amber (slow down to be reduced). The Agriculture Agreement has no Red Box, although domestic support exceeding the reduction commitment levels in the Amber Box is prohibited. Instead there is a Blue Box and 'Special & Differential (S&D) Box' for developing countries. Questions have arisen as to who can use Amber Box. It will be useful to glance over the composition of the boxes and WTO agreements for the usability in agri-business.

WTO/Sanitary and Phyto Sanitary measures (SPS) Agreement

In view of the WTO and SPS agreement, the trade among the countries is likely to increase as a result of which pesticides residue certificate on agricultural commodities would become unavoidable. The pesticides residue are required to be monitored and certified both before export and before allowing import. Yet, there is no programme for certification of pesticide residues on agricultural commodities. Similarly, pesticide residues are covered by the Ministry of Health under PFA Act. This is an area which needs immediate attention as there is need for establishing the facilities for pesticide residue testing in agricultural commodities before import and export.

The issue of human and animal health and plant protection is high on the agenda of several developed countries, fueled by recent cases of food poisoning, the spread of pests among animals, and environmental contamination. International trade is perceived as a magnifier of such problems. Developing countries appreciate that, in several cases, these concerns are genuine, but they fear that developed countries may use sanitary and phytosanitary (SPS) measures for protectionist purposes. Their concern is well founded, since the major difficulty in dealing with SPS measures is likely to live in distinguishing those measures that are justified by a legitimate goal, and have a scientific justification, from those that are applied to shield domestic producers from other country agricultural exports.

The need for specialist scientific or technical knowledge makes restrictions imposed for health and safety reasons much more difficult to challenge than some other barriers to trade. While the requirement that SPS measures be based on scientific evidence helps secure trade policy objectives, it is perceived by some environmental and consumer protection groups in some developing countries as a dangerous limitation on the right of governments to take precautionary measures to protect their citizens and the environment against risk that can be irreversible effects. Differences between "sound science" and the "precautionary approach" to health and safety are causing acute tensions among countries.

B. WTO- AGREEMENT ON AGRICULTURE (AOA)

We note that much has been said about the Agreement on Agriculture, some to it either misleading or wrong. Certain negotiators and officials have found this agreement as a reform of the world agricultural trade. Scrutiny of the details, how ever, shows that it is something considerably less. We agree that the agreement does represent a significant reduction in border made and a major increase in access to protected markets, even though it may involve major changes in the rules for border protection. Wrong criticism has been leveled against this Agreement. First, it is claimed that the agreement requires developing countries to throw open their market uncontrolled imports from the developed countries. We have seen that this is grossly incorrect. The second charge of the critics is that the agreement will sharply increase the world prices creating problems for food importing countries. Given the modest policy adjustments only a marginal change can result at most. This charge is also wrong. Thirdly, critics of the agreement have asserted that reduction in domestic subsidies in industrial subsidies will reduce the quantum of food aid available. This charge is also hopelessly out of place.

The final agriculture agreement that emerged from the Uruguay round was shaped largely by the fact that the European Union and United States were the chief negotiators. Despite rhetoric about ridding, the world of trade – distorting subsidies, the United States had its ultimate objective for effective international control over the European unions ever expanding export subsidies. The Cairns group hope to control or eliminate export subsidies used by the European union and the United States. The European Union and Japan had, as their prime objective, the continuation of their strong protection and their isolation from world market forces. There's been a defensive strategy, and to a large extent it worked. Despite the political furor the agreement created in those countries still be heavily shielded from the international competition.

Developing countries outside Cairns group had a limited impact on the agenda for the agricultural negotiation and the outcome. Provisions in the Dunkel text allowed many to escape tariffication and to maintain high levels of protection. Thus most of the distortions that a developing country imposes on its economy through agricultural policy will remain largely untouched if the country chooses.

The revised rule for agriculture, which clarify the Limits on export subsidies and provide uniform methods of border protection, should shoot tension in GATT over agricultural trade issues. This, together with the ceasefire should remove agriculture as one of the major questions about the trading system functions. If countries fail to comply with their commitments, the system's functioning will resurface as an issue. The agricultural agreement calls for discussions at the end of five years on the need for further reform. It remains to be seen whether the major stakes holders in world agricultural trade wants to pursue real liberalization. The following sections are required boxes of the AOA measures.

BLUE BOX

The Blue Box is an exemption from the general rule that all subsidies linked to production must be reduced or kept within defined minimal (de minimis) levels it covers payments directly linked to acreage or minimal numbers, but under schemes which also limit production by imposing production quotas or requiring farmers to set aside part of their land. Countries using these subsidies – and there are only a handful-say they distort trade less than alternative Amber Box subsidies, currently the only members notifying the WTO that they are using or have used the Blue Box are: the EU, Norway, Japan, and Slovak Republic (so far only in 1995-97).

At the moment, the blue Box is a permanent provision of the agreement. Some countries want it scrapped because the payments are only partly decoupled from production, or they are proposing commitments to reduce the use of these subsidies. Other say the Blue Box is an important tool for supporting and reforming agriculture, and for achieving certain 'non trade' objectives, and argue that it should not be restricted as it distorts trade less than other types of support. The EU says it is prepared to consider negotiating restrictions on the Blue Box although they oppose scrapping it completely.

The Blue Box is an exemption from the general rule that all subsidies link to production must be reduced are kept within defined minimal levels. It covers payments directly link to acreage or animal numbers, but under schemes that also limit production by imposing production quotas or requiring farmers to set aside land. Only the EU, Iceland, Norway, Japan, the Slovak Republic, Slovenia, and US have use these subsidies. The distinguishing feature of Blue Box policies is payments based on fixed acreage, yields, or live stock numbers on no more than 85 percent of base line production. Blue Box Measures are direct payments under production limiting programmes. Such payments are exempt from the reduction commitments if:

- Such payments are based on fixed area and yield; or
- Such payments are made on 85 percent or less of the base level of production; or
- Live stock payments are made on a fixed number of head

GREEN BOX

In order to qualify for the Green Box, a subsidy must not distort trade or at the most cause minimal distortion. These subsidies have to be government-funded (not by charging consumers higher prices) and must not involve price support. They tend to be programmes that are not directed at particular products, and include direct income supports for farmers that are not related to (are decoupled' from) current production levels or prices. Green Box subsidies are therefore allowed without limits, provided they comply with relevant criteria. They also include environmental protection and regional development programmes. Canada has proposed setting limits on all 'boxes' combined, which would mean limits on Green Box subsidies as well. Some countries say they would like to review the domestic subsidies listed in the Green Box because they believe that some of these, in certain circumstances could have an influence on production or prices. Some others have said that the Green Box should not be changed because it is already satisfactory. Some say the Green Box should be expanded to cover additional types of subsidies.

Green box Policies include decoupled payments (which purportedly do not effect production decisions) and general policies such as environmental programmes, research, food aid, crop insurance, and income safety net programmes to correct for market failures. These policies are general taxpayer – funded and do not involve consumer transfers. Green box policies are suppose to meet the criteria of "no, or at most minimal, trade distorting effects or effects on production". It will be shown that the Green Box also encompasses some policies that are not fully decoupled.

The Green box also includes programmes that are not directed at particular commodities or products, such as income insurance programmes, as well as environmental protection and regional developments.

Green box measures include:

- General services, including research,
- Pest and disease control
- Training and extension
- Inspection, marketing and promotion services
- Infrastructural services;
- Food security stocks,
- Domestic food aid; and direct payments to producers, including decoupled income support
- Income insurance and safety net programme
- Disaster relief,
- Producer or resource retirement schemes
- Investment aids
- Environmental programmes, and
- Regional assistance programmes

Food Security Box

Food security is an issue normally associated with developing countries where food supplies are inadequate because of low production or inability to import and distribute adequate amounts. Perhaps somewhat surprisingly, food security is also an issue in developed countries that can readily afford to import much of the food they consume.

Food security can be defined as a situation in which "all households have both physical and economic access to adequate food for all members, and where households are not at risk of losing such access.

The Amber Box

For agriculture, all domestic support measures considered to distort production and trade (with some exceptions) fall into the Amber Box. The total value of these measures must be reduced. Various proposals deal with how much further these subsidies should be reduced and whether limits should be set for specific products rather than having an 'aggregate' limit.

C. WTO- TBT

TBT agreements is intended to ensure that WTO members do not use technical regulations and standards as disguised measures to protect domestic industries from foreign competition. In international trade law, health and environmental standards and regulations, labelling, symbols and packaging markings can be considered as technical barriers to trade.

D.WTO-TRIPS

Designed to enhance the protection of intellectual property rights, the TRIPS agreement makes explicit reference to the environment, which allows members to exclude from

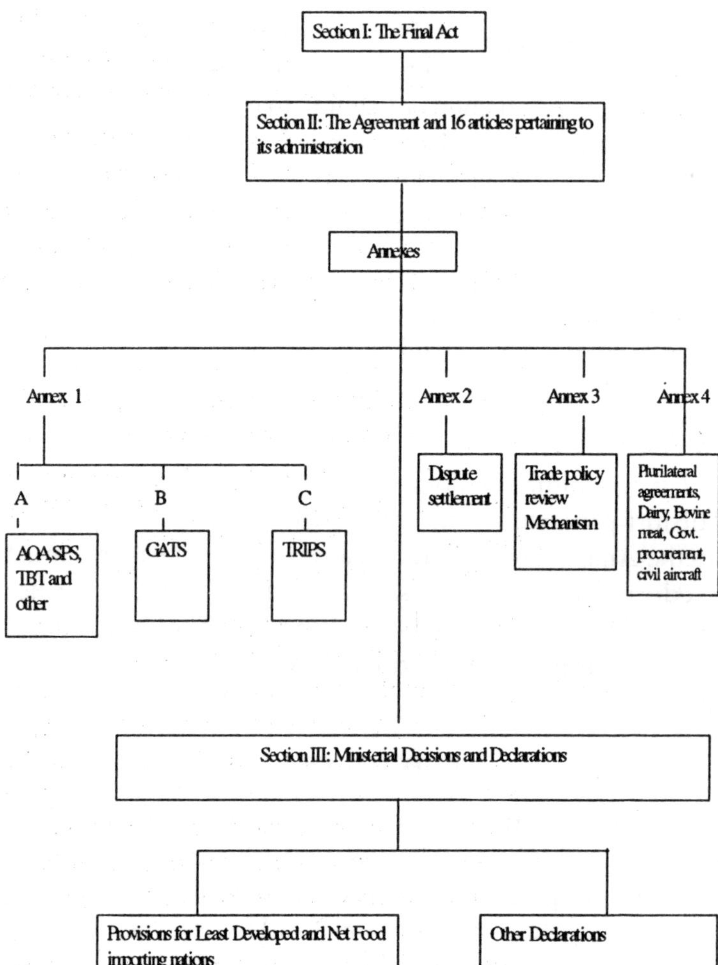

Fig. 1: The WTO Document Structure

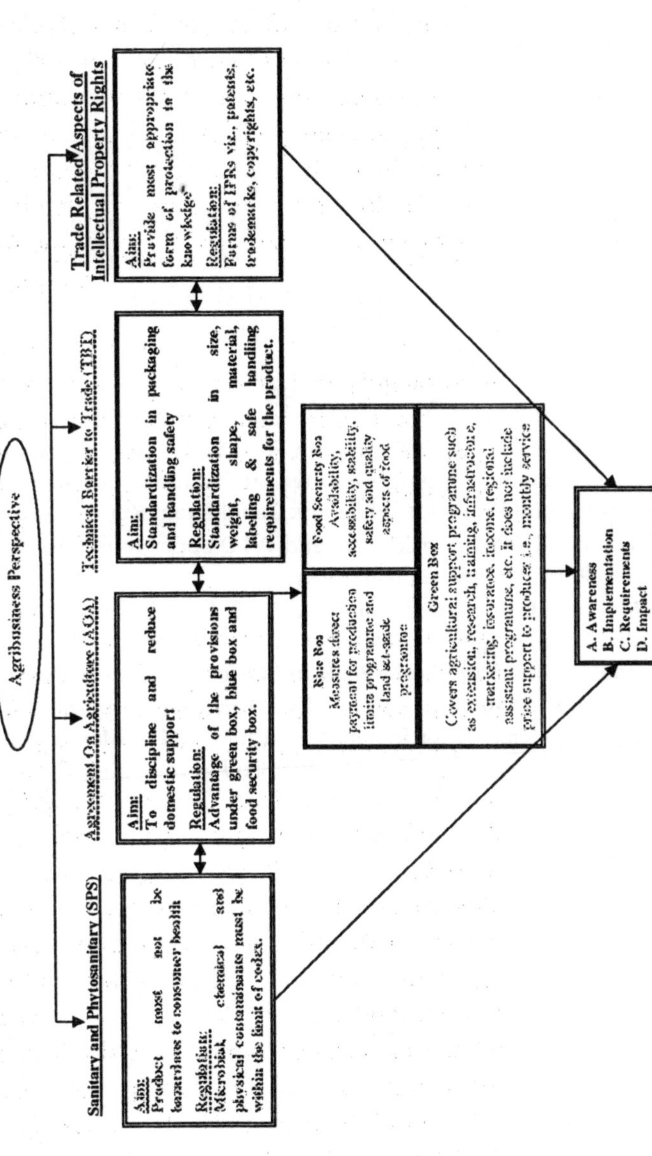

Fig. 2: Conceptual Framework to Understand interrelationship of WTO-SPS-AOA-TBT-TRIPs Agreements & Its Relevance in Agribusiness Sector

patentability invention the prevention of whose commercial exploitation within their territory is necessary to protect human, animal and plant life or health or to avoid serious prejudice to the environment.

Conclusion

Post WTO era has brought different standards and limits to the agriculture production system. Decision making body of agribusiness units should be aware of these standards for proper planning and implementation. Different stakeholders should be trained in SPS-TBT-AOA -TRIPS in relevance to agribusiness sector.

REFERENCES

1. Dhanakumar, V. G. 2005. IPR for Food Safety Technology and Management. Paper presented at National Seminar on Intellectural Propety. 6-7 January. Gandhigram Rural Institute.
2. Jayanta, B, 2003. Agriculture and WTO opportunity in India, Samskriti Publication, New Dlehi.
3. Merlinda D. Ingco and John D.Nash, 2004. Agriculture and the WTO, Creating A Trading System for Development, A Co-publication of the World Bank and Oxford University Press.
4. Samar K. Datta and Satish Y. Deodhar, 2001. Implication of WTO agreements for Indian Agriculture, CMA Monographs No.191, Oxford ad IBH publication Co Pvt Ltd, New Delhi.

14

Ready to Eat Food Technology

India is the largest producer of fruits and vegetables, spices, plantation products and food grains. India is one of the world's major food producers but accounts for less than 1.5 per cent of international food trade. This indicates a vast scope for both investors and exporters. As a result of several policy initiatives undertaken since liberalization, the industry witness fasts growth in most of the segments. Government has approved proposals for joint ventures, foreign collaboration, industrial licences and 100 per cent export oriented units. The consumer food industry consists of ready to eat products such as Encapsulation (or) Micro Encapsulation products, fabricated foods, nutraceutical foods, weaning food, fortification etc.

Ready to eat foods serves the following purpose:

Dietary diversification: Consuming foods rich in micronutrients and applicable on long term basis.

Supplementation: Administering oral doses of these micronutrients and applicable in short term basis.

Food fortification: Adding micronutrients to the food products and applicable in medium term and most sustainable approach.

Four Types of Modern Foods

(A) Encapsulation (or) Micro Encapsulation

(B) Fabricated Food

(C) Nutraceuticals

(D) Fortified Foods

a) Encapsulation (or) Micro Encapsulation

Droplets of liquids, solids or gases are coated by thin films. Droplets can be released under different conditions. This technique is applied to preserve and/or protect numerous ingredients from fruits, vegetables and grains.

Different Encapsulated Products

(1) Encapsulated Acids

Eg., Ascorbic Acids (Vit. C) used as an oxidation agent in the strengthening and conditioning of bread. Encapsulated form of products protects the acid from the environment and released when it is most needed.

(2) Encapsulated Natural Colours

Eg., Turmeric. Extended self-life, which can exceed two years, compared to 6 months.

(3) Encapsulated Flavours

Eg., Natural and artificial flavours viz., oleoresin and essential oil.

(4) Encapsulated Vitamins and Minerals

Added to nutritional dry mixes to fortify variety of food like breakfast, cereals, dairy products, and infantile formulas.

b) Fabricated Foods

Fabricated foods (or) instant foods that have been designed, engineered or formulated from various ingredients. Provide a scope for incorporating minerals and vitamins. Fabricated foods are limitation of natural foods

E.g., Snacks, cookies, prepared cereals, and cakes & roll miles. Advantages of Fabricated (or) Instant Foods are free of toxin and anti nutritioned actors, fortification of nutrients, high food value and Foods made for convenience

For example Vit C are fabricated in different forms (or) sources as indicated in Table below:

Natural Vit .C	*Vit.C Tablets*
Orange juice	**Chewable**
Sukee- more ascorbic acid	
Amla powder	Celin
Amla powder	Citravite,Limcee
Non-chewable,	
Celin&redoxin	

Ingredients used in Fabricated (or) Instant Foods

Soyabean Protein - variety of products

Cotton Seed Protein - additives for cookies, biscuits and speciality breads

Peanut Protein - tonned in milk and atta

Sunflower Seed Protein - high quality protein

Coconut Protein - residue (after extraction of oil)

Sesame Seed Protein - used in other cereal flavour

Need for Fabricated (or) Instant Foods

Convenience

Protein derive

Preservation

Technology

Palatability and nutrition

Soyabean Proteins are best for Instant Foods because of

Emulsification

Whipping ability

Foaming

Water holding capacity

Processed soyabean raw materials

Product	Uses	Process
Soyaflour with fat	Beverages, baby food removed	Beverages, Oil is not
Soyaflour, defatted	Bakery & meat products	Oil is removed
Soya protein breads	Beverage & fortified Carbohydrates are	Oil and soluble removed
Soya milk	Commercial soya beverage	Extraction of cooked bean at higher temperatures followed by clarification

c) Nutraceuticals

Nutraceuticals are processed food that are fortified with ingredients that have either fruit / vegetable / animal basis that offers health benefits. Milk, vegetables and fruits, grains, etc contains disease-preventing substance. Nutraceuticals food that have developed with a specific aim of reducing fat, prevention or reduction of diseases and acceptable to our regular diets.

Examples of Nutraceutical Products

Ingredients	Found in	Used in	Advantage
Pyruvate (Carbohydrate) s	Fruits and Vegetables	Used in beverages	Weight reduction& energetic
Lactinol	Milk	Chocolate, jams, ice cream	Reduced calorie sweetness used in sugar free products
Vit. C.	Fruits & Vegetables	Bakery products	Protecting against cataracts, bronchitis, asthma, etc
Zinc	Minerals	Chewing gums, breath mint	Appetite & normal growth

d) Weaning Food

Introduction of food as secondary source to Mother's milk during the weaning period of 4 to 6 months. Infant cannot drink the volume of milk necessary to fulfil energy requirements without the addition of other foods in the diet. Ingredients of weaning food are cereal grains (wheat, rice, millet & jowar) Skimmed milk and corn soya milk. The process of infant food preparation is illustrated below:

Infant Food Production

Milk or Water

↓

Mixing
(Ingredients can be added wholly or partly

↓

Heat Treatment
(150°C - to obtain product of high bacterological standard)

↓

Drying
(Spray drying system)

↓

Dry Mixing
(20-30% of the ingredients mixed after drying)

↓

Agglomeration
(Thorough Mixing)

e) Fortification

Supplementation of staple food with vitamins and micronutrients. The vehicles selected should ideally be the staple food like rice, wheat flour, oil, sugar, salt, tea, etc. The fortified food must be stable under normal conditions of storage and use. The nutrients must be physiologically bio-available should not produce undesirable changes in the physical properties like taste, smell, colour, texture, etc. Advantages of Fortification are most efficient and cost-effective, simple and affordable for rectifying the deficiencies, impact can be detected in 1-3 months and covers a large section of population.

Types of Fortification

1) Mandatory Fortification

   Vanaspathi ghee with vitamin A

2) Voluntary Fortification

   Milk, Wheat flour, salt etc.

Different food and micro nutrient added

Food	*Micro-nutrient*
Wheat Flour	Vitamin A with Folic acid & Iron
Sugar	Vitamin A
Milk	Vitamin A
Rice	Vitamin A
Oil	Vitamin A

Different companies

Name of the Company	*Products*
Advanced Bio-chemicals Ltd. Thane	Neutraceuticals
DuPont Protein Technologies Gurgoan, Harayana	Soya Protein & Dietary Soya Fibre
Venkatesh Food Industries Chinndwar (MP	Food Powders & Herbal Extracts
Shreyas, Baroda, Gujarat	Milk Products / baby Foods
Vital Flavour & Fragrances	Flavours for Foods & Beverages

Conclusion

Ready to eat food industry currently focuses on minimizing food preparation cycle time, convenience and accessibility to suit the current lifestyle of the consumers. However, efforts should be focussed towards the development of technology for commercialization of ready to eat traditional Indian foods meeting the international standards of food safety and hygiene. Nutraceuticals, fortified foods, weaning food and fabricated foods provide nutrition with vitamins, minerals for human health. The future focus on ready to eat food should concentrate on the area of baby food, teenage, patients within the framework of WHO & codex standards to meet felt needs of the special group. The ready to eat product must have a well-known certification for authenity of foods and standards for the target sector.

REFERENCES

1. Von Loesecke, W.H. (2001). *Outlines of Food Technology*. Agrobios (India). Jodhpur.
2. SBP. *Hand Book of Food and Agro Based Industries*. SBP consultants and Engineers Pvt Ltd.
3. Cost of fortification of foods (2004). *Times Food Processing Journal*. Oct-Nov. Pp.35-39.

15

Production and Manufacturing Technology for Bio-fuel

Introduction

India is home of billion people. Economic liberalization and post-WTO era has opened up Indian economy to the world market. Currently, India is the fifth largest economy with potential future market. But one factors which hinders economic growth is import of about 70% of its petroleum demand. Periodic increase in crude oil price has created a lot of socio economic problems in the country. Major solutions to these problems can be foreseen from extraction of oil or bio diesel from petrocrops like jatropha, pongamia, neem, mahua etc.

Characteristics of Biodiesel

Bio diesel chemically referred as Mono Alkyl Ester (MAE). Biodiesel contain oxygen in their molecular structure. This characteristic is advantageous to the burning process in an internal combustion engine but also reduces the release of harmful pollutants. It is eco-friendly, nontoxic, bio degradable and free from carcinogenic pollutants. Its energy is equivalent to fossil counterpart and higher burning efficiency (centane number) makes bio fuel alternative to fossil fuels. Pure biodiesel is essentially sulfur free and results in a total reduction of SO_2 emission as well as sulfate aerosols in particulate matter. These reductions should assist in increasing both vehicle and catalyst life over time.

Standards and Grades of Biodiesel

A working group of Austrian standardization institute issued the first Biodiesel fuel standard in 1991, as ONC 1190 for RME or Rapeseed-oil-Methyl Ester. This is followed by 011C1191 for FAME or fatty acid-methyl ester in July 1997, later, the DIN E 51606 was published in Germany, while other national standards were established in France, Italy, Sweden and the USA. American biodiesel standard is ASTM D6751. The most recent development is the completion of CEN draft standard for biodiesel with validity all over the Europe. Popular grades of Biodiesel are:

- B100- Pure form of biodiesel
- B20-Blended fuel with 20% biodiesel and 80% diesel
- B10- Blended fuel with 10% biodiesel and 90% diesel

  Biodiesel mixes easily in any proportion with conventional diesel and by virtue of its high density can be easily mixed in a tank containing petroleum diesel.
- Generally blend of 5% to 30% is used in most countries.

Biodiesel is normally extracted from crops like Pongamia, Jatropha , Mahua, Neem and other non edible oils. Production aspects of these important crops are given in the below table No. 1.

TABLE. 1

Best Production Technology (BPT) for Important Bio-fuel Plants

Production Characteristics	Neem (*Azadirachta indica*)	Pongamia (*Pongamia Pinnata*)
Area of Cultivation	Bihar, West Bengal, Orissa, Gujarat, Maharashtra, Karnataka, Tamilnadu & Assam	Bihar, West Bengal, Uttar Pradesh & Madhya Pradesh
Climate (Maximum Temperature)	30°C to 48°C	37°C to 49°C
Rainfall (mm)	480 to 1000	500 to 2000
Irrigation	Drought tolerant & low moisture preference	Abundant water requirement (1.30 water/g/biomass)
Soil Type	Black cotton soils, alkaline soils, dry stony shallow soil and well drained loamy soils	Deep Sandy loam
Soil pH	7 - 8.5	7 - 8.5
Plant Spacing	Alley cropping system 4m x 4m	
Seed Collection period	June - August	March - May
Seed life span	3 - 5 weeks	1 year
Seed Management	• Depulping of fruits • Seeds dried (2 days) under shade to bring down the moisture level of 5 percent • Seedlings of 10 - 15 cm height planted in the main field • Seed stored for long time will be contaminated with aflatoxin	

Pre-sowing treatment	Hot water treatment		Soak in water
Sowing Season	July-August		July-August
Pit Size	45 or 60 or 90 cm^3		45 or 60 or 90 cm^3
Fertilizer application while planting	Gypsum 2-3 kg/pit FYM 2.5 kg/pit		Gypsum 2-3 kg/pit FYM 2.5 kg/pit
Flowering period	March to May		April to June
Pollination	Cross pollination by honey bees (*Apis florea Apis, Cerana, tregona sp and ceratina spp*)		Honey bees
Pest & Disease	Tea mosquito bug - Thrips Root grub Termites-Scales & Mealy bug	Dimethoate (0.01-0.2%) Aderex Monocrotophos (0.01 - 0.02%)	

Transcertification Process

Bio diesel is made by transcertification of vegetable oils and/ or animal fats in the presence of catalyst and glycerine, which are obtained as by product. Majority of biodiesel produced today is based on catalyst transcertification as illustrated below:

$$100 \text{ kg plant oil} + 10 \text{ kg Alcohol} \xrightarrow{\text{Na OH}} 10 \text{ kg Glycerine} + 100 \text{ Kgs of Biodiesel}$$

Biodiesel Manufacturing Process

The different types and models on manufacturing of biodiesel are furnished in the following sections viz., A to F.

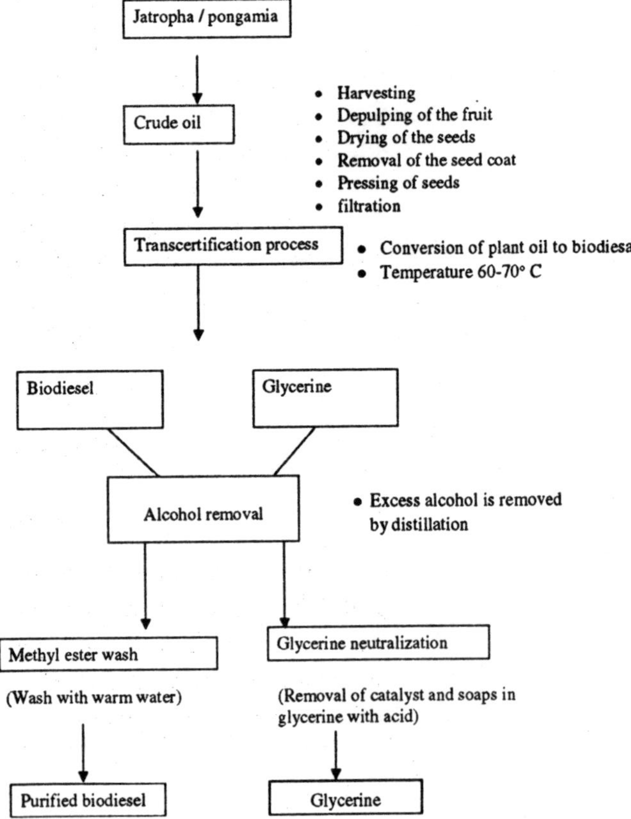

B) A model case of Jatropha plantation / processing

Jatropha Plantation

Number of trees-	2500 trees/hectare
Jatropha seed production –	1.5 - 2 kg /tree/ annum
Total amount of seeds/annum/hectare-	4000-5000 kg /ha

Project on wasteland of 500 ha

Land-	500 ha
Seeds produced per ha. –	4000 kg/ha
Seeds produced for 500 ha-	20, 00, 000 Kg

Seedling cost:	Rs.4/- seedling
Cultivation Cost:	Rs.30,000/ ha.
500 ha.	Rs.1,50,00,000

Jatropha oil Extraction unit

Transesterifiation process (90%)

· Jatropha oil-	2000 t/annum
· Methanol –	100t/annum
· Sodium hydroxide-	29t/annum

Jatropha Oil - 1800 t/annum

Glycerine-810 t/annum

Community lands	no investment
Factory building	10,00, 000
Plant and machinery	25,00, 000
Miscellaneous expenditure	15,00, 000
Total	50,00, 000

Jatropha oil sold at the rate of –	Rs.4 / kg
1 tonne- 1000X Rs.4 =	Rs. 4000
2000X 4000=	**Rs. 80,00,000**

Bio diesel Extraction Unit

Land	No Investment
Factory cost-	20, 00, 000
Jatropha Oil	No Investment
Methanal- 13/ liter-	13, 00, 000
Sodium hydroxide 12 / kg-	3, 50, 300

E. Present model of operations

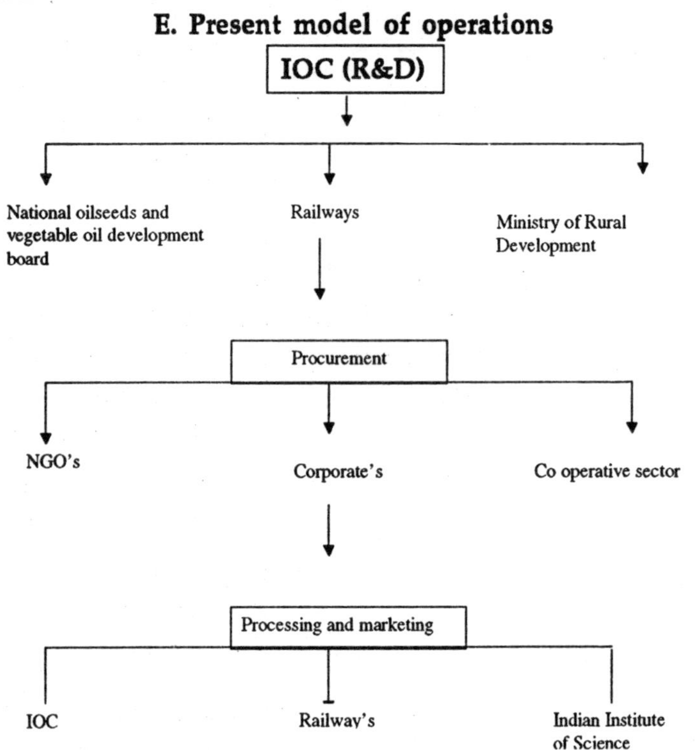

F. Model Appropriate proposed for Bio diesel Business

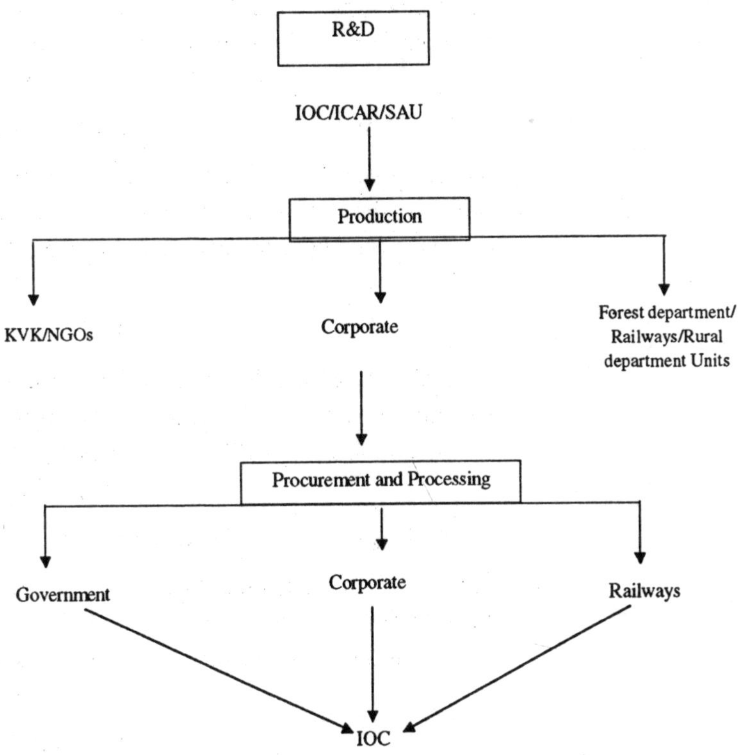

Conclusion

Consumption of petroleum diesel in India contributed several million tonnes per annum and it is anticipated a higher level of demand at a significant level. To minimise overall dependence on crude oil, it is recommended to promote bio diesel based crops viz., Jatropha, Mahua, pongamia based diesel as appropriate solution for Indian condition. This chapter also illustrated different model for bio diesel business with reference to production, processing, procurement, value addition and marketing. An institutional framework for the sustainability of bio diesel business is also illustrated in this chapter. The further detail related to bio diesel business can be obtained from Australian bio fuel institute at www.biofuel.com

REFERENCES

1. Anonymous. 1990. *Plants for Reclamation of Wastelands*. CAIR. New Delhi.
2. Bedell, P.K., 1998, *Seed Science & Technology*. Allied Publishers Limited, New Delhi.
3. Dhanakumar, V.G., 2003., Boon for Bio fuel., *Wastelands News*, pp. 36-41.
4. Jha, L.K. 1995. *Advances in Agro Forestry*. APH Publishing Corporation, New Delhi.
5. Jha, L.K., 1995, *Advances in Agroforestry*. APH Publishing Corporation, New Delhi.
6. Troup, R.S, 1986, *The Selviculture of India Trees*. International Book Distributors, Vol.II, Dehradun.
7. *Investment Opportunity in Jatropha Based Biodiesel Project* - 2004, Nandini Consultancy Center Pvt ltd. Madras.

AROMEDIC PLANTATION FOR AGRI-BUSINESS

Introduction

Interest in agro-ecological based plantations are increasing rapidly, which shows that the area of plantation increased over six times between 1965 and 1990, and the rate of planting in the 1980s was double that of the 1970s. The countries such as Fiji, Malawi, and Swaziland undertake plantation programmes covering tens of thousands of hectares, and millions of hectares being planted in China, India, and Brazil. In India, for example, not only are government and parastatal bodies involved but nearly 10000 non-government organizations (NGOs) are concerned to promote planting of one kind or another. The interest in aromatic & medicinal (Aromedic) sector in developing countries are heavily dependent on planting, but many countries with large natural reserves are also implementing major projects. For example,

Brazil, with one of the largest remaining areas of natural forest in the world – the Amazon rain forest – in 1966 embarked on a planting programme which reached a planting rate of nearly half a million hectares per year during the late 1970s and early 1980. Papua New Guinea has about 75 per cent of its land surface covered with forest and plantation per person than any other country (about 600 m^3 per person), yet much of the annual budget is used for establishment and maintenance of plantations.

In seeking to answer the question of why plantations of aromatic & medicinal, World Health Organization (WHO) says that more than 1 billion people rely on herbal and medicinal plants to manifest the harmony between the plant kingdom and the human world. The WHO has listed 21,000 plants that have reported medicinal uses around the world. India has rich medicinal plant flora of some 2500 species. Of these, 2000 to 2300 species are used in traditional medicine while at least 150 species are used commercially on a fairly large scale. India and China are the largest exporters of medicinal plants. Medicinal plants in India are estimated to be worth Rs.550 crores, ayurvedic ethical formulation contribute the remaining sum. Cosmetic industry as well as aromatherapy are two important areas where Indian medicinal plants and their extracts, essential oil can contribute globally. Medicinal and aromatic plants have a high market potential with the world demand of herbal products growing at the rate of 7 percent per annum.

Resourcing the Sources of India

India is bestowed with a wealth of medicinal and aromatic plants, most of which have been traditionally used in Ayurveda, Yunani system of medicines and tribal healers for generations. India is rich in agri-biodiversity. Many valuable and rare medicinal and aromatic plants have been identified from different parts of state. India is rich in herbs useful in treatment of common ailments to lethal diseases like blood cancer. Bhramar mar for cancer, Satawar, Safed Musli, Kali Moosli, Asgandh as promising tonic, Kukronda and Adusa for respiratory trouble, Gudmar and Sadasuhagan for Diabetes, Bramhi and Bach for Memory, Kalmegh for Chronic fever, Sarpagandha and Arjun for heart troubles are some example of miracle herbs found in Chhattisgarh.

Inspite of huge agri-biodiversity and traditions of use of medicinal and aromatic herbs, we have not been able to utilize opportunities and exploit its hidden potential. Many of the potential herbs are not known to the scientific world and of those known many are overexploited leading to their extinction or listing them as endangered or threatened plants. (Indian Herbal Research Message Board – 12/18/2002). A way has to be found to domesticate and cultivate such herbs within the concepts of Production and Operations Management.

Review of Literature on the use of Aromatic & Medicinal Plants

Human beings have used perfumes, cosmetics and flavors from the very beginning of human civilization. The ancient man used pastes and water extracts of roots, stems, leaves, flowers to beautify. This was replaced by scented waters and finally essential oils, as part of modern perfumes and cosmetics. Essential oil is a concentrated aromatic liquid substance extracted from flowers, fruits, leaves, bark, roots, seeds and gums. These oils are utilized in high volume consumer products like soaps, cosmetics, confectioneries, beverages, ice creams and baby foods etc.

The use of essential oils in cosmetics and perfume has increased progressively due to non-health hazardous in nature and cost effectiveness compared to synthetic sources. Herbal preparation are generally non-less toxic compared to synthetic (Yoganarasimhan, 1996). There is a definite trend to adopt plant based product due to cumulative derogatory effects of antibiotics (Farooqi and Sriramu, 2001).

Recently, consumer magazine Insight 2002, has exposed deleterious affect of industrial chemical Phthalates in cosmetics and perfumes. Phthalates are extensively used in perfume to make scent linger. Phthalates can be metabolized by the human body once inhaled as fumes, ingested or absorbed through the skin. Phthalates can damage the liver, kidney, lungs and reproductive system. European Union have banned the usage of Phthalates. (Refer:www.nottoopretty.org). According to Balz, 1999, the anthroposophical approach reveals through the following diagram to illustrate a complementary interactions between human being and plants.

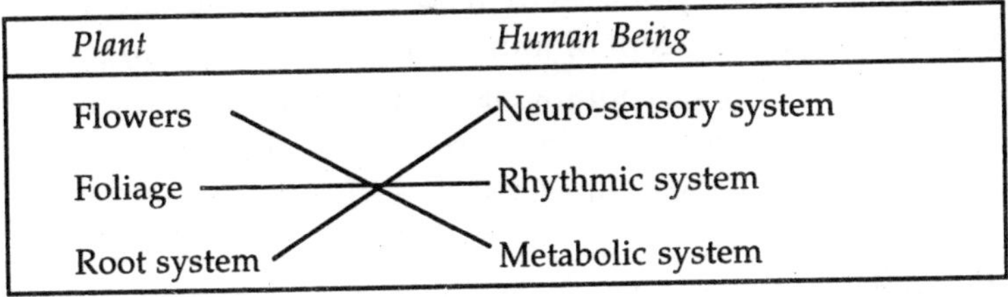

Haley, 2002 reported that all synthetic cosmetic articles contain preservatives and or disinfectants that impair or even eliminate the effectiveness of any natural substances they may contain. These agents are foreign substances (e.g., formaldehyde, hexachlorophene, and quarternium) that are known to damage the skin's flora and protective acid mantle. Moreover, they promote aging of the skin by reducing its water-absorbent capacities. As they penetrate the skin's layers, such substances remove the skins elasticity. The wrinkles resulting from this process are then likely to be treated with some anti-aging cream that is likely to contain harmful preservatives.

There is a need to introduce aromatic crops into the cropping systems of the country in large scale (Farooqi and

Sriramu, 2001), to propagate and promote aromatic products to the next generation.

Future of Aromedic

The growth in demand of the perfumery raw materials is very fast in the world trade. It is estimated that the total world production of essential oils, aroma, chemical flavours and fragrance compounds are of the value to 3600 US$ in 1978, which rose to 1.65 billions US$ in 1983 and reached 7 billion US$ in 1987.

India produces and exports few aromatic plants like peppermint, sandalwood, lemongrass etc. India's major production comes from forest areas. Ninety five percent of the raw materials come from wild plants (Chauhan, 1990). Establishing the concept of Joint Forest, Planter and Marketer approach (JFPM), Corporate farming or Contract Farming of Medicinal and Aromatic plants to improve the areas of plant conservation, propagation, value addition, supply chain, assured buy back to the producers and to meet essential demand are the policy dimensions of the country. Need based production require critical management practices for productivity, quality and value-addition. An understanding on "Critical Management Practices" within the guidelines of Good Agricultural Practice (G.A.P.) of Medicinal and Aromatic Plants should also be intended to meet the demands of National, European and US regulations.

A main aim is to ensure that the plant raw material meets the demands of the consumer and as such the standards of the highest quality, especially important aspects are that they:

- are produced hygienically, in order to reduce microbiological load to minimum,
- are produced with care, so that the negative impacts

affecting plants during cultivation, processing and storage can be limited

The details related to GAP on seeds propagation, cultivation and value addition, refer to www.ienica.net/policy/goodagpracherbs.htm. It is suggested that the producer, trader, processor of medicinal and aromatic plants should comply with GAP guidelines to meet the demands of the consumers.

The majority of the rural and urban population have made a paradigm shift in using synthetic cosmetic to herbal medicines and perfumes i.e., shift from Business of Synthetic to the Business of Aroma from nature. Resurgence of interest in aromatic and medicinal plant product in business has created a market niche. The parameters for the production, processing and value addition for the important medicinal and aromatic plants are illustrated in table No.1. Development of aromatic product parameter has to be assessed in pilot scale to upscale in the industrial sector.

Constraints

The UNIDO has suggested the following constraints related to production of medicinal and aromatic plants within industrial utilization perspective.

- Poor agricultural practices
- Poor harvesting (indiscriminate) and post-harvest treatment practices
- Lack of research on development of high-yielding varieties, domestication etc.
- Poor propagation methods
- Inefficient processing techniques leading to low yields and poor quality products
- Poor quality control procedures
- High energy losses during processing
- Lack of current good manufacturing practices

- Lack of R & D on product and process development
- Difficulties in marketing
- Lack of trained personnel and equipment
- Lack of facilities to fabricate equipment locally
- Lack of access to latest technological and market information

Source: UNIDO

Moreover, exploitation of important aromatic and medicinal plants had increased natural population due to biotic pressure and increasing dependency of pharmaceutical companies leading to habitat destruction and they are on the verge of destruction. In order to meet an urgent need to conserve these species in natural habitat, the Government of India, SAU, Central Institute of Medicinal and Aromatic Plants have proposed the following strategies.

1. A strategy to develop appropriates extension system for non-conventional crops like aromatic & medicinal plants to disseminate appropriate technology to the farmers and industry.
2. Establish region-wise demonstration to take cultivation practices of aromatic plants.
3. Market led extension system to network through Cooperatives and self help groups to realize remunerative price.
4. Establishing Contract Farming and Grower's-cum-Marketing Cooperatives Societies.

Conclusion

The Division of Extension Management (DEM) of IIPM, demonstrate the hidden potential of medicinal and aromatic plants with special reference to industrialization, R&D and Quality Management. The principle author has identified nearly 250 medicinal and aromatic species in the Nilgiris with help of primitive tribes as part of workshop organized by ICAR-UPASI-KVK in Coonoor during 1996-97. An association with the Cornell Plantation of Cornell University during his tenure on doctoral programme in 1986-87, had influenced his interest in wildscience in the area of essential oils of wild and its use in aromatherapy. Currently, a course on Plantation Technology of PGD-ABPM of IIPM allows the students to learn the area of Aromatic and Medicinal Plants viz., identification, propagation & production management, processing of essential oils, Supply Chain Management (SCM), Contract-cum-Corporate Farming, Value-addition and to built an institution on enterprenurship in aromatherapy. Due to well known properties of aromatic plants, quality has to be built into whole process of production to consumption. The elements of quality such as Total Quality Management (TQM), ISO 9000, 14000, HACCP, GAP and GHP have to be incorporated in the production system of aromedic.

Aromedic plantation is a growing resource and central to its operations management. Appropriate and timely intervention & the pattern of crop production management can be manipulated to modify both quality and the quantity of the end-product. An orderliness, regularity and relative agri-ecological simplicity show that the "aromedic plantation" to be manmade (naturally inhospitable) and clearly distinguish it from habitat. The economic advantage of these qualities are greater efficiency in many operations, and a more uniform product, all of which be saleable.

The challenge facing the industry is to harness these opportunities in ecologically sound ways to achieve sustained yield, not only for aromatic, but as one important ingredient of wise stewardship of land i.e., sustainability in aromatic, land and in service.

TABLE 1

Production, Processing and Value Addition (PPV) of Important Aromedic Plants

Sl. No. Common Name (Scientific Name)	*Production Management*				*Processing Management*			*Value Addition*	
	Nutrient (Organic in nature)	*Irrigation*	*Harvesting*	*Economic*	*Pre – extraction*	*Type of Extraction*	*Components of Essential Oil and its Characteristics*	*Uses*	*Oil Yield kg/ha*
of Extraction	Components of Essential Oil and its Characteristics				Uses	Oil Yield kg/ha			
1. Palmrosa (*Cymbopogan martini*)	· 60:50:40 kg/ NPK/ha · FYM – 10t/ha	4 – 6 irrigation	· Harvest 7-10 days after opening of flowers · Cut floral shoot at full flowering stage at the ht. of 10-15 cm above ground	Floral shoots and above ground level parts	· Semi-dry produce for 4-6 hrs and stock in shady cool place for few days	Steam distillation (2 to 3 hrs)	Geraniol (Rose like aroma)	· Perfumes · Soaps · Tobacco flavouring	60-80

Sl. No.	Common Name (Scientific Name)	Production Management				Processing Management		Value Addition		
		Nutrient (Organic in nature)	*Irrigation*	*Harvesting*	*Economic*	*Pre – extraction*	*Type of Extraction*	*Components of Essential Oil and its Characteristics*	*Uses*	*Oil Yield kg/ha*
2.	Patchouli (*Pogostemon cablin*)	· 150:50:50 kg/NPK/ha · FYM – 12t/ha	3-4 irrigation	· Cut, when foliage becomes pale green and light brown · Cut young shoots of 10-20 cm below the apex	Foliage	Shade drying for 8 days	Steam distillation (6 to 24 hrs)	Patchouli alcohol and patchoulene (Strong fixative proportion to prevent rapid evaporation of perfumes)	· Perfumes · Soaps · Flavouring (Alcoholic and non-alcoholic beverages) · Uplifting effect for depression & anxiety	16-20
3.	Davana (*Artemisia pallens*)	· 120:40:40 kg/NPK/ha · FYM – 6t/ha	5-6 irrigation	· Harvest when majority of flower buds open · Cut 5-6 cm above ground in blossom	Leaves and flowers	Shade drying for 2-3 days	Steam distillation (5 to 6 hrs) 15-16	Davanone (Sweet and pleasant odour)	· Flavouring cakes · Beverages · Confectionaries	

Components of **Nitrogen:** Dried blood, Fish manure, oil cakes. **Phosphorous:** Bone meal, oil cakes. **Potassium:** Wood ash, oil cakes.

4. Lemon Grass (*Cymbopogan flexuosus*)	· 450:100: 125 kg/ NPK/ha · FYM – 10t/ha	3-4 irrigation	· Harvest 10-20 cm above the ground and essentially of radical leaves · Harvest at night increase the oil yield	Leaves and shoots	Wilting of grass under shade for 48 hrs.	Steam distillation(2 to 4 hrs)	Citral (Lemon like odour)	· Perfumery · Hair oils · Scents · For sore throats and respiratory problems	50-100
5. Geranium (*Pelargonium gravolens*)	· 40:40:40 kg/ NPK/ha · FYM – 10t/ha	6-8 irrigation	· Harvest, when leaves turn light green and changes from lemon like odour to rose of terminal branch with 10-12 leaves	Leaves	Drying for 12 hrs in shade	Steam distillation	Geraniol and citronellol (Rose like odour with fruity minty undertone)	· Perfume · Scenting soaps · Talcum powder · Treating nervous tension & depression	26-50
6. Sweet Basil (*Ocimum basilicum*)	· 120:300:60 kg/NPK / ha · FYM – 15t/ha	Once in a month	· Harvest during flowering and seed setting stage · Lower leaf start turning yellow · Harvest at 15-20 cm above the ground level	Leaves and tender parts of the shoot	Distill in fresh leaves within 6-8 hrs after harvest to retain quality	Steam distillation	Linalool and methyl-chavicol	· Perfume · Flavouring of food · Ideal as nerve tonic to lift fatigue, anxiety & depression	32-35

Sl. No.	Common Name (Scientific Name)	Production Management			Processing Management			Value Addition	
		Nutrient (Organic in nature)	*Irrigation*	*Harvesting*	*Economic Part Used*	*Processing Techniques*	*Chemical components*	*Uses*	*Oil Yield* kg/ha
7.	Senna (*Cassia angustifoliu*)	· 80:40:40 kg/NPK/ha · FYM – 10t/ha	Initially, irrigate at 6-7 days interval. Later at 15-20 days interval	· Harvest when leaves fully grown & bluish in colour · Pods turn to golden yellow colour	Leaves and Pods	Leaves dried for 3 to 5 days	Sennosides	· Important source of organic laxatives · Effective drug of habitual constipation	2000 kg/ dry leaves 800-1000 kg pods
8.	Aloe (*Aloe vera*)	· 50:50:50 kg/NPK/ ha · FYM – 15t/ha	One irrigation per month	· Greyish green to dirty white in colour with bright yellow flower	Leaves & flower	Optimum drying	Barbalorin	· Give cooling effect & act as moister-ing agent · Rejuvena-tion of ageing skin	10,000 to 12,000 kg/fresh leaves
9.	Fox glove (*Digitalis lanata*)	· 150:50:30 kg/NPK/ha · FYM – 40t/ ha	3 to 4 Irrigation per month	· Leaves har-vested on midday have high glyco-side content	Leaves	· Proper & fast drying of leaves prevent loss of glycosides · Leaves sun dried at 30-40°C	Glycoside	· Used as a myocar-dial stimulant in congested heart failure, auricular flutter & rapid auri-cular fibrill-ation	3000 kg/ dry leaves

REFERENCES

1. Akhtar Husain (1994). Status Report on Aromatic & Essential Oil-Bearing Plants in NAM countries. Centre for Science and Technology of the Non-aligned and other countries. Publication and Information Division (CSIR), New Delhi.
2. Annonymous (2002). Indian Herbal Research Message Board – 12/18/2002. info@econbot.org.
3. Annonymous. (2002). Phthalates in Cosmetics. Insight. P 20-21.
4. Balz, Rodolphe (1999). The Healing Power of Essential Oils. M.B.P. Private Ltd. New Delhi.
5. Carole McGilvery and Jime Reed. (1995). Essential Aromatherapy. Ultimate Editions, Canada.
6. Chandha, K.L. and Rajendra Gupta (1999). Advances in Horticulture. Malhotra Publishing House, New Delhi.
7. Chauhan, N.S. (1990). Medicinal and Aromatic Plants of Himachal Pradesh. Indus Publishing Company, New Delhi.
8. Dhanakumar, V.G. (1996). Indigenous Knowledge System. Kisan World, Vol.(23): 12th Dec.
9. Dhanakumar, V.G. (1997). Indigenous Knowledge System (IKS) in Medicinal Plants. The Planter Chronicle, Vol.92(2) Feb.P.91.
10. Dhanakumar, V.G. (2000). Indigenous Knowledge System Management (IKSM). Training Manual, IIPM, Bangalore.
11. Farooqi, A. A., Khan, M.M and Vasundhara, M. (1999). Production Technology of Medicinal and Aromatic Crops. Natural Remedies Pvt. Ltd, Bangalore.
12. Farooqi and Sreeramu, B.S. (2001). Cultivation of Medicinal & Aromatic Crops. Universities Press (India) Ltd, Bangalore.
13. Julian Evans. (1996). Why Plantations. Plantation Forestry in the Tropics. Clarendon Press, Oxford. P-12.
14. Katie Haley. (2002). Skincare for a New Age. Cosmicflower@angelfire.com.
15. UNIDO (1981). Industrial Utilization of Medicinal Plants in Developing Countries. Amruth, Vol. 4 (6); P.3-9.
16. Yogonarasimhan, S.N. (1996). Medicinal Plants of India Volume-I Karnataka. Interline Publishing Pvt. Ltd, Bangalore.

Annexures

ANNEXURE 1

APPROPRIATE TECHNOLOGY FOR TEA PRODUCTION & MANUFACTURING

Taxonomy of Tea Plant

Tea belongs to the genus *Camellia* and family *Camelliaceae*. The Jats which produce Tea are C *.assamica* (Assam Jat), C *.sinensis* (China Jat) and Hybrid C *.assamica* ssp *lasiocalyx*

Characteristics of Assam and China Jats Can be Distinguished as Follows

Characters	*Assam*	*China*
Habit	Tree	Shrub
Branches	Few, robust	Abundant, whippy
Leaves	Large, glossy	Small leathery
	Light green	Dark green
Yield	High	Low
Quality	Medium	Superior
Pests and Diseases	Susceptible	Tolerant

Varieties

UPASI has released 27 clones, where as Tocklai had 29 clones.

Climatic Factors

Suitable climatic factors for Tea are as follows.

pH- 4.5-5.0

Temperature- 16-32° C
Rainfall- 125-130 cm

Nursery Practices

Sleeve size of 30cmx10cmx150cm gauge is used for filling. Top 8 to 10 cm is filled with rooting medium (red /sub soil: sand) at the rate of 1:1 and bottom 20-20cm with growing medium in the jungle/top soil sand at the ratio of 3:1. Sieve soil and sand before use with 6 mesh x 16-gauge sieve. Heat treatment of moist soil at 60-80° C for Eelworm.

Preparation of Cuttings

Establish mother bushes near the nursery. Collect cuttings from pruned bushes. Approximately 100-150 cuttings could be collected/bush/year. Take about 3 cm long cuttings with healthy mother leaf having active auxiliary buds. Punch holes in the centre of the sleeves and insert the cuttings. The sleeves are then covered with polythene sheets over the G.I. wire arches.

Common Maladies in Tea Nursery are Given Below the Table

Problems measures	*Reasons*	*Preventive/curative*
Club callusing	High soil pH, clay/ sandy texture	Check the soil pH and texture before use
Chlorosis and stunted growth	Manganese toxicity due to over heating of soil	Avoid over heating of soil
Stunted growth with vague chlorosis and rosetting	Zinc deficiency	Spray 2% Zinc sulphate with Managanese and Boron

Planting

Tea is planted in a strongly acidic soil (around pH of 5) with soil depth of minimum 1 meter. Soil and water conservation was followed to minimise loss of valuable topsoil and conserving moisture in marginal rainfall areas. Important soil and water conservation structures are boundary drain, leader drain, and contour stone wall. Boundary drain prevents water entering into the field from the upper reaches. Leader drain should be taken along the natural fall with inward slope. Planting weeping love gross (*Erogrostis curvula*) along the sides prevents caving in of soil Contour stone wall helps in retaining soil and draining the excess water.

Contour planting single hedge and double hedge:

Contour planting single hedge: 1.2 x 0.75 m
11,111 plants/ha (4498/ac)

Contour planting double hedge: 1.35 x 0.75 x 0.75 m
13,333 plants/ha (5397/ac)

TRAINING OF YOUNG TEA

1). Centering

Cut as low as possible leaving 8-10 mature leaves below the cut and Centering usually done 4-6 months after planting.

2). Tipping

First plucking of the aperiodic shoot after centering/ pruning and Two tiers tipping for proper spread is practiced. First tipping is done at 35-cm height to induce the tertiaries and second tipping at 50-cm height for increasing the density of plucking points

Fertilizer Recommendations

Fertilizer Recommendations for North-East India & South India as Follows

North India

Yield in KG per ha	*N Kg/ha*	*P_2O_5 Kg/ha*	*K_2O kg/ha Soil Available Potash*		
			Low	*Medium*	*High*
Up to 1500	Up to 90	Up to 20	Up to 90	Up to 70	Up to 50
1500-2000	90-110	20-30	90-110	70-80	50-70
2000-2500	110-140	30-50	110-140	80-120	70-100
2500-3000	140-165	50	140-165	120-140	100-120

South India

For soils with pH between 4.5 and 5.5

Composition:		*60:90:Nk_2O*
Ammonium Sulphate	-	300 parts
Muriate of potash (or)	-	150 parts
Urea	-	132 parts
Muriate of potash	-	150 parts

RATES OF APPLICATION

Age of the clearing	*Kg/ha/annum* $N : K_2O$	*No. of applications*
1st year	180 : 270	5
2nd year	240 : 360	6
3rd year onwards upto 1st pruning	300 : 450	6

Apply phosphorus at 90 kg P_2O_5/ha every year in one application (23 g of Rock phosphate or 35 g of Mussoorie phosphate/plant)

Calculated for a bush population of 13,000/ha. Always apply fertiliser dose based on soil test results.

Shade Management

Tea requires filtered shade and of it is exposed to direct sun, its growth is affected. In North East India, *Albizzia chinensis* and South India, *Grevillea robusta* is grown as shade trees. Comparative shade tree management practices followed in both north and south india is given in the table.

a. Permanent shade tree	*North East India (Albizzia chinensis)*	*South India (Grevillea robusta)*
1. Importance	• Shade trees Sautree *(Albizzia chinensis)* add 2500 - 5000 kgs organic matter/ha to the soil	• Evergreen tree • Filtered shade and withstands frequent

	annually by dropping of leaves, twigs and pods. • Shade trees regulate temperature for photosynthesis (Photosynthesis activity in tea declines rapidly above 35^{0}c)	looping
2. Spacing	10.9 - 12.7 m	6 m x 6 m
3. Pest and disease	Psyllids & leaf eating caterpillars	Die back
4. Shade management	Lopping • Unwanted lower branches should be removed. • Underplant plants of permanent species well ahead of the removal of old shade trees.	Pollarding • Cutting the main stem with the object of deve loping lateral branches when the tree attains height of 8 - 9m Annual Lopping· • Cutting the erect branches on the laterals
b. Temporary shade tree	*Acacia mearnsii* *(Black Wattle)*	*Acacia mearnsii* *(Black Wattle)*

WEEDS IN TEA

Weed is a problem in young and pruned fields. Different weeds are found in North-East and South India. Common weed species and recommended weedicides are given in the table.

	North East India	*South India*
1. Common weed species	• *Axonopus compressus* • *Cynodon dactylon* • *Digitaria sanguinalis* • *Imperata cylindrica* • *Paspalum scrobiculatum* • *Polygonum perfoliatum* • *Setaria palmifolia* • *Arundinella bengalensis* • *Polygonum chinense* • *Saccharum spontaneum*	• *Mitracarpus verticillatus* Resistant to weedicide (Broad leaf button) • *Ageratum conyzoides* (Goat weed) • *Bidens biternata* (Spanish needle) • *Conyza ambigua* (Spanish needle)

2. Weedicides		
Pre-emergent weedicides	• Simazin (1.5-2 kg/200 ltr/ha) • Diuron (1 kg/200 ltr/ha) • Oxyflurofen (0.5 ltr/200 ltr/ha)	• Simazin • Diuron (1 kg/200 ltr/ha)
Post-emergent weedicides	• 2,4 - D (500 gm/200 ltr/ha) • Dalapon (1.75 kg/200 ltr/ha) • Glyphosate (2 ltr/200 ltr/ha)	• Paraquat (2.25 ltr/200 ltr/ha) • 2,4 - D (1.5 ltr/200 ltr/ha) • Dalapon • Glyphosate

Micronutrients

Micronutrients are important for Tea. Sulphur and Zinc are the essential micronutrients for Tea. The recommended doses are given below:

Importance	*Deficiency*	*Control measures*
Sulphur		
Sulphur increases amount of theafl-avins which en-hance tea quality	• Leaves are yellow and smaller in size. • In severe deficiency, the leaves may curl up and their edges and tips turn brown	• Periodic use of Ammonium sulphate fertilizer. • Annual application 40-50kg S/ha (*South India*) and 20kg S/ha (*North India*) for high yield.
Zinc		
Synthesis of Indole acetic acid (IAA)	Reduced leaf size, rosetting, chlorosis formation of more banji shoots.	• Zinc sulphate 6-8kg/ha/yr. • Combination of Magnesium sulphate (15.5g/10lts) & boric acid (5.5g/10ltrs) with zinc sulphate

PRUNING

Pruning is cutting of branches of Tea bush to maintain

convenient height for plucking, more vegetative growth, minimise banji formation and control crop during rush periods. Different type of pruning is given below:

Sl. No.	*Type of pruning*	*Pruning height (cm)*	*Season*	*Remarks*
1.	Rejuvenation pruning	20 - China Jat 30 - Assam Jat	Apr-May	Done in old bushes affected with canker and wood rot to invigorate the new healthy branches. Not done regularly.
2.	Hard pruning	30 - 45	Apr-May	First formative pruning done to a young tea.
3.	Medium pruning	45 - 60	Aug-Sept.	Normal pruning wherever frames are healthy.
4.	Light pruning	60 - 65	Aug-Sept.	Normal pruning wherever frames are healthy.
5.	Skiffing	65	Aug-Sept.	Mainly to postpone pruning and to encourage better frame development.

Types of Pruning

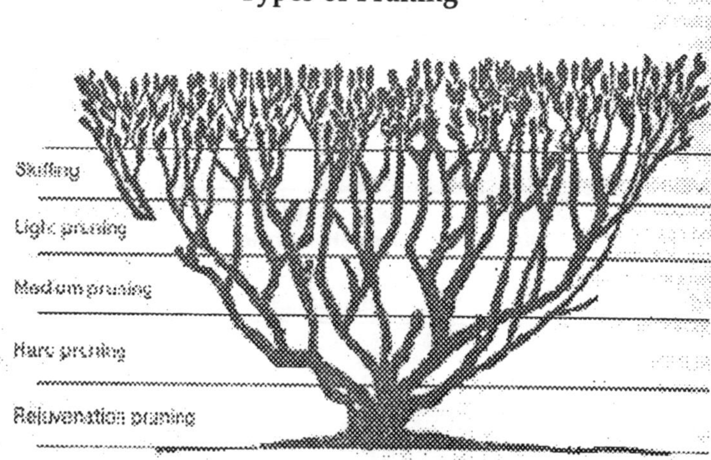

Plucking

Harvesting of 2 to 3 leaves and a bud/or single and two leaf banjis. When the shoot is plucked upto mother leaf, it is known as light plucking and if it is plucked below the mother leaf is called hard plucking.

IMPORTANT PEST AND DISEASE IN TEA

Many pests and diseases are known to infect the tea bushes and cause economic losses. The important pests and diseases, their typical symptoms and chemical control measures are furnished below.

Common Name	*Scientific Name*	*Symptoms*	*Control Measures*
The Pink Mite	*Acaphylla theae*	Leaves turn pale,curl upwards and latter becomes leathery	Dicofol (18.5 EC) or Ethion 50 C-1 ltr/ha
The Purple Mite	*Calacarus carinatus*	Copper brown dis-colouration in the leaves	Dicofol (18.5 EC) or Ethion 50 C-1 ltr/ha
The Red Spider Mite	*Oligonychus coffeae*	Ruddy bronze foliage	Ethion 50 EC-750 ml/ha
The Tea Mos-quito Bug	*Helopeltis theivora*	Leaf curl, deforma-tion & shoots dry up	Endosulfan-(35EC) 1 ltr/ha
Tea Thrips	*Scirtothrips bispinosus*	Leaf surface uneven, curled and matty	Endosulfan (35 EC) 750 ml/ha
Flush worms	*Cydia leucostoma*	Leaves become rough, crinkled and leathery	Endosulfan (35 EC) or Phosalone (35 EC) 1 ltr/ha
Shot Hole Borer	*Xyleboris fornicatus*	Grubs make a typical shot-hole on the branches and gallaries	Fenvaleate 20 EC @ 500 ml/ha

DISEASES

Common Name	*Scientific Name*	*Symptoms Measures*	*Control*
Blister Blight	*Exobasidium vexans*	Infects tender leaves and develops transl-ucent spot	Copper oxychloride 350 g in 67 ltr of water
Black root disease	*Rosellinia arcuata*	Infected roots show black mycelium on the roots, white star sha-ped mycelium betw-een bark and wood	Drenching with Moncogeb-30 g/10 l of waterr
Red root disease	*Poria hypolateritia*	Infected roots exhibit blood red mycelium on washing	1. Uprooting and burning of affected bushes.
Brown root disease	*Fomes noxius*	Infected root wood turns soft and spongy	2. Drrench the soil either with calium/ Cont of @ 0.5% concentration
Charcoal stump rot	*Ustulina zonata*	White fan shaped mycelium between bark and wood. Charcoal like encrus-tation on bark	Uproot the lightning affected bushes immediately
Collar canker	*Phomopsis theae*	Chlorosis, cessation of growth, profuse flowering and canker on stem	1. Removal of affected portion. 2. Copper fungicide application.

TEA MANUFACTURING

Two main manufacturing process in India are: CTC (Crush, Tear, Curl) Tea Manufacture and Orthodox Tea Manufacture. Green tea processing is commonly done in China.

(a) CTC Tea Processing (Crush ,tear and curl) involves the following steps, machinery's and factors

Withering

(10-12% removal of moisture)

Physical Withering
Weathering period - 16 -20 hrs
Initial period - (first 10-12 hrs)- loss of moisture was rapid
Later period - (next 10-12 hrs)- slow moisture loss.

Rolling

(Pre-conditioning)

Green leaf shredder
Green leaf shifter
Roller/Rotarvane $< 35^{\circ}C$

Fermentation

(Oxidation process)

Floor
Drum
CF Machine

Temp - $27^{\circ}C$
RH - 95%

Drying

(Moisture of tea leaf reduced to 2 to 3 %)

Sorting

(Removal of stalks and fibers)

Grading

(b) Orthodox Tea Processing

Common in North- East India involves the following steps, machinery's and factors.

Withering

Weathering period - 16-20 hrs
Initial period - (first 10-12 hrs) - loss of moisture was rapid
Later period - (next 10-12 hrs) - slow moisture loss.

Rolling

Twist is produced in the leaf and the juice or sap mixed in the presence of air.

Rolled leaf sifting cum roll breaking

Temperature
- 27-32^{0}c.

Period and Number of Rolling
Highly withered - 2-5 rolling
North-east Indian plains - 2 roll
Darjeeling, Srilanka and South India - 3 rolls

Fermentation

(Optimum temperature around 28°C)

Drying

Air Temperature

Normal range of drying temperature is 82^{0}c - 99^{0}c
Exhaust temperature of 49^{0}c - 54^{0}c

Double firing in North-eastern India
First firing - 93.3^{0}c - 104^{0}c
Second firing - 71 - 77^{0}c

Sorting and Grading

Different grades
Pekoe (P)
Flowery Pekoe (FP)
Orange Pekoe (OP)
Souchong (S)
Pekoe Souchong (PS)

Brokens
Broken Orange Pekoe (BOP)
Broken Pekoe (BP)

Fannings (F)
Dust (D)

Green Tea Processing

Common in China where polyphenal content is presented without breakage. This type of processing involves following steps, machinery and factors.

Steaming

(Inactivate the enzymes & helps to stop the oxidation process)

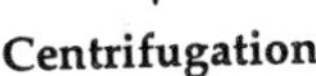

Centrifugation

(Removal of excess moisture)

Rolling

(Rolled in the roller for 10 to 30 minutes without pressure)

Dryer

(Removal of 40% of its moisture content)

Rolling

(Semi-dried leaf is rolled again with medium pressure for 20 minutes)

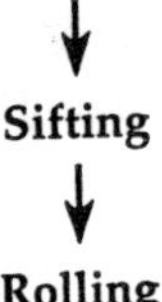

Sifting

Rolling

(With medium heavy pressure for about 40 minutes)

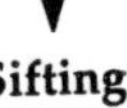

Sifting

(To break leaf balls)

Drying, graded & packed

Green Tea Classification

PAN (or) Chinese Green Tea

SENCHA (or) Japanese Green Tea

a) Chinese Green Tea

Sencha (Not fermented)	*Pan (Half fermented)*
Dis-similarities	
Green leaf is steamed to inactivate the enzyme (poly phenol oxidase) and late dried until moisture of percentage of 3	Slightly fermented and roasted in hot pan to arrrest enzymic activity
When infused, tea produces pale greenish yellow colour	Tea prroduces a light orange liquorr
Similarities	
In both teas the green colour of leaf is preserrved durring manufacturre and end product will be in green.	
Both teas can be consumed without milk or sugarr. Usually a lemon slice is added to enhance flavourr.	

b) Japanese Green Tea

1. GYOKURO : Special and expensive tea cultivated under heavy shade & plucked once a year.
2. SENCHA : Normal green tea graded further into superior, medium and low grades.
3. BANCHA : Lowest grade of green tea recovered from SENCHA. BANCHA may also be made from coarse leaf & prunings.
4. MACHA : Cultivated under shade like GYOKURO. But, not rolled during manufacture. The open leaf is grounded into fine powder and sold at high price. MACHA is used in "*Japanese Tea Ceremonies*".

Oolong Teas

- Withered semi-fermented teas of orthodox type

  Manufacturing Process
- Green leaves - withering - shaking - panfiring - rolling - drying
- Shaking - carefully rubbing the leaves against each other without breaking the leaf view
- Tea leaf turn red

White Teas

- Whole withered teas of orthodox type

  Manufacturing Process: Withering and drying
- Withering - 20-30% moisture removal
- Infusion almost colourless

Dark Green Teas

- After fermented teas of orthodox type
- Colour black green
- Infusion - red yellow to brown red
- Key process -piling after fermentation

INSTANT TEA

Dust grade Tea is commonly used for Instant tea extraction. Normally done under automated machinery set up. Instant tea production involves following steps, machinery and factors.

Co-current flow (water & leaf more together)

Counter Current flow (water & leaf more in opposite directions).

Tea Extraction Process

(Extract leaf by using hot water)

↓

Vaccum Pan Evaporation

Freeze Concentration

Membrane Technology

Separation of Leaf and Liquid

("Decanter used to separate leaf & liquid by centrifugation process)

↓

Concentration of Tea Extracts

(Removal of water)

REFERNCES

1. Arunachalam. K. 1995. *A Hand Book on Indian Tea*. Arunachalam Associates (Plantation Consultants).
2. Banerjee. B. 1993. *Tea Production and Processing*. Oxford & IBH Publishing Co. Pvt. Ltd. #
3. Barbora. B.C. 1996. *The Planters Handbook*. Tea Research Association, Tocklai.
4. Barbua. D.N. 1989. *Science and Practice in Tea Culture*. Tea Research Association, Tocklai.
5. Dhanakumar. V.G. and Abdul Kareem. A. 1997. *Tea Nursery Management*. UPASI-Krishi Vigyan Kendra. #
6. Dhanakumar. V.G. and Kumaravadivelu. P. 1997. *Tea Productivity and Quality Management*. UPASI-Krishi Vigyan Kendra. #
7. Dhanakumar. V.G, Kumaravadivelu. P, Ramamoorthy. G. and Durairaj. J. 1997. *Ready Reckoner on Tea*. UPASI-Krishi Vigyan Kendra.
8. Dhanakumar. V. G. 2002. *Total Quality Management in Tea through Quality, Safety and Risk Management: An HACCP Perspective*. International Journal of Tea Science (2001-02 Issue).
9. Ghosh Hajra N. 2001. *Tea Cultivation Comprehensive Treatise*. International Book distributing Company, Lucknow.
10. Hudson. J.B., Durairaj. J., Muraleedaran. N. and Dhanakumar. V.G. 1997. *Guidelines on Tea Culture in South India*. UPASI-Krishi Vigyan Kendra. #
11. Jain. N.K. 1999. *Global Advances in Tea Science*. Aravathi Books International (P) Ltd.
12. Mulky, M. J and Sharma, V.S. 1993. *Tea Culture, Processing & Marketing*. Hindustan Lever Research Foundation. Bombay.

ANNEXURE: 2

COFFEE PRODUCTION & MANUFACTURING

Coffee belongs to the genus *Coffea* of the family *Rubiaceae*. There are more than 70 species under the genus *Coffea*, most of which are native of Africa including the two species viz., *Coffea arabica* and *Coffea canephora* which are commercially cultivated in India. The important difference among these two species with respect to soil and climatic factors are as follows.

Particulars	*Coffee arabica*	*Coffee canephora*
	Arabica	*Robusta*
1. Elevation	1000-1500 m MSL	500-100m MSL
2. Annual Rainfall	160-250 cm	100-200 cm
3. Soil pH	pH 6.0 to 6.5	6 to 6.5
4. Blossom Rain	Mar-Apr (2.5-4.0 cm)	February-March (2.0-4.0 cm)
5. Backing Rain	Apr-May (5-7.5 cm)	April-May (5-7.5 cm)
6. Shade	Medium to light shade	Uniform thin shade
7. Temperature	15-25^{0}c(ideal) (cool equable)	20-30-25^{0}c (ideal)

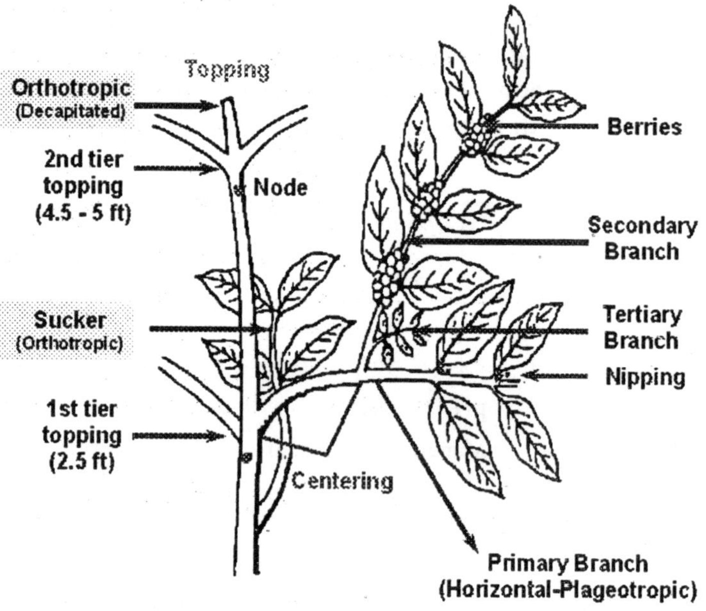

Topping: Arabica: 75 cm, Robusta: 110-120 cm (single stem system)

Nipping: Growing tip of primary branches is removed to encourage secondaries & territories

Centering: Removal of veg. growth upto 15cm radius from the center & upto the 1st node of all primary branches.

Handling: Removal of small sprouts arising from the axis of the leaves which otherwise grow towards the inner side and cause shade & become unproductive wood.

Desuckering: Removal of orthotropic sucker branches arising from the main trunk

PROPAGATION

Vegetative Propagation is by cuttings and seed propagation (Shoot, leaf and roots)

Preparation of Cuttings by

Single node cuttings

Terminal cuttings and

Mallet cuttings

1. Single Node Cuttings

Select pencil thickness orthotropic shoots (Suckers) from 3 to 6 months old mother plants. Prepare single node cuttings of 10 cm length with a pair of leaves. Cut the leaves to half their size. In each cutting, make a basal slant cut and top horizontal cut.

2. Terminal Cuttings

The terminal portion of the orthotropic shoots can be used for planting as terminal cuttings.

3. Mallet Cuttings

Mallet cutting is a young sucker of 45-60 day old, detached from the main stem along with a piece of woody bark.

Cuttings must be planted in punched polythene bags (size 23x15cm). Filled with well seived jungle soil, sand and FYM in the ratio of 6:3:1. These bags will be placed in trenches of 1m width, 0.5m depth and 2-6m length and covered with a transparent polythene sheet (500 gauge). The entire structure should be provided with over-head coir mat shade. Watering is done once a day during morning hours in cool season and second round of watering may be given in afternoon hours during dry season. Cuttings will root in three months under trench condition. After rooting the cuttings should be hardened for 2 months under coir mat shade. Rainy season (June - August) gives a good percentage of success (above 95%) in rooting.

Planting and Aftercare

Soil Conservation Measures (Shade Tree)

Coffee plantation should be protected with lower canopy (upper foliage) shade tree of dadap and silver oak and top canopy with Ficus sp (Attis, Basris) and Albizzia sp.

Ideal Type of Planting

Square system is found to be ideal in flat to gentle sloppy area and steep slopes for contour planting.

Spacing for Different Coffee Species

(Rows & Spacing of plants) The following are the optimum spacing for different coffee species/varieties.

- Arabica

    Talls - 1.8 x 1.8 m
    2.1 x 1.8 m
    2.1 x 2.1 m

    Dwarfs - 1.5 x 1.5 m

- Robusta

1.8 — 1.8
1.8 — 1.8

S. 274; old Robusta - 3 x 3 m; 3.6 x 3.6 m

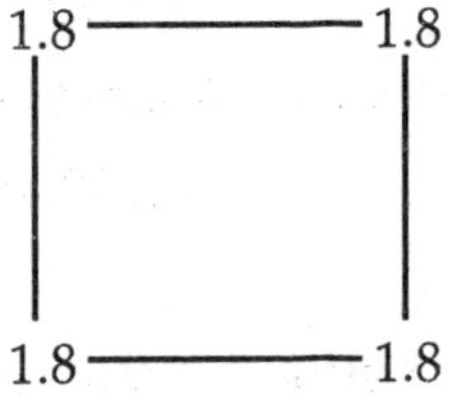

Pits for Planting

Pits are usually opened during March/April. Pit size - 45 x 45 x 45 cm of Length Breadth Height (LBH) are preferred. Addition of compost or FYM @ 1-2 kg/pit along with 20 - 30 g of Rock phosphate.

Planting in the Field

Seedlings raised in secondary beds (age about 16 - 18 months) are planted at June (commencement of South West Monsoon) and polybag nursery seedling (6 - 8 months old), August - September.

Planting shade Trees

Dadap is commonly used as Lower canopy shade. During dry season Dadap young are planted between two coffee plants. Silver oak can be planted as shade belts at 6m x 12 m while permanent shade trees are planted at wider spacing 9 -12 m.

Interplanting Varieties

Plant Cauvery variety in Robusta coffee due to more spacing (3.6 x 3.6). Interplanting cauvery within and between the robusta rows, the plant population is substantially boosted.

TRAINING, PRUNING & REJUVENATION

Training

The plant management involving training and pruning is an essential maintenance operation for achieving potential yields in coffee. Training of bush is important to give proper shape and desirable height and production of bearing wood.

Generally two types of training methods are adopted.

- Single stem system - most suitable to Indian condition.
- Multiple system - practiced in Kenya & Tanzania.

Single Stem System

Height of the bush restricted at convenient height by topping / capping. Topping helps in diversion of food material to thicken the main stem and primary branches and facilitates lateral spreading of plants.

The vertically growing main stem is cut two inches above the node near the prescribed topping height.

Varieties	*Topping Height*	*Time required to reach the topping*
Tall Arabica	First Tier - 0.75m (2.5ft) Second Tier - 1.4-1.5 (4.5 - 5ft)	9 - 12 months
Dwarf Arabica	Single Tier - 0.9 - 1.5 m (3-5 ft)	- do -
Robusta	Single Tier - 1.0 -1.2m (3.5-4ft)	18 - 24 months

Pruning

Pruning is essentially a thinning process to remove of old, unproductive branches, criss-cross branches, lean lanky and whippy wood, diseased and damaged branches as well as branches growing towards main stem & ground etc.

1. *Handling:* New flush arising after the main pruning is thinned out to a desired number of well spaced branches during during early monsoon (June-July) and August - September.
2. *Centering:* Removal of new shoots arising within 15 cm radius of the main stem & upto 1st node of primary branches (Plageo - tropic).
3. *Desuckering:* Removing the suckers growing from the main stem (Ortho - tropic).

Rejuvenation

Coffee bushes, which are badly damaged by falling branches during shade regulation or irregular pruning, can be rejunuvated by collar pruning / stumping. Collar pruned / stumped at about 30 cm from the ground level at 45° sloping angle facing towards East or Northeast direction. The cut surface is treated with Bordeaux paste (1 kg CuSo4 and 1 kg lime dissolved in 4.5 ltrs of water).

IRRIGATION

Coffee being an evergreen plant requires maintenance of soil moisture during dry months. For successful establishment of young coffee, 1 inch water at 15 days is required during dry months. Irrigation for blossom and backing, 1.5 inch water during second fortnight of February to second week of March. Followed by 1 inch backing irrigation, 15-20 days after flowering. Irrigation of mature coffee during dry months (winter irrigation), first irrigation of 1-1.5 inches of water immediately after 15-20 days of cessation of north -East rains. Next irrigation at an interval of 15-20 days upto the end of December. Winter irrigation + timely blossom + backing irrigation = Double yield.

NUTRIENT MANAGEMENT

Variety	*Yield*	*N*	*P*	*K*
Arabica	< 1000 kg/ha	120-190	80-90	120-140
	> 1000 kg/ha	160-175	90-120	160-175
Robusta	< 1000 kg/ha	80-120	60-90	80-120
	> 1000 kg/ha	120-175	90-120	120-175

B.N: Place around the plant (drip circle) and covered with leaf mulch

WEEDS

Common Weeds

Ageratum conzoides
Bidens pilosa
Cyperus difformis
Amaranthus spinosus
Eupatosium odaratum
Vernonia cinera

Common Weedicides

Paraquat-di-chloride 24% EC @ 1.33% a.i. (e.g., Gramoxone @ 1000 ml per barrel)

Glyphosate 41% EC @ 2.27% a.i. (e.g., Round up or Glycle @ 1200 ml per barrel)

Drought Management

In the absence of water resources and irrigation facilities, it is recommended to spray the following nutrient mixture (one liter solution mixture per plant) as a drought amelioration measure to minimize the adverse effects.

Nutrient Mixture Per Barrel of Water

Urea (0.5%)	-	1 kg
Superphosphate (0.5%)	-	1 kg
Muriate of Potash (0.375%)	-	750 g
Zinc Sulphate (0.5%)	-	1 kg

Spray Schedule

1st spray : 45 days after the last rain fall (2nd fortnight of January)

2nd spray : 30 - 45 days after the first spray

Soil Management Practices

1. *Soil Conservation Measures*

Contour planting (Areas with 10 - 20% sloping)

Terracing (Slope of more than 20%)

2. *Soil Moisture Conservation Measures*

Digging practiced in new clearings, depth of 30 - 45 cm to conserve water during the end of monsoon (Oct - Nov).

Cover digging: Weeds are completely turned and buried in soils.

Scuffling: Soil stirring at the end of monsoon to control weeds and soil moisture.

3. *Mulching*

Mulch the soil around the coffee plants after digging / scuffling operations

4. Trenches / Pits

Across the slope during post-monsoon period. Staggered manner in between the rows of coffee all along the contour. Trenches of 30cm wide, 45cm deep and of any convenient length and Cradle pits, short trenches of 1 to 1.5 m long

PHYSIOLOGICAL & STRESS DISORDER AND MANAGEMENT

1. Dieback

This disorder occurs due to adverse environmental factors such as high temperature, exposure to high light intensity, low soil moisture and low relative humidity etc. leads to the death of young branches.

Remedial Measures

Providing optimum shade (50%) and conserving the soil moisture status by think mulch

2. Premature Fruit Drop

90-120 days after blossom reasons due to field conditions (wet feet-water logging & continuous heavy rainfall) and physiological status (hormonal imbalance & nutrient deficiency).

Remedial Measures

Good drainage, cradle pits etc and post blossom (15 days after blossom)

HARVESTING

Variety	*Harvesting Season*	*Duration*
Arabica	November - January	8-9 months
Robusta	December - February	10-11 months

Fly Harvesting

- First picking consists of selective picking of ripe berries seen in nodes.
- Main picking - 4-6 main picking at 10-15 days interval.

IMPORTANT PEST AND DISEASE IN COFFEE

PESTS

Common Name	*Scientific Name*	*Symptoms*	*Control Measures*
White Stem Borer	*Xylotrechus quadripes*	External ridges around the stem Wilting & yellowing of leaves	Provide good shade, burn the infested plants in situ and swap with Lindane 20 EC @ 1300 ml in 200 ltrs of water along with 200ml of any wetting agent
Coffee Berry Borer	*Hypthenemus hampei*	Typical pin hole at the top of the berry fall of infested tender berries	Timely harvest, minimize glenings, spray endosulfan 35 EC @ 340 ml in 200 ltrs of water
Shot Hole Borer	*Xylosandrus compactus*	Attacked plants dry up. The terminal leaves wilt, droop and dry up	Prune and burn the affected branches
Mealy bugs	*Planococcus citri*	Mealy bug attack nodes, spikes, berries tender branches, leaves and roots leading to debilitation of the plant and crop loss	Maintain optimum shade, control ants and spray with quinalphos 25 E or fenitrothion 50 EC @ 300 ml each
Green Scale	*Coccus viridis*	Debilitation of the old plants and death of nursery plants	Maintain optimum shade. Spray 200 ml of malathion 50 EC or 120 ml of quinal-phos 25 EC
Root Lesion Nematode	*Pratylenchus coffeae*	Affected young plants become unhealthy with lean & lanky stem. Older leaves become yellow and drop	Uproot and burn the affected plant. Dig and expose the soil to the sun.

DISEASES

Common Name	*Scientific Name*	*Symptoms*	*Control Measures*
Leaf rust	*Hemileia vastatrix*	Yellow to orange spots on the lower surface of leaves. Severe attack results in defoliation, die-back	Bordeaux (1 kg $CuSo_4$:1 kg Cao:200 l of water) mixture 0.5% or Plantavax 0.03% (300 ml / 200 ltrs of water) or Bayleton 0.02% a.i. (160 g/200 ltrs)
Black rot disease	*Koleroga noxia*	Blackening & subsequent rotting of affected leaves, berries and young shoots	1% Bordeaux mixture or Bavistin 0.03% a.i. (120 g/ 200 ltrs of water)
Root Diseases Brown root disease	*Fomes noxius*	Internal portion of the roots show dark brown to black wavy lines	1. Uproot the affected coffee plants and burn it.
Red root disease	*Poria hypolateritia*	Root system shows red encrustation covered with soil and gravel	2. Add agricultural lime (1-2 kg) 3. Drench the soil with Bavistin 0.4% @ 3 l plant (24 g/3 l of water) or Vitavax 75 WP 0.3% @ 3l/plant (12 g/3 l of water) in the initial stage of wilty.
Black root disease	*Rosellinia aicuate*	Black fungal or wooly mycelium on the affected roots. On stem near the ground level fan-shaped fungal mats with pellet like fruitification	
Santavery root disease	*Fusarium oxysporum*	Sudden wilting yellowing of leaves. Transverse section of the roots shows brown discolouration	4. Soil application of bio control agent Trichoderma

COFFEE MANUFACTURE

Method of Coffee Processing

The wet processed coffee is superior in its quality compared to dry processed coffee.

A) WET METHOD

SORTING BY FLOTATION

(Syphon system to segregate the light and heavy fruits using clean water)

↓

PULPING

(Mechanical removal of outer skin of coffee berries)

Disc pulper common in India

The cherry is squeezed between a fixed pulping bar or chop.

↓

FERMENTATION

(Break down the thick mucilage layer on the parchment in to simple non-sticky substances, which are easily washed off.)

Optimum temperature 300 - 350°C. The depth of the fermentation 75 cms.

Fermentation duration- 24-36 hours for arabica and 72 hours for robusta.

↓

POST WASH SOAKING

After washing soak the parchment under clean water for a period of 12 hours.

↓

DRYING

(Moisture content of 50-55% brought down to 10% for safe storage)

Trays kept at a height of 75 cm above the ground.

- Parchment spread on clean concrete of tiled floor to a thickness of 5 cms.
- Stir the coffee mass 12-15 times a day - during initial 5 days of drying.

B) DRY METHOD

PREPARATION OF CHERRY

Sorting and spreading

(Greens, under ripe fruits sorted out: Dried separately to a thickness of 7-8 cm)

↓

Stirring

- Stirred and ridged at least once every hour
- Coffee heaped up and covered daily in the evening

↓

Drying

(Drying period 12-15 days under bright weather condition).

COFFEE PROCESSING AT CURING WORKS

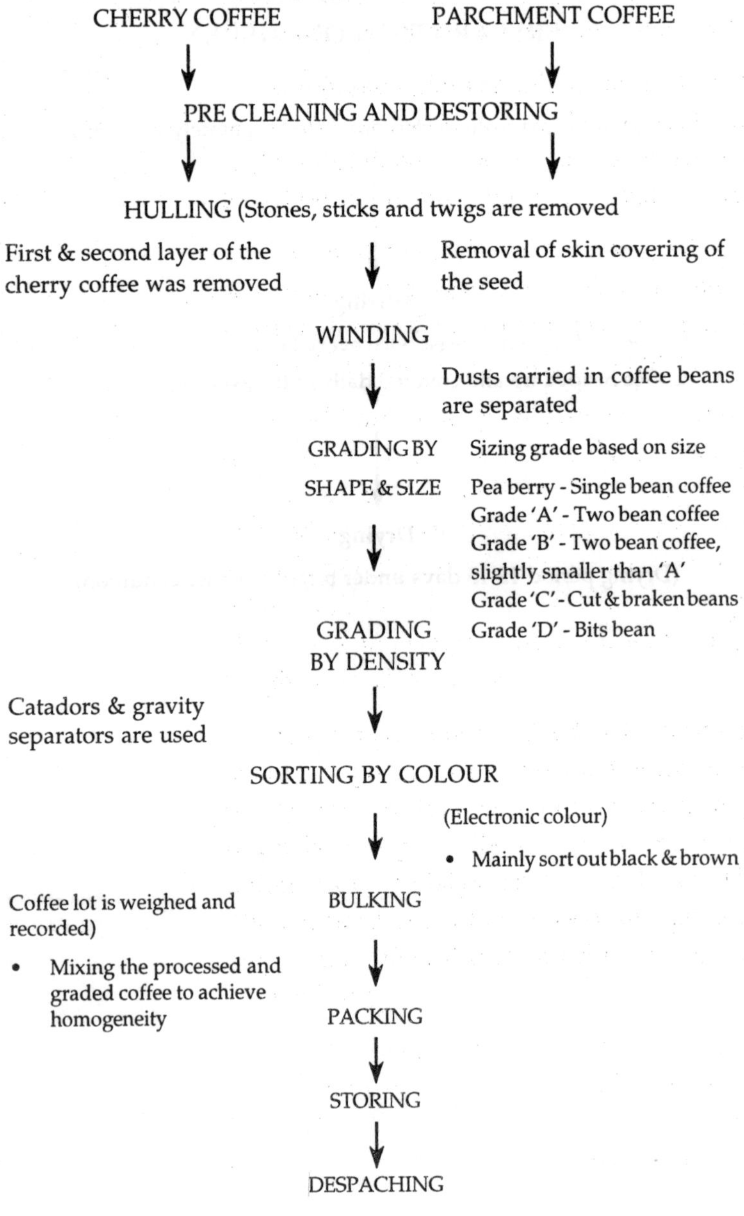

CHERRY COFFEE ↓ PARCHMENT COFFEE ↓

PRE CLEANING AND DESTORING

↓

HULLING (Stones, sticks and twigs are removed

First & second layer of the cherry coffee was removed

Removal of skin covering of the seed

↓

WINDING

↓

Dusts carried in coffee beans are separated

GRADING BY SHAPE & SIZE

Sizing grade based on size

Pea berry - Single bean coffee
Grade 'A' - Two bean coffee
Grade 'B' - Two bean coffee, slightly smaller than 'A'
Grade 'C' - Cut & braken beans
Grade 'D' - Bits bean

↓

GRADING BY DENSITY

Catadors & gravity separators are used

↓

SORTING BY COLOUR

(Electronic colour)

- Mainly sort out black & brown

↓

BULKING

Coffee lot is weighed and recorded)

- Mixing the processed and graded coffee to achieve homogeneity

↓

PACKING

↓

STORING

↓

DESPACHING

SPECIALTY COFFEES PROCESSING

Harvesting

(Selective harvesting - careful hand picking of just ripened berries)

↓

Natural Fermentation

(Flavour development & high quality)

↓

Soaking

(Soaking the washed beans under fresh water overnight)

↓

Slow Drying

(Under natural sunlight)

INSTANT COFFEE PROCESSING

Grading, storage, blending of green coffee

↓

Roasting and Grinding

(Eg., 50-100 gm coffee at 205oC)

↓

Pre-wetting

(Danish Manufacturers recommend for percolation)

Extraction

1. Atmospheric Extraction (Water temperature around 100o C for 10-15 minutes
2. Autoclaved Extraction (Water temperature around 170oC (90 minutes for Extraction)

Drying

* Freeze drying (for granules only)
* Spray (powder or granule formation)

Decaffination in Coffee

Swelling the raw beans with water

(Solublize the caffeine and make Caffeine available for extraction)

Extraction of caffeine with a solvent

(Methylene Chloride or ethyl acetate to absorb caffeine)

Steam stripping to remove all solvent residues

Drying the decaffeinated coffee

FLAVOURED COFFEE

Common Fragrances

Vanilla, Nut, Fresh Cream, Chocolate, Almond, Coconut, Cinnamom & Chocolate Raspberry

Flavouring Process

Thorough mixing of a liquid additive with the whole roasted bean (or) mixing of the powdered flavoring agent with grounded coffee

Mild arabica are strongly preferred

Roasting slightly darker to deepen the coffee flavour

Brewing for extreme temperature (> 95°C) & extended time evaporates flavour

ESPRESSO COFFEE

Espresso is a brew obtained by percolation of hot water under pressure through a cake of roasted ground coffee, where the energy of the water pressure is spent within the cake.

The range of the parameters is:

Ground Coffee portion	6.5 + 1.5 g
Water temperature	90 + 5°C
Inlet water pressure	9 + 2 bar
Percolation time	30 + 5 sec.

SPECIALITY COFFEE

Decaffeinated Coffees

Coffee with caffeine removed artificially are known as decaffeinated coffee.

Organic Coffees

Coffee grown without using chemicals & pesticide.

High Grown Coffees

The coffees grown at higher elevation i.e., 4000 ft. Distinct flavour and acidity in cup due to slower development of beans. Coffees are of high quality with densed beans.

Estate Coffees (Single origin coffees)

Production of good quality coffee by highlighting the special feature of the estate - elevation, variety, cultural practices and special processing techniques. Estate coffees are those that originate on a single farm.

Varietal Coffees

Some of the varieties are known to possess good inherent quality. For example: Kents, Agaro & Cloccie for cup quality. Fruits from such varieties can be harvested and processed.

Separate processing of these variety help in processing them to get intrinsic quality.

Monsooned Coffee

Monsooned Coffee is prepared at the curing works situated on the West Coast. 'A' grade of Arabica and Robusta Cherry are used for monsooning. Monsooned coffees are popular in 'Scandinavian' market for their natural mellow flavour in the cup.

Mysore Nuggets (EB)

These coffees are prepared from washed Arabica grown in the region of Mysore, Coorg. The cup ensures full body, soft, smooth and mellow flavour.

REFERENCES

1. Anonymous. *A Guide to Coffee Quality*. Coffee Board.
2. Dhanakumar V.G. 2003. *Biological Risk Management (Biosecurity) in Coffee: An HACCP Perspective.* Indian Coffee (April 2003).
3. Naidu. R. 2000. *Coffee Guide.* Central Coffee Research Institute.#
4. Naidu, R. 2000. *Package of Practices for Organic Coffee.* Central Coffee Research Institute.
5. Naidu, R. 1998. *A Compendium on Pests and Diseases of Coffee and their Management in India.* Central Coffee Research Institute. #
6. Wilson. K.C. 1999. *Coffee, Cocoa and Tea.* CABI Publishing.

ANNEXURE 3

APPROPRIATE TECHNOLOGY FOR RUBBER PRODUCTION AND MANUFACTURING

Taxonomy

Hevea brasiliensis is the most important commercial source of natural rubber. Genus Hevea, belong to the family Euphorbiaceae. Sturdy perennial tree with height about 30 m. Leaves are arranged in-groups or storeys and it is trifoliate with long stalk. Monocieous flower and pollination is by insects. Fruits mature about five months after pollination. Three seeded & burst when mature. Normal annual leaf fall during (Dec - Jan - South India). Refoliation and flowering follow wintering.

Latex are present in almost all parts of the plant. Laticifers commercially exploited from bark (latex vessels). Latex vessels - activity of vascular cambium.

May - Jun : Low rate of cambial growth.

Nov - Jan : Highest growth.

PROPAGATION OF RUBBER

Budding Grafting

Bud grafting contents of replacing a strip of bark containing a dormant bud (bud patch) taken from the scion plant and bandaging it. The tissues of the bud patch and the seedling become firmly united within three or four weeks after grafting.

Depending on the colour and age of buds, two types of budding are recognized, brown budding and green budding. A patch of the bark of the seedling plant (stock) is replaced by a patch of bark with a dormant bud taken from the clone (Sion) to be multiplied.

Common Budding Techniques

(a) Brown Budding

Brown coloured buds - bud wood (1 year old). Stock plants (10 months old) of girth 7.5 cm & bark peels easily.

Stock Plant

Two parallel vertical cuts, 2.5 cm above the collar are made. Horizontal cut, joining the bottom ends. Latex allowed to ooze completely. Flap of bark gently lifted and peeled upwards.

Bud Patch

Bud patch - Length of about 5 cm and width of 1.5 cm.

Budding

Bud patch placed in the budding panel after lifting the flap. Bandaging from bottom to upwards using polythene strips.

(b) Green Budding

Comparatively new method of vegetative propagation. Stock plant - 2 to 8 months old, girth (2.5 cm), brown bark upto a height of about 15 cm. Buds - 6 to 8 week old bud wood.

Stock Plant

Two vertical incisions, 5 cm long & 1 cm apart, from a point about 2.5 cm above the collar region. The lower ends of these cuts are joined by a horizontal cut. The flap gently lifted upwards and cut off leaving a short "tongue".

Bud Patch

Bud patch separated from the wood. Bud patch - length of 5 cm and width of 1 cm. Upper end of the bud patch gently inserted under the tongue. Bandaging with thin polythene strip (25 cm long & 2 cm wide).

PREPARATION OF NURSERY

Digging the soil to a depth of 75 cm and remove stumps and stones. Bed size of 60-120 cm width and convenient length.

Spacing

Seedling stumps - 23 x 23 cm, 30 x 30 cm, 34 x 20 cm. Budded stumps - 30x30 cm (or) staggered pairs of rows 60 cm apart & 23 cm between plants. Stumped buddings - 60 x 60 cm. Budwood nurseries - 60 x 90 cm (or) 60 x 120 cm.

Land Preparation

Rubber plantation in India are mostly situated on sloping and undulating lands. In Southindia, June/July is the best season for planting and so all preparation should be completed before that period. Cleaning, lining, terracing and drainage activities should be done on appropriate time.

The planting density recommended is 420 to 445 plants per hectare (170-180 per acre) in the case of budding or plants proposed to be field budded and 445 to 520 plants points per hectare (180-210 plants per acre) in the case of seedling. Pitting is necessary to provide favorable contribution for the easy establishment and growth of young plants. The size of the pits depends upon the type of planting material and the nature of the soil. For example the standard pits recommend are of 90x90x90 cm or 75x75x75 cm sizes.

Planting should be carried out during favorable weather. Seedling stumps and budded stumps are used for planting. It is advisable to plant stumps soon after pulling out from nursery. While planting budded stumps, the budpatch should be just above the ground level. About 5 cm of surface soil is first removed from an adequate area around the planting pounds to accommodate the lateral roots.

TAPPING

Tapping is a process of controlled wounding of the bark to extract latex. Tapping was done for seedlings plants of 50 cm ht and 55cm girth. For the budded plants, girth of 50 cm at the height of 125 cm from the bud union. Seventy percent of the trees in the selected area should have attained the standard girth. Best period for opening new fields for tapping is Mar - Apr. Tapping cut is opened along the uppermost template marking. Panels are marked on the trees by using templates and marking knife. Template marking-Slope of the cut for budding - 30^0.

Type of cut :
S - Spiral Cut
V - V Cut
C - Circumference cut

Length of Cut

Length of cut is the relative proportion of the trunk circumference that is embraced by the tapping cut.

E.g., 1/2 S = One half spiral cut.

Frequency of Tapping

- d/1 : Daily tapping
- d/2 : Alternate daily (once in two days)
- d/3 : Third daily (once in three days)
- d/4 : Fourth daily (once in four days)
- d/0.5 : Twice a day

Common Tapping Systems in India

- Budded trees - (1/2S d/2) system
- Seedlings - (1/2S d/3) system
- D/3 - To avoid the incidence of panel dryness

Average amount bark consumption on half spiral cut of different types:

Alternate daily	:	2 - 23 cm
Third daily	:	16 - 18 cm
Fourth daily	:	14 - 16 cm

Time of tapping: Morning is the best time for tapping.

Tapping Task

Number of trees allotted to a tapper for a day's tapping.

In India, task varies from 300 - 400 trees.

Tapping Implements

1. *Knives* - Two types of tapping knifes commonly used.

Michie Golledge - Popular and common knife used for tapping in india.

Jebong knife - Common in Malaysia, but slightly higher bark consumption. Other knife like modified gouge is used for controlled upward tapping (CUT)

2. ***Spout***--V- shaped and used to guide latex into the collection cup

3. *Cup hangers* - To place latex collection cups.

4. *Collection cups* - Plastic cups of varying capacity (400-900 ml).

5. *Scrap baskets* - Collection of lace, cup scrap etc.

6. *Templates* - Template panels are marked on the trees selected for tapping by using marking knife.

- 16 to 18 cm wide for seedlings
- 20 to 23 cm for budding

Different Types of Tapping

1. Intensive Tapping

Generally done in old rubber tress. Increasing the number and length of tapping cut or/and frequency.

2. Slaughter Tapping

Last stage in the tapping cycle (2 or 3 years before replanting). New cuts are opened in the high panel.

3. Puncture Tapping

Extract latex through punctures made on the bark. Ethephon based stimulant is applied to a strip of scraped bark (1.5 to 2 cm wide & 50 -100 cm long). On each tapping day, four to ten punctures are made, at equal spacing in the stimulant bark and latex is collected.

4. High Level Tapping

Tapping of renewed bark on basal panel becomes uneconomic. New cuts opened at higher level (180 cm from bud union).

5. Control Upward Tapping (CUT):

Longer exploitation of the virgin bark above the basal panel. Long handled modified gauge knife is used.

CUT - Applications

Low yield from renewed bark. Renewed bark is unsuitable for tapping. Too early completion of tapping on virgin bark and prolonged exploitation of high panel.

Method

Tapping cut on the virgin bark above renewed bark of the base panel. Tapping cut - 1/4 spiral & angle 45^0. Rest the panel during rainy season. One high panel can be tapped for 3 years. Tapping cut in the high panel can be stimulated using 5 % ethephon . 3 - 5 monthly applications - 1/2 spiral cuts. Monthly application - 1/3 and 1/4 cuts. Tapping frequency, d/3 frequency for high yielding clones and d/2 frequency for medium to low yielding clones. 50 % increase in yield can be achieved.

Advantages of CUT is to

Minimise bark consumption. Reduce injury to cambium and spillage.

Tapping Panel Dryness

Commonly known as Brown Blast

Initial stage: Prolonged flow of watery latex

Advanced Stage

Latex flow completely stops

Brownish discolouration as streaks or patches

Bark cracking, flaking and development of burs and nodules

Reasons

Inherent susceptibility of certain cultivars

Intensive tapping

Control measures: Tapping rest

Bark Difference in Seedling and Budded Trees

Seedling trees	*Budding trees*
1. Bark thickness and number of latex vessels/rows	
More towards the base	Uniformly distributed
2. Bark	
Less thinner	Thinner

Tapping

- A thin layer of bark - hard bast & major part of soft bast is removed.
- The phloem tissue, including latex vessels is regenerated by the activity of vascular cambium.

Climatic Conditions

Rainfall

2000 mm or more.

Evenly distributed without any marked dry season.

125 to 150 rainy days per annum.

Temperature

Maximum temperature of about 29 to 34^0c.

Minimum of about 20^0c.

Monthly mean of 25 to 28^0c.

Relative Humidity

High atmospheric humidity - 80 percent with moderate wind.

Sunshine

Bright sunshine - 2000 h per annum (6 h per day throughout all the months).

Name of the Disease	*Casual agent*	*Symptoms Measures*	*Control*
Abnormal leaf fall	*Phytopthora*	Leaves fall in large numbers prematurely either green or after turning coppery red	Bordeaux mixture
Powdery mildew	*Oiduim heveae*	Spots of ash colour appear on newly formal leaves	Sulphur dust 11-15kg/hectare
Pink disease	*Corticuim salmonicolor*	Cobweb like mycelial growth occurs on bark surface	Bordeaux parte application

PROCESSING OF RUBBER

Marketable Forms of Natural Tubber

1. Sheet rubber
2. Crepe rubber
3. Preserved field latex and latex concentrates
4. Block rubber

Sheet rubber: Latex is coagulated in suitable containers into thin slabs and sheeted through set of smooth rollers, grooved and dried to obtain sheet rubber. Depending upon the drying method, sheet is classified as ribbed smoked sheet (RSS) and air-dried sheet. Six grades are RSS-IX, RSS-1, RSS-2, RSS-3, RSS-4 and RSS-5.

Crepe rubber: Processing of earth scrap, shell scrap, tree laces to upgrade low quality field coagulum materials.

Preserved field latex: Field latex preserved with suitable preservatives is termed as preserved field latex. E.g., Calculated quantity of diammonium hydrogen orthophosphate (DAHP) is added at a 10% solution.

Composition of Latex is as Follows

Rubber	30 - 40%	Resin 1 - 2%
Protein	2 - 2.5%	Sugar 1 - 1.5%
Ash	0.7 - 0.9%	Water 55 - 65%

Fresh Latex from the Tree

Slightly alkaline or neutral.

Become acidic rapidly due to bacterial action.

Fresh latex cannot be kept for long without coagulation.

Anticoagulants

It is a chemical added to latex to prevent pre-coagulation before it is processed.

Anticoagulant Chemicals

Ammonia, sodium sulphite and formaline.

- Ammonia recommended for preserve latex or latex concentrate.
- Sodium sulphite is preferred for sheet rubber processing.

DRC (Dry Rubber Content)

DRC is defined as the mass in grams of rubber present in 100 g of latex.

DRC of Field Latex Depends on

1. Age of the tree
2. Tapping intensity
3. Season
4. Climate
5. Soil conditions, etc.

Different Methods of Estimating DRC

1. Hydro-metric (metrolac) method
2. Standard laboratory method
3. Rapid method
4. Microwave technique.

(a) Latex Concentrates: Good market for preserved latex concentrates are concentration by creaming and concentration by centrifugation.

Concentration by Creaming: The processing of latex into creamed concentrates involves the *mixing of a creaming agent* such as *ammonium alginate or tamarind seed powder.*

Concentration by Centrifugation: The processing of latex into latex concentrates by centrifugation involves the *separation of preserved field latex* into two fractions one containing the concentrated latex of *more than 60% dry rubber* and the other containing *4-8% dry rubber*.

(b) Crepe rubbers are classified into:

1. Latex Crepe
   - Pale latex crepe (PLC)

     E.g., High quality products, pharmaceutical articles, adhesives, tapes.
   - Sole crepe (SC)

     Translucent shoe soling materials
2. Field Coagulum Crepe

1. Latex Crepe

Pale latex crepe (PLC)

Latex - free from yellow pigment. Addition of anticoagulant - sodium sulphide. Seiving and bulking - latex seived through 40 and 60 mesh seives. Standardization of latex (Dilution) - latex is diluted to a standard DRC of 25 percent. Addition of chemicals. Sodium bisulphite or sodium metabisulphite - to prevent enzymatic darkening. Removal of pigments. Fractional coagulation - small amount of oxalic or acetic acid. Bleach - xylyl mercaton was widely used. Coagulation - Formic acid - 3.3 to 4.4 ml/kg dry rubber. Crepe making - battery of machines consisting of two course macerators, one intermediate and three sets of plain roller. Drying - air drying sheds or in heated drying chambers.

Sole Crepe (SC)

Any speak of impurities, discoloured parts removing on the surface are removed. Crepe cut into the required length. Placed on a metal - topped laminating table and heated by circulating hot water. Laminator - too heavy plain rollers.

2. Field Coagulation Crepe

Estate Brown Crepe

Cup lump and tree lace - better quality. Earth scrap, bark scrap, smoked and dried cup lump - low quality materials. Process: Soaking - field coagulation soaked in water for atleast one day. Crepe making - machinery consist of a macerator, crepe roller and one finishing machine. Drying - wet crepe dried in air shade or heated drying chamber.

(c) Sheet rubbers are classified into:

1. Ribbed Smoked Sheets
2. Air Dried sheets

Processing into Sheet Rubber (Ribbed Smoked Sheet)

Straining

(Latex strained through 40-60 mesh stainless steel sieves)

↓

Dilution

(Latex is diluted in bulky tanks)

↓

Coagulation

- Formic acid

Acid requirement for coagulation of 4 liters (Pan)

- Formic acid - Next day sheeting - 1.5 ml diluted to 300 ml with water

  Same day sheeting - 2 ml diluted to 400 ml with water

↓

Washing

- After coagulation, coagulum removed from the pans & thoroughly washed in running water.

↓

Sheeting

- Sheeted with sheeting battery or smooth rollers to a thickness of 3 mm.

↓

Dripping

- The wet sheets are allowed to drip for 2-3 hours in a well-ventilated dripping shed.

↓

Smoking

- Temperature in the smoke house - 40 to 60^{0}c.
- Smoke the sheets on the first day - low temperature (40-43^{0}c).
  Subsequent days (2nd to 4th day) - high temperature
  (not exceeding 60^{0}c)
- Smoking period - Normal condition - four days
  Rainy season - five to six days.

Flow Diagram for Processing Field Coagulum and Latex into Technically Specified Rubber (TSR)

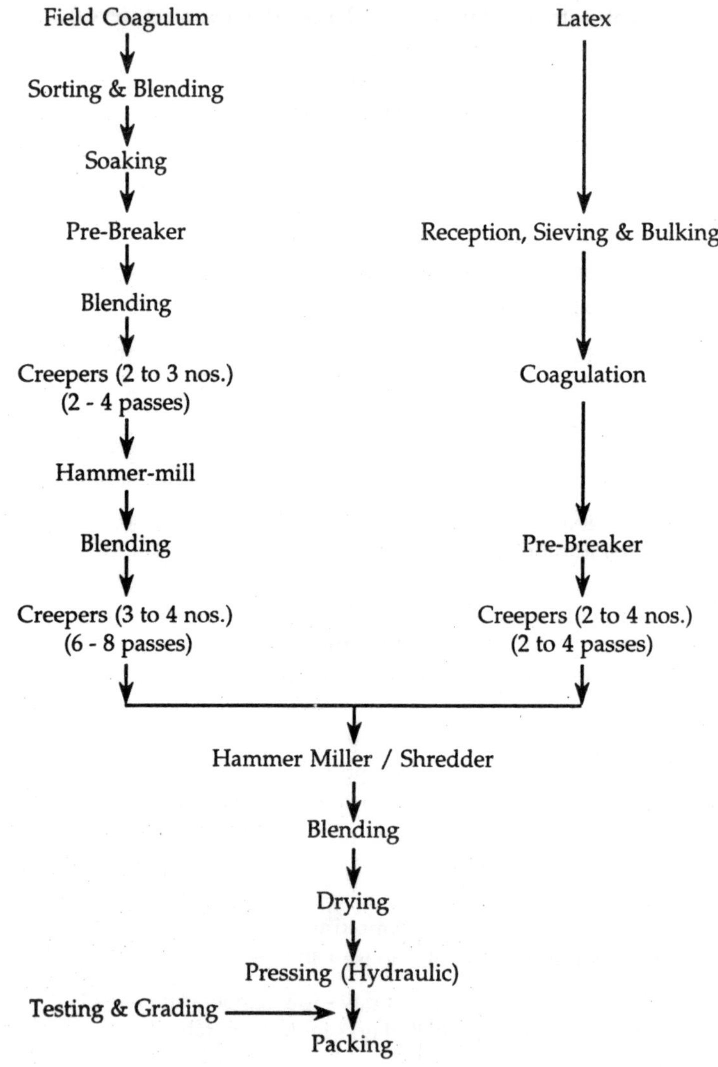

REFERENCE

George. P.J. and Kuruwilla Jacob. C. 2000. ***Natural Rubber - Agro Management and Crop Processing***. Rubber Research Institute of India. #

ANNEXURE: 4

APPROPRIATE TECHNOLOGY FOR SPICES PRODUCTION AND MANUFACTURING

Cardamom

Two Major Cardamom

Large cardamom (*Amomum subulatum*)

Small cardamom (*Elettaria cardamom*)

Small Cardamom (*Elettaria cardamom*)

Mature plant height is 2 to 4 mts. Flowers are bisexual, anther, stigma and well-developed labellum. Stigma positioned above anther. Labellum is a leaf like structure modified for the insect entry. The foraging activity leads to pollination in flower. No synchronized flowering. Flowering occurs from Apr - Oct and coincide with southwest monsoon. No insecticide should be applied to avoid poor pollination and fruit set. Bees are generally active during forenoon. Schedule the insect applications only in the afternoon.

Cardamom strives well at the altitude of 600-1200mts MSL. Optimum rainfall required for cardamom growth is 1500-4000 mm. It requires optimum temperature of 10-30° C. Forest loamy soil with pH of 4.2 to 6.8 is suitable for successful cardamom cultivation.

Propagation

Aerial shoot with some underground stem.

Fruit mature within 90 - 120 days. Maturity period of plant is 20 - 22 months. Economic yield starts 3rd year onwards and continues upto 8 - 10 years. Flavour in cardamom is due to presence of essential oil (1-8-Sinone).

DIFFERENT CULTIVARS IN CARDAMOM

Features	*Malabar*	*Mysore*	*Vazhukka*
1. Size :	Medium (2-3 mts height)	Robust (4 mts)	Hybrid (Malabar x Mysore) Robust
2. Panicle Flowers:	Prostrate (lying face downwards)	Erect	Semi-erect
3. Flavour:	Camphorous odour	Fruity odour	--
4. Fruits/capsule after curing:	Coorg green	Allepey green	--
5. Environment:	600 - 1200 mts elevation, low & seasonal rainfall conditions	900 - 1200 mts, assured and well distributed rain-fall conditions	900 - 1200
6. Pest & disease:	Less susceptible to thrips	--	--
7. Area under cultivation:	Karnataka	Kerala	Kerala & Tamil Nadu

Nursery

Planting material: Seedling or suckers.

1. Primary Nursery

Gentle sloppy area with perennial water source. Bed size of 1 mt width, 20 cm height & required length (generally 6 mts). Place jungle top soil 2 to 3 mts on the beds. Fumigate raised nursery beds with Methyl bromide (45 g per bed). Air tight with polythene sheet. Treated bed kept open for week before sowing.

Seed collected are cleaned with water and dry them on shade. Take the seed in glass jar and place in cold water. Slowly pour acid in the jar. Stir gently for about 2 minutes. Drain the acid using stainer. Transfer the seed immediately to a large volume of water. Wash seed free of acid in running water. Later soak in water and keep overnight. This process is called scarification.

(a) Sowing

Seed normally viable for 3 months but newly harvested seeds are best suited for sowing. Seeds sown at a row distance of 10 cm. Seed rate of 30 -50 gm and for 6x1 m size bed. Dibbling is the recommended method, cover the seeds with thin layer of fine soil. Germination commences 20 to 25 days after sowing and continues for further 30 to 40 days.

2. Secondary Nursery

(a) Bed Nursery

Layer of cattle manure and wood ash are spread and mixed with soil. Transplanting at 3-4 leaf stage from primary to secondary nursery at a distance of 20 - 25 cms.

(b) Polybag Nursery

Black HM/HDP bags of size 20x20 cms, and of thickness 100 gauge with 3-4 holes at the bottom. Fill the bags with potting mixture in the ratio of 3:1:1 (jungle top soil, cowdung and sand) and arranged in rows. Seedlings of 3 to 4 leaf stage can be transplanted into each bag (one seedling/bag).

3. Propagation by Suckers

Clump sections having 1 to 2 old suckers with 2 or 3 new shoots.

Field Planting and Management

Shade regulation, terracing & preparation of pits during summer months.

(a) Field Preparations

Sloping Areas

Width of the terraces across the slope is between 1.5 to 1.8 m.

Pit Size

90 x 90 x 45 cm.

1/3 of the pit - top soil.

1/3 of the pit - 1:3 mixture of organic manure & top soil.

Plant (Spacing)

Mysore - 3 X 3 m.

Vazhukka - 2.4 x 2.4 m.

Weed Control

Two or three rounds of handweeds are applied during the months of May, September & December/January.

Irrigation and Soil and Water Conservation

Irrigation generally required from Feb to Apr. Planting in trenches across the slope, Mulching of soil, Diagonal planting, Rectangular silt pit opening (1.8 x 0.5 x 0.6 m) in between 4 plants and Steep slope are the important soil conservation practices followed in Cardamom.

Forking and Mulching

Forking the plant base to a distance upto 90 cm and depth (9-12 cm).

Trashing

Removing old tillers, dry leaves and leaf sheaths.

Earthing Up

Earthing up of the plant base with top soil December to January.

Manuring

Irrigated areas - 125:125:250 NPK (3 split application).

Rainfed areas - 75:75:150 NPK (2 split application).

Micronutrients

Zinc - Enhance cardamom growth, yield and quality.

Zinc sulphate application - 250 gm/100 ltrs of water during Apr/May and Sep/Oct.

IMPORTANT PEST AND DISEASE IN CARDAMOM

PESTS

Common Name	*Scientific Name*	*Symptoms*	*Control Measures*
Cardamom thrips	*Sciothrips cardamomi*	Sucking the plant sap.Injury to panicle - stunted growth. Flower - flower dropping.Capsules - malformed, shrivelled.	Monocrotophos 0.025%
Shoot/ panicle/ capsule borer	*Conogethes punctiferalis*	Infested shoot show dead heart symptoms and capsules become empty	Monocrotophos or Fenithion 0.075%
Early capsule borer	*Jamides alecto*	Circular hole on the emptied capsule turn yellowish brown, decay and drop off in rainy season	Methyl parathion or Monocroto-phos 0.05%
Cardamom whitefly	*Kanakarajiella Cardamomi*	Crawls on the leaves. Black sooty mould growth on the lower	Neem oil & Triton (500 ml) in 100 litres of
water			
Root grub *fulvicorne*	*Basilepta*	Yellowing of leaves in nurseries	Drenching with Chloropyriphos (0.04%)-3-4 litres/ clump Phorate 30-40gm per clump

DISEASES

Common Name	*Scientific Name*	*Symptoms*	*Control Measures*
Katte disease	*Cardamom mosaic virus*	Youngest leaf-spindle shaped chlorotic flecks. Later, develop into slender discontinous stripes of pale green and dark green areas parallel to the veins.	Constant surveillance, healthy seedling and regular rouging
Nilgiri necrosis disease	*Rod shaped virus*	Alternate light green and whitish to yellowish streak in the form of mosaic.Later reddish brown necrotic areas. Leaves are crinkled with wavy margin.	Plant sanitation-rouging
Kokke kandu	*Cardamom vein clearing virus*	Mottling on the foliage. Yellow stripes or streaks parallel to the side veins. Leaves are arranged in Rosette manner.	Plant sanitation
Azhukal or capsule rot disease	*Phytophthora meadii*	Young leaves - water soaked lesions.Mature leaves - necrotic, areas shrivel and remain hanging.Capsules-decays and falls.	Phytosanitory Bordeaux mixture 1 % or Alliette 80 WP (0.3 %) 300 gms/100 litre of water or Akomin (0.4%-4 ml/litre of water)
Clump rot or rhizome rot	Pythium vexans *Rhizoctonia soloni*	Yellowing of leaves. Decay of tillers starting from collar region.	Plant base drenched with 2-3 litres of copper oxychloride (COC) (0.25%)

PROCESSING OF CARDAMOM

Harvesting

↓

Pre Drying Treatment

(Capsules treated with 2% washing soda for 10 minutes)

↓

Curing

(Moisture content of green cardamom reduced to 12% at an optimum temperature of 50^{0}c)

Natural sun drying (5-6 days)

Electrical drier (10-12 hours at 45-50^{0}c)

Pipe curing (18-22 hours at 45-50^{0}c)

↓

Garbling

(Process of separating the awn)

Manual-capsules are heated to the temperature of 60-65^{0}c and rubbed over an wiremesh platform

Mechanical methods-shaft with wire mesh

↓

Sorting & Grading

BLACK PEPPER

Black pepper is obtained from the perennial climbing vine. It grows to the height of 10m or more. Pepper is a plant of humid tropics requiring adequate rainfall and humidity. The hot and humid tropical climate of submountaneous tracts western and eastern ghats is ideal for its growth. The crop tolerates the temperature between 10^{0}c - 40^{0}c. A well-distributed annual rainfall of 125-200cm is ideal for pepper. Pepper can be grown in a wide range of soils such as clay loam, red loam and sandy loam with soil pH of 4.5 to 6.0

Important Cultivators

Kerala - Karimunda, Koltanandan, Narayakkodi

Karnataka - Malligesara and Uddagare.

Hybrid - Panniyur-I.

Propagation

Common propagation techniques are cuttings. Cuttings are secured mainly from the runner shoots. After trimming the leaves, cuttings of 2-3 nodes were used. Lower half of north and northeastern slope preferred for avoiding sun scorching. *Erythrina sp, Garuga pinnata* (India Coral Tree), *Grevillea robust*a (Silver Oak). are the common shado trees. The stems planted in the edge of the pits dug for pepper wines.

Planting

Planting is done during onset of monsoon. 2-3 rooted cuttings of pepper planted individually on the pits with a spacing of 2.5x2.5 m. As the cuttings grow, the shoots are tied to the standards.

Aftercare

Regulation of shade by lopping the branches of standards. Excessive shading during flowering and fruiting encourage pest infestation.

Nutrient Management

140:55:270 gms of NPK/vine is recommended 1/3 of this dosage applied in the first year, 2/3 in the second year and full dose from the 3rd year onwards. Applied in 2 split doses during May-Jun and Aug-Sep. Fertilizer applied at a distance of about 30 cm all around the vine and cover with thick layer of soil.

Harvesting

Pepper flowers in May-Jun. Crop takes 6 to 8 months

from flowering to harvest. Whole spike is hard picked when one or two berries in the spike turn bright orange or purple.

IMPORTANT PEST AND DISEASE IN BLACK PEPPER

PESTS

Pests	*Causal agent*	*Symptom*	*Control Measure*
Pollu beetle	*Longitarsus nigripennis*	Grubs bore into the berries, cause black colour and crumble when pressed	Spray endosulfan (0.05%)
Top shoot borer	*Cydia hexidoxa*	Caterpillars bore into the tender shoots turning them to black and drying up	Spray endosulfan (0.05%)
Leaf gall thrips	*Liothrips karnyi*	Leaves become malformed and crunkled	Spray monocrotophos
Scale insects	*Lepidosaphes piperis*	Drying of the infested portion of the wine	Spray dimethoate (0.05%)

DISEASES

Disease	*Causal agent*	*Symptom*	*Control Measure*
Quick wilt	*Phytophthora capsici*	Pathogen infects leaves, spikes, collar region and roots. Collar infection causes sudden collapse of the vine.	Removal of the infected dead vines and burn them.Spray vine with 1% Bordeaux mixture and 0.25% Ridomil Ziram alternatively.
Pollu disease	*Colletotrichum Gloeosporioides*	Brown sunken patches in young berries and berry splitting.	Spray 1% Bordeaux mixture.
Slow decline or slow wilt	Fusarium sp	Dry months- foliar yellowing defoliation and dieback symptoms appear in vines.	Treat the plany pit with phorate (15g) or carbofuran (50g).

PROCESSING OF BLACK PEPPER

Harvesting

(Harvested spikes kept in bag for 12 to 24 hours)

↓

Despicking

(Separation of berries)

Trampling (or) Thresher

↓

Blanching

(Dip in boiling water for one minute)

↓

Drying

(Drying of pepper to the moisture level of 8-10%)

Drying process

1. Sun drying: Period of 4-7 days (or)

Use of polythene sheets paste watered bamboo mat

2. Hot air drying

3. Solar drying process

↓

Cleaning and Grading

(Removal of extraneous material)

Winnowing and hand picking

Pneumatic separators

Multiple sieve cum air classifier

PROCESSING OF WHITE PEPPER

Harvesting

Spikes with fully ripe berries are filled in gunny bags.

Steeping

Steeped in flowing water for about 7 days.

↓

Rubbing

Outerind of the berries removed by rubbing in water.

Further cleaning with fresh water.

↓

Drying

Cleaned seeds are dried for 3-4 days.

Winnowing & Polishing

Further winnowing and polishing then by rubbing with cloth.

"Decordictated white pepper" - produced mechanically by rubbing the black outer layer of the black pepper berry.

DIFFERENCE BETWEEN BLACK AND WHITE PEPPER

	Black Pepper	*White Pepper*
1. Harvest	Spikes with 1 or 2 ripe berries	Spikes with fully ripe berries
2. Colour	Black to dark brown	Half white to gray
3. Corn	Shriveled	Smooth

Condiments and Seasonings

Condiments are compounds containing one or more spices, or spice extractives, which when added to a food, after it has been served enhances the flavour. E.g., Clery salt - sprinkled on fish, egg dishes, salads, etc. Garlic salt - sprinkled on fish and other sea foods. Onion salt - sprinkled on sea food and chicken dishes. Tomato, chilli and meat sauces - sprinkled on fried foods.

Seasonings are compounds containing one or more spices, or spice extractives, which when added to a food during preparation enhances natural flavour of the food. E.g., Gravy mixtures, Masala mixtures

REFERENCES

- Extension Floders, 2003 Indian Cardamon Research Institute (Spcies Board). Myladumpra. Kaelsanadan.
- Kumau N. JBM Md Abdul Khaden, Ramgaswami, P and Jrulappan. 1. 1997. Introduction to Spices, Plantation Crops, Medicinal and Aronatic Plants. Oxford and IBH Publishing Co. Private Ltd.

VANILLA

(Vanilla Planifora)

FIELD PRODUCTION AND PRACTICES

Vanilla is a tropical orchid, which is cultivated for its pleasant odour. It belongs to the tropical genus of the family orchidaceae. Vanilla needs warm and moist condition with well distributed rainfall of 150-300 cm with a temperature range of 25-32° C and comes well from sea level to around 1500m above mean sea level.

Ideal Condition is moderate rainfall evenly distributed throughout 10 months of the year, dry periods during flowering and harvesting period, soil of high organic matter content, loamy texture and sloppy land and flourishes well under 50 percent shade. Common support trees are Casuarina, Mulberry and Erythrine lithosperma plants.

Propagation

Shoot cuttings. Vines cut into pieces of about one meter with the bottom 3 or 4 leaves removed at the node.

Planting

Laying the 3-4 basal nodes from where leaves have been removed on the soil surface. The top end of the cuttings is to be tied to the base of the support. Ideal time for planting when the weather is neither too rainy nor too dry. Planting in August or September.

After Care

Manuring

17:17:17 NPK complex to give a full coverage of the foliage

Irrigation

During, initial 2 to 3 years, weekly irrigation with 2 to 3 ltrs of water/plant. Nipping of the tip of vines produce more number of shoots. Vines are allowed to grow up to a height of 1.2 to 1.5 meters and allowed to hand down on the branches.

Flowering

Flowering commences in the third year after planting. Artificial pollination is commonly practiced by skilled labour at the rate of 1000 flowers per day. Beans mature in nine to eleven months. Pale yellowing at the distal end indicates the fruit maturity.

IMPORTANT PEST AND DISEASE IN VANILLA

Pest

Lamellicom beetles, Ash-gray weevil and Vanilla bug.

Disease	*Control Measure*
Shoot tip rot stem and bean rot	1 percent Bordeaux mixture. Indofil M-45 (200 g in 100 litres of water.

Flower of Vanilla

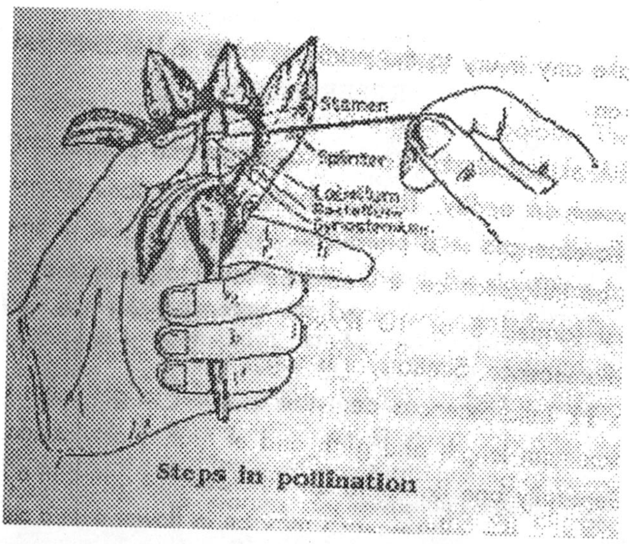

PROCESSING

Killing

(Beans dipped in hot water (63 to 65°C) for 3 minutes)

↓

Sweating

(Beans are made to sweat by exposing to sunlight for about 1-1 1/2 hrs during day time)

↓

Slow drying

(Spreading beans on wooden racks at ambient temperature)

↓ (Duration of 20 to 25 days).

Conditioning

(Beans sorted or graded)

Followed by wrapping woolen blanket and storing in air tight. wooden boxes during night time.

Repeated for 10-12 days.

REFERENCES

1. Dhanakumar V.G. 2004. *Techno Risk Management in spices: SPS Aspects of HACCP*. Spices Week.
2. Krishnamurthy K. and Melanta K.R. 2002. *Vanilla-A Fragrant Crop for Export*. Geetanjali Graphics, Bangalore.
3. Kumar. N. JBM Md. Abdul Khader, Rangaswami. P. and Irulappan. I. 1997. *Introduction to Spices, Plantation Crops, Medicinal and Aromatic Plants*. Mohan Primlani for Oxford and IBH Publishing Co. Private Ltd.
4. Sanjeev Agarwal et.al. 2001. *Seed Spices-Production, Quality, Export*. Pointer Publishers. Jaipur.
5. Singh. V.B. and Kirti Singh. 1996. *Spices*. New Age International (P) Limited Publishers.#

ANNEXURE: 5

APPROPRIATE TECHNOLOGY FOR GRAPES PRODUCTION AND PROCESSING

Grapes

(*Vitis vinifera*)

Grapes grown mostly in the states like Maharashtra, Karnataka, Tamil Nadu, Punjab, Andhra Pradesh, Haryana and Uttar Pradesh. Hot and dry climate is suitable for grapes production. It comes well under ideal temperature of 15-35°C and rainfall not exceeding 900 mm. Loamy and sandy loam soil with soil pH of 6.5 to 8 are suitable for grape cultivation.

Varieties

	Table Grapes	*Raisin Grapes*	*Wine Grapes*
Characteristics	Thin & soft skin, crisp pulp & few seeds	Seedless, high sugar content	
Varieties	World: Ahmeria, Calmeria, Cardinal	Thompson seedless, Black Corinth, black Momikka	White Riesling, chardonnay, Cabernet Sauvignn
	India: Anab-e-shahi, Bangalore Blue, Bhokai, Gulabi, Thompson seedless	Thompson seedless and Arakavati	Bangalore Blue, Thompson seedless & Arka Kanchan

Propagation: Most commonly propagated by Hardwood cuttings.

Best cuttings from healthy, vigorous wines and well matured canes. Cuttings of 0.75-1.00 cm and length of 30-45 cm with atleast 3 nodes to be selected.

Callusing, soaking in water prior to planting and soaking in auxin solutions for 12 to 48 hours.

Planting

Planting either in the nursery bed or in the polybags.

Nursery bed of 1.2m width and convenient length. Furrows of 15-20 cm depth are opened 30 cm apart. Superphosphate was applied at the rate of 3 kg/100m^2 and Heptachlor 5 g/m. Basal portion of the cutting pushed inside the soil to bury atleast two nodes in the soil. Leaving one or two apical buds above the soil surface. Poly bag planting - Poly bag of 25 cm x 15 cm. and thickness of 150x200 gauge was used. Superphosphate 20 g & Chloridane or heptachlor dust was applied at 2 g/bag.

Erection of Trellis

Grapevine stem being weak, it needs support in the early years. Structures used to support grapevines are referred as trellis. Most commonly used trellis in India are overhead arbour. It helps to develop highest number of fruiting units per unit area of vine spread. Trellis consists of vertical posts, galvanized iron wire and turning bucks. Granite stone pillars are used as vertical posts. Spacing of the vertical posts depend on the spacing of wines.

Vineyard Establishment

Plot Size

Surface irrigation - 60 m x 90 m.

Drip irrigation - 90 m x 120 m.

Row direction - North-South direction (Sunlight equally on either side of the rows).

Vine Spacing: varies with varieties and region.

Thompson Seedless - 1.65 x 3.3 m (Karnataka).

1.2x 3.6 m (or) 1.8 x 2.4 m (Maharastra & North Karnataka).

Anabe-Shahi - 3.3 x 6.6 m (South Karnataka).

Bangalore Blue - 3.2 x 5.0 m (or) 3.3 x 6.6 m (South Karnataka).

Row width are fixed at intervals equal to the spacing of vines in a row.

Training Practices

Grapevines are trained when they are young to develop the permanent framework of the vine. Grapevine training should be varied out meticulously in the first year of planting itself. Growing short apex is pinched to promote the development of lateral branches.

Different System of Training

Bower system.

Kniffin.

Telephone.

Head system.

Bower system is found suitable for all the commercial grown varieties in India. Shoots start growing from the newly planted cuttings in the main field. Only the best shoot growing vertically is allowed to grow upto the bower height. Vertically growing shoot is topped 20-25 cm below the bower height. Thickness of the shoot should be atleast 6 mm thickness. The two laterals arising from the main stem are called primary branches and allowed to grow in opposite direction either east -west or north-south. Primaries growing on either side of the main stem are cut at a point slightly (about 5cm). Shoots arising from each topped primary, terminal one should be allowed to grow in the direction of the primary. While the second and third should be allowed to grow in the opposite direction. Approximately 12-15 territory branches (canes) developed on each secondary branches.

Pruning

Double Pruning-Single Cropping

Predominantly followed in Maharastra, Karnataka & Andra Pradesh.

Foundation Pruning

After harvest in summer, the vines are forced to undergo

rest for about a month. All the fruiting canes are pruned back to spurs retaining only one basal node.

Forward Pruning

Buds on the shoots growing from these spurs differentiate into floral primordia. The shoots mature in about 5 months. These mature shoots are pruned for fruiting before the onset of winter (Sep/Oct).

Shoot Pinching

Elimination of unwanted shoots and shoot thinning during the growth period would promote fruitfulness in grapevine. Shoot pinching is done during the growth as well as fruiting seasons in peninsular India, but only during the fruiting season in North India.

Manuring

Pre-bearing age (Karnataka)

More N and comparatively less P & K.

100 g urea (monthly interval).

100 g SOP (quarterly interval).

1 kg Superphosphate (6 monthly interval) + 20 kg FYM and 1kg of oil cake.

Bearing age (kg/ha)

		N	*P*	*K*
Anaebe-shahi	North India	600	300	1200
	Karnataka	500	500	1000
Thompson	Maharashtra	1000	500	800
Seedless	Karnataka	300	500	1000

Placement Methods

Broadcasting, ring placement, band, placement and pocket placement.

Fertigation - application nutrients, mainly N, through trip irrigation is also followed.

Irrigation Practices

Newly Planted Vineyards

In case of young wines irrigation was done in the form of circular basin of 50 cm radius made around it once in three days whereas in case of grown up wines the size of the basin is 2m.

Weeds

North India	- Altermanthera sessils Cannabis sp
Maharashtra & North Karnataka	- Argemone mexicane Asistolochia bractata

Harvesting

Normally selective picking is followed. Before a day of picking remove the broken, decayed, deformed, green or poorly coloured undersized berries. Harvesting is noramlly done during the early hours before the berry temperature rises above 20^{0}c. While picking, the pickers should hold them by stems only, without touching the berries by hand and erasing the waxy coating called "bloom". Wear rubber gloves while harvesting. Care must be taken to avoid exerting pressure on berries.

Grading

Grading based on size and colour of the berry.

Post-harvest Management

Take care not erase the thin coating of natural bloom. Subject the grapes to pre-cooling 4-6 hours after harvest. Put "grape guard" inside the filled curton, seal it and put in the cold storage (temp ±0.5 and RH 85-90%). Palletize the boxes after they are cooled adequately. Use refrigerated containers for shipment to overseas to market.

Storage Spoilage

1. Desiccation

Desiccation is caused due to moisture loss in the fruit to avoid this relative humidity in the storage room should be increased.

2. Decay

Decay of grapes is caused during storage due to fungus like Botrytis, Cladosporium, Alternaria. Fumigation with sulphur dioxide prevents fungus attack on fruit.

3. Biochemical Deterioration

Pre-harvest treatment

Fungicides: Spraying of fungicides like Capton (0.2%) 3 to 4 days before harvest reduce the decay of berries in storage.

Growth Substances: NAA and Kinetin extend the storage life of grapes.

Calcium: Preharvest spray of calcium as calcium nitrate prolong the storage life of grapes.

ENOLOGY

Enology in India

In India, commercial viticulture has emerged as one of the most important horticultural industry in recent years. Large scale cultivation of grapes spreading over nearly 50,000 hectares with a total annual production of over 12 lakhs metric tones provides a great scope for utilization of grapes for diversified used like wine, juice and raisins. Although more than 80 per cent of the grapes produced throughout the world are used for wine making, only limited quantity is crushed in India. This is mainly due to the non availability of suitable wine grapes for quality wine production, lack of proper technological facilities and limited market potential for this group of beverages in this country. Few wineries such as Shaw Wallace Company Ltd., Hyderabad, Hindustan Export Corporation, Bangalore, Baramathi Winery, Champagne India Ltd., Narayanagao and Nashik Co-operative Winery in Maharashtra and few other small scale processing units produce the bulk of Indian wines. Production of quality wines offers good prospects for increasing the national wealth through export as well as domestic trade.

Wine Classification

Wines are classified based on their colour, sugar and alcohol content, presence of CO_2, time of consumption etc. Besides, there are speciality wines such as Sherry (acetaldehyde flavour), Port (Fortified dessert), Champagne (Sparkling wine with CO_2), Muscatal (Muscat flavoured dessert wine) and Wine coolers (low alcohol blend of wine and fruit juices).

Raw Material

The characteristic composition, flavour, colour and other qualities of grapes largely determines the wine quality. Grape varieties with high sugar (19° Brix and above); moderate acidity (0.5 to 0.7%), pH 3.2-3.5, good flavour and stable colour are generally preferred for production of standard quality wines. Many typical wines require one or more specific grape varieties which contributes distinctiveness to the wine.

Winery Equipment

The production of wines demand selection of suitable grape variety for crushing, skill and control over fermentation; but not necessarily large or expensive establishment. A small winery with a crushing capacity of 50-100 tons/year required the following equipment with a total investment of Rs.40-50 Lakhs excluding building.

1. Grape crusher/Stemmer.
2. Press for Juice extraction.
3. S.S. Fermentation tank with cooling facility.
4. Controlled temperature rooms.
5. Mixing tanks.
6. Transfer pulps (Must and wine).
7. Filters.
8. S.S. Storage tanks.
9. Centrifuge.
10. Bottling, Labeling and corking machine.

Wine Making Process

Although traditionally wine making process was considered as an art, now it has developed into a science involving precise control over processing operations right from the selection of grapes to bottling of wine. Harvesting wine grape cultivar at optimum maturity, use of best yeast strain, adoption of standard fermentation techniques, careful handling of wine during cellar operations, close monitoring of free and total sulphur dioxide levels in wine are the critical steps in wine making process. Appropriate aging is essential to produce wine with desirable levels of maturity and complexity of flavour.

Composition and Yield

During the alcoholic fermentation, the yeasts converts sugar into alcohol. The range of values for different composition are as follows: alcohol 9-12%; acidity 0.5-0.7%; total phenols 250 mg/1 (white wine) and 1000 mg/1 (Red wine) as galic acid; acetaldehyde 100 mg/1; Ethyl accelate 200-300mg/1. Total and free SO_2, 100 and 25 ppm respectively. Depending on the juice content of grape variety used for crushing, the wine yield varies from 50 to 65% (vol/wt).

Production of Speciality Wines

Besides dry table wines (Red and white) other wine types are commercially produced throughout the world. Examples are vermouth, sherry, port, sparkling wines etc.

Vermouth: Vermouth is prepared by flavouring the fortified base wine with a mixture of herbs and spices which impart characteristic aromatic flavour, odour and bitter taste. Sweet vermouths of Italian type contain 15-17% alcohol and 12 to 13% reducing sugar where as French dry types have 10% alcohol and 4% sugar. Herbs and spices are introduced directly along with the fermentation or in the form of concentrated alcohol extract to the base wine.

Sherry: Sherry is a fortified wine with characteristic accetaldehyde flavour. It is produced either by baking fortified wine with 17% alcohol in wooden or S.S. tanks at 60-80°C for 1-6 weeks of fermentation using *Sacch. Fermentatii* which is allowed to grow on the surface of wine fortified to 16% alcohol and develop floor character.

Portwine: Port wine is a fortified red dessert wine usually produced by crushing dark coloured grapes with stable colour. The fermentation is arrested at 10^{oB}, the base wine is fortified, sweetened and blended for uniform quality.

Sparkling wines: Since direct carbonation of wine is not acceptable, champagne process is developed. Base wine is converted into 'Cuvee' by addition of 20g/1 hydrolysed sugar to provide 4-6 atmosphere pressure of CO_2. This is achieved by bottle fermentation using Champagne yeast. After secondary fermentation the yeast sediment is removed by a special technique and wine is bottled.

TABLE 1

Principal Wine Regions of the World

Europe	Australia, Bulgaria, Czechoslovakia, France, Germany, Greece, Hungary, Italy, Portugal, Rumania, Switzerland
South Africa	Argentina, Brazil, Chile, Peru
North America	Canada, U.S.A., Mexico
Africa	Algeria, Morocco, S. Africa, Tunisia
Asia	Cyprus, Isreal, Japan, Turkey
Occenia	Australia, Newzealand

TABLE 2

Classification of Wines

Character	Wine type
Colour	Red, rose and white wine
Alcohol	Natural and fortified wine
Sugar content	Dry, semi dry and sweet wine
Time of consumption	Table wine, Appetizer and dessert wine
Presence of CO2	Still wine and sparkling wine
Presence of herb and flavouring components	Vermouth (sweet and dry)

TABLE 3

Grape Varieties Recommended for Quality Wine Production

Type of wine	Grape variety
Dry white Table wine	Bayan Sherei, Chenin Blanc, Excelsior, Feteasca Alba, Ova Pagola, Sauvignon, White Riesling, Sheridon, *Arka Kanchan, *Arkavati, *Arka Soma, Thompson Seedless.
Red dry table wine	Black Champa, Black Muscat, Cabernet Suvignon, Feteasca Neagra, Gamsa, Red Prince, Rubired, Sapervi, Tievoasa, Zinfandel, *Arka Shyam.
White desert wine	*Arka Kanchan
Red desert wine	*Arka Shyam, Rubi red.

* IIHR recommended varieties

Popular Wine Varieties of the world

Sl.No.	*Red Wine*	*White Wine*
1.	Bastardo	Chardonnay
2.	Bonvedro	Chasselas
3.	Cabernet Franc	Chenin Blanc
4.	Cabernet Sauvignon	Clairette
5.	Carignan	Doradillo
6.	Insaut	Melon
7.	Durif	Muller Thurgau
8.	Gamay	Muscadelle
9.	Grenache	Muscat Gordo Blanco
10.	Malbec	Palomino
11.	Mataro	Pinot Blanc
12.	Merlot	Riesling
13.	Pinot Noir	Sauvignon Blanc
14.	Rubired	Semillon
15.	Ruby Cabernet	Solvorino
16.	Sangiovese	Sylvaner
17.	Shiraz	Traminer
18.	Tinta Amarella	
19.	Touriga	
20.	Zingandel	

WINE EVALUATION

1. Standark Davis Score Card System

   Colour = 2

   Appearance = 2

   Aroma x bouquet = 4

   Acidity = 2

   Volatile acidity = 2

   Flavor = 2

Sweetness, Body, Bitterness & Astringency = 1 each (4)

Overall quality = 2

Total Scores = 20

Rating: Superior (17-20); Standard (13-10); Below Standard (9-12); Unacceptable (1-8)

2. Hedonic rating
3. Ranking test

Fig.1. Operations in White Wine Making

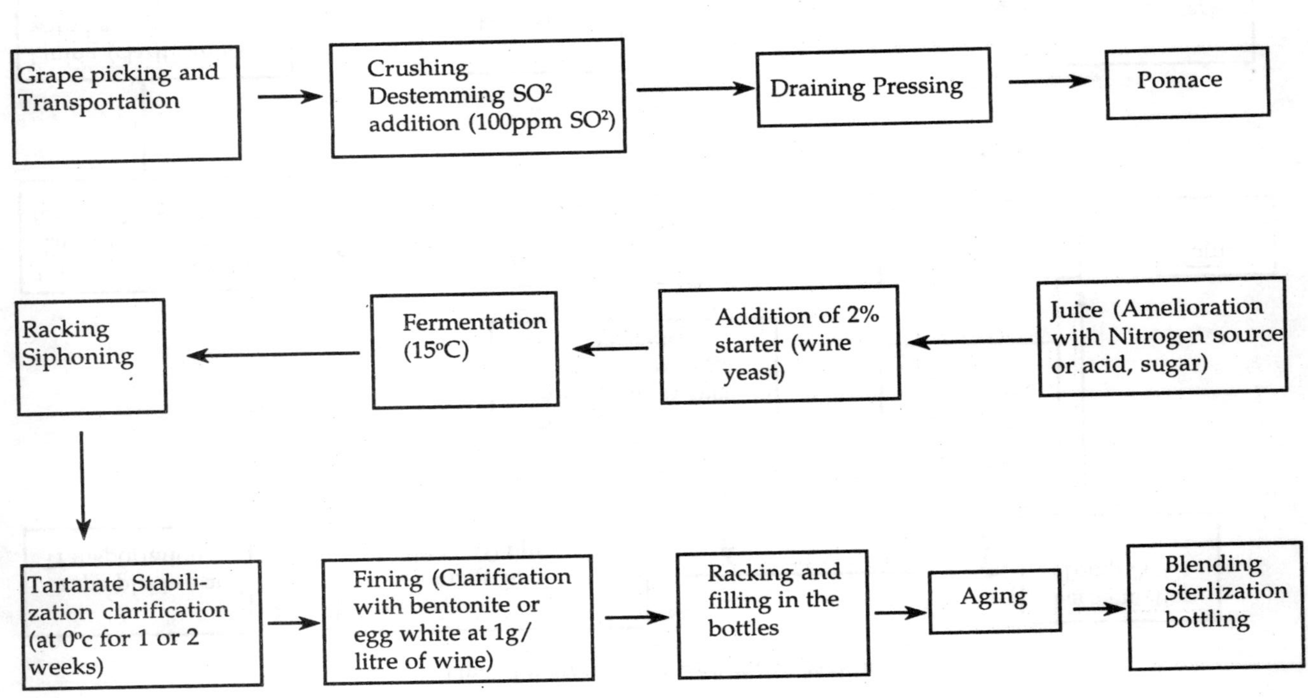

Fig.2. Operations in Red Wine Making

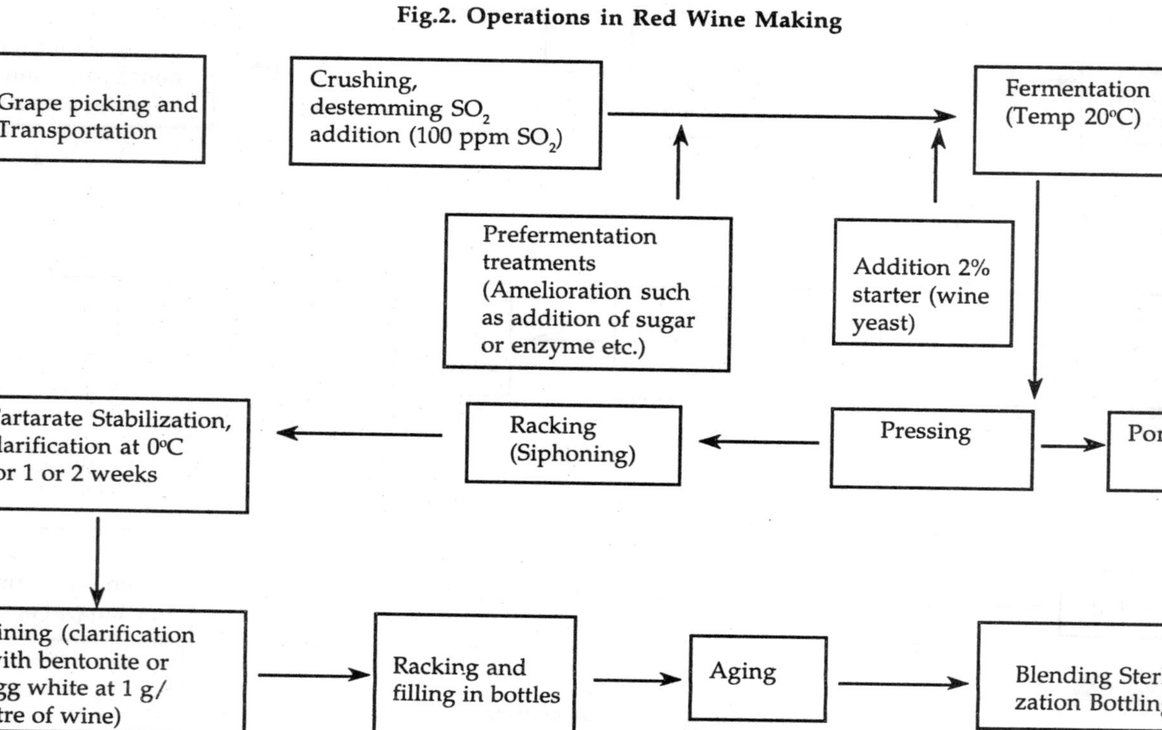

REFERENCES

1. Chadha, K.L., and Shikamany, S.D. 1999. The Grape - Improvement, Production and Post-Harvest Management. Malhotra Publishing House, New Delhi.
2. Pandey, R. M. and Pandey, S.N., 1996. The Grape in India, ICAR Publications, New Delhi.
3. Shanmugavelu, K. G., 1998. Viticulture in India. Agro Botanixa., B. Kaner.
4. Suresh, 2004. Enology. Indian Institute of Horticultural Research, Hessarghatta, Bangalore.

ANNEXURE 6

APPROPRIATE TECHNOLOGY FOR OIL PALM PRODUCTION AND MANUFACTURING

(Elaeis Guineensis)

Origin

Oil Palm is native of Guinea in coast of West Africa. Introduced to India by the National Botanical Garden, Kolkata in the 19th century. It grows to the height 30 m at the rate of 30-60 cm per year. Life span of Oil Palm tree is 200 years.

Agronomical Practices

Grown in variety of soils with moist, deep, well drained and medium textured soils. Very cold (or) dry spell affect growth. Griws wekk ub 2000 mm rainfall area. Temperature below 19°c reduces the growth rate. 5 hours bright sunlight is required per day. 1800-2000 sunshine hours is necessary for good growth.

Varieties

Dura	Shell is 2.8 mm thick mesocarp is 35-50 with 17 18% percent of oil
Pisifera	Mesocarp and oil content is high (crossing dura with pisifera type)
Tenera	Produced by crossing Dura and Pisifera. Mesocarp is 60-96 per cent oil content is 22 to 24 per cent
American oil palm	Dwarf - more oil, persistent resistant to bud rot and wilt disease

Land Preparation

Make circular platforms with 3-4 m diameter and terracing in slopes over 20°.

Plant Density

Triangular method - 9mx9mx9m spacing & plant population of 43 per ha.

Seedlings of 12-14 months, 1-1.3 m height and having more than 13 functional leaves are best for planting.

Planting

Pits size - 60x60x60 cm.

Filled with 20 kg FYM and 200 g phosphate/per pit along the soil.

Irrigation

Good moisture level throughout the growing period. 90 liters of water per palm required during dry months.

Planting Material

Collection of Seeds

Only tenera hybrid are commercially planted. After harvest, fruits are removed by retting for 5-10 days & repeated washing. Seeds are dried in sun for a day to bring the moisture upto 18 percent. Seeds may be stored for 6 months.

Germination Techniques

Heat treatment was followed for better germination by using a seed germinatar chamber with a thermostat controlled temperature of 38 to 40^{0}c. Pack seeds in thick polybag (500 seeds in a pack) kept in the chamber for 40 days for preheating. Preheated seed soaked in water for 2 to 3 days to increase moisture content to 22 percent. Seeds are returned to sealed polythene bags and kept in ambient conditions. Germination starts (80 to 90%) in 7-10 days and continue for 30-40 days.

Growing Seedling

Germinated seeds stored in black poly bag (23x13cm) filled with mixture of sand, silt and manure. Plants are shifted to secondary nursery with wider spacing with larger polybags after 8 weeks at 5 leaf stage.

Nursery Manuring

NPK at 0.6 g, 0.5 g and 1.5 g/plant at 3 times in 3 month stage and 4 times at 6 month stage.

MANURES AND FERTILIZERS

Age	*(Nitrites gms/palm/year)*		
	N	P_2O_5	K_2O
First year	400	200	400
Second year	800	400	800
Third year onwards	1200	600	1200

Additionally 20,30,50 kg FYM may be added in pits, in 1st year, 2nd year and 3rd year respectively.

Fertilizer is spread in a 2m circle around trunk during May-June and September-October.

Inter crop - Maize, cassava & elephant foot yams

Cover crop - Calopogonium mucunoides or Pueraria phaseoloides

Fruit set - Fruit set could be increased by introduction of a weevil (Elaedobipus camerunicas) which helps in pollination

Harvest

Bunch ripen in 6 months after *anthesis*. Ripeness is determine by the degree of detachment of fruits from bunches, change in colour and texture. Fruit ripen and get detached from tip downwards in 11-20 days. Harvesting is done in frequent rounds at 7-10 days interval. Important Pest and Disease in Oil Palm.

IMPORTANT PESTS AND DISEASES

PESTS

Common Name	*Symptoms*	*Control Measures*
Spindle bug	The nymph and adult bug sucks saps from the spindle and unfolding leaves at nursery stage	Endosulfan 1.5 ml
Rhinoceros beetle	Adult beetle pores into the unopened fronds and spathes	Place 3 to 4 naphthalene balls in the youngest spear axils at weekly intervals
Red palm weevil	Presence of hole, oozing out of viscous brown fluid, longitudinal splitting of leaf bases and wilting of inner leaves	Injection of pyrithrin piperonyl butomide 10 ml in one litre of water per palm through a hole above the infested portion

DISEASES

Common Name	*Symptoms*	*Control Measures*
Spear rot	Yellowing of youngest whorl of unfolded followed by browning and drying	Roguing of affected palm and burning
Bud rot	Rotting starts at the basal part of spear close to meris tem and gradually extends to whole spear	Carbendazym 1 g/litre of water
Crown disease	Brown lesions with water soaked margins appear on middle portion	- -

Quality Standard and Grades for Export

FFA	-	<5 percent.
Moisture content	-	0.5 percent.
Dirt	-	0.5 percent.
Grade I	-	under 9 percent FFA.
Grade II	-	9-18 percent FFA.
Grade III	-	18-27 percent FFA.
Grade IV	-	27-36 percent FFA.
Grade V	-	over 36 percent FFA.

Advantages/ Nutritional Properties of Palm Oil

Good resistance to oxidative deterioration. Better ability to withstand high temperature. Palm oil readily absorbed and shows a digestibility of 97 percent.

Nutritional properties of palm oil. Provide energy efficiently. Supply the essential linoleic and linolenic acids. Carry the fat soluble vitamin A, D and E.

Improve the palatability of food.

Palm Oil in the Food Industry

1. Frying Fat and Oils

To improve the heat and oxidation stability.

2. Hard Butter

Palm oil contains 2-oleoyl 1,3-dipalmitin (POP) for chocolate production. Hard butter prevents blooming of chocolate products and changes during transportation or in the shops due to frequent change of temperature and humidity in Japan.

3. Ice Cream and Mayonnaise

Palm oil or a mixture of POP can be used in ice cream and milk product. Super olein can be used in mayonnaise.

FLOW CHART OF PALM OIL AND KERNEL EXTRACTION PROCESS

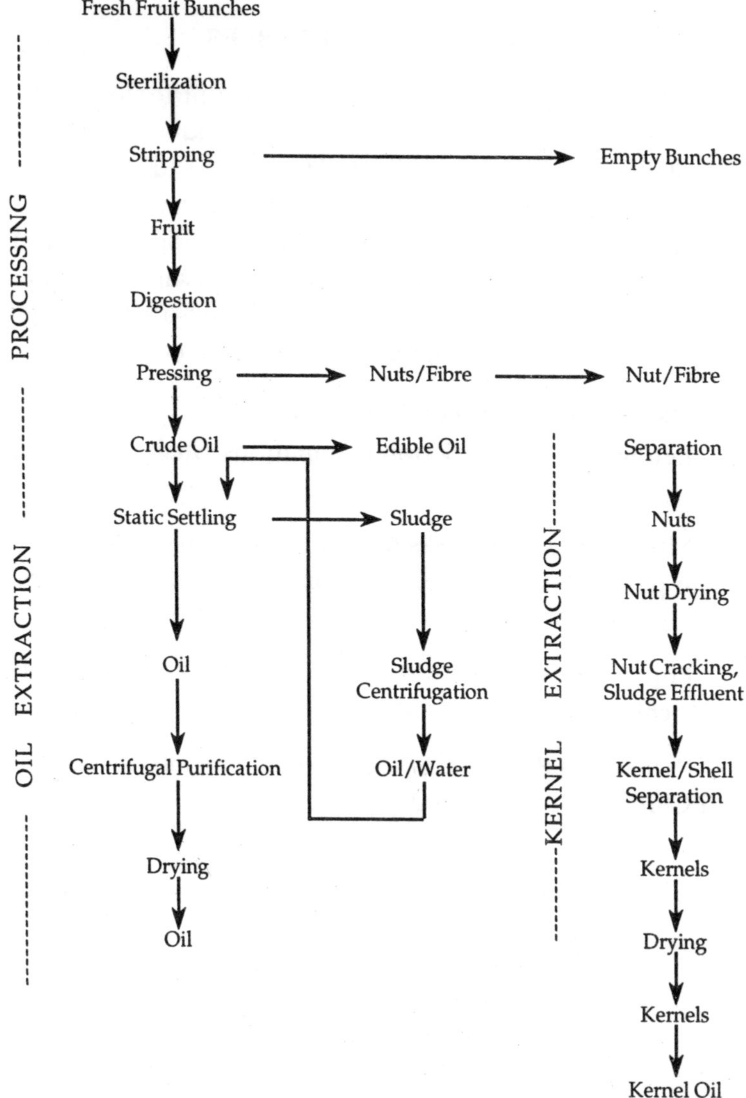

REFERENCE

1. Dhanakumar, V.G. (2005). PGDABPM Reading Manual.IIPM, Bangalore.

ANNEXURE 7

ORIENTAL VEGETABLES

Collection of crops of Asian Origin (East) countries like Japan, China, Hongkong, Singapore, Indonesia, India and Korea. Oriental or specialty vegetables and fruits are odd sized (baby size) (or) shaped (or) coloured, out of season (or) origin, Miniatures (or) heirlooms, command a higher price (or) prized by gourmet cooks and had demand in wholesale, retail and direct sales. Eg. Cripsy Choy - Chinese loose leafed cabbage; Chinese broccoli; Mizuna; Oriental Radishes; etc.

Popular Speciality/Oriental Products

Peppers: Jalapeno; Serrano; Tomatillos; Shallots; Pasilla; Prickly pearcactus.

Mini/Baby sized: Beaks & egg plants; Corn & fillet beans; Pelite pois (peas); Lettuce/leeks/onions; Potatoes/summer squash; Cherry tomatoes.

Popular Miniature: King Richard Leek; Parmex carrot; Garlicchieve flower bud stalks (Chinese-American).

Production Practices for the Oriental Vegetables - Lettuce and China Cabbage is produced hereunder:

	Lettuce	*China Cabbage*
Countries grown	Spain, Italy, France, U.K., Germany, Greece, Belgium and Netherlands.	California, New Jersey, Hawaii and Florida.
Types	Crisphead, Butterhead Cos, Leaf and Stem	Heady types and Leafy types
Suitable Temperature	Prefers relatively cool and mild temperature 18°C - 25°C	Cool temperature
Soil pH	6.5 to 7.2	5.5 to 7.6
Propagation	Seed	Seed
Plant Spacing	25 cm x 36 cm	25-46 cm x 46-91 cm
Fertiliser	Nitrogen - 245 kg/ha.	49.5 kg. N & 67.5 kg/ha.
Duration	Summer lettuce - 50-65 days Winter lettuce - 110-120 days	50-80 days
Stage of Harvesting	Full Rosette and well filled heads	Heads fully developed, firm and free from discoluration.
Common Disease	Downy Mildew, Powdery Mildew, Anthranose and Worky shoot	Turnip Downy Mildew, Powdery Mildew, Leaf spots and Diamond black moth Nematode.

REFERENCES

1. Harrington, G. 1978. *Grow Your Own Chinese Vegetables.* Garden Way Publishing: Pownal, Vermont, pp. 286.
2. Ryder, E.J. 2000. *Lettuce. Endure and Chicory.* CABI Publishing. London, pp. 97-117.
3. Shattuck, V. and B. Shelp. 1986. *Chinese Cabbage Production in Southern Ontario.* Ministry of Agriculture and Food. Factsheet, pp. 86-90.

Index

❑❑❑